PeopleSoft Application Development Tools

PeopleSoft Application Development Tools

Jami Clott

Stephen Raff

McGraw-Hill
New York • San Francisco • Washington, D.C.
Auckland • Bogotá •Caracas • Lisbon • London
Madrid • Mexico City • Milan • Montreal
New Delhi • San Juan • Singapore • Sydney
Tokyo • Toronto

McGraw-Hill

A Division of The **McGraw-Hill** Companies

1 2 3 4 5 6 7 8 9 0   AGM/AGM   9 0 4 3 2 1 0 9

ISBN 0-07-135569-3

The sponsoring editor for this book was Simon Yates and the production supervisor was Clare Stanley. It was set in Janson Text by Patricia Wallenburg.

Printed and bound by Quebecor/Martinsburg.

To Jeffrey, Jacob, Beth, Joshua and Benjamin—
Who kept wondering when we would ever be finished.
We thank you for your support and patience.

Acknowledgments

There are many people to thank for their assistance in the development of this book. First, there are a few people at the firm of Ernst & Young LLP who deserve particular mention. Thanks to John McCreadie, partner and Chief Information Officer of the firm, for his support of this effort. Additionally, we appreciate the encouragement we received from Lynn Anderson, partner in our firm's PeopleSoft consulting service. We thank our colleagues, Heidi Kaufman and Dawn Merolli for their careful review of the entire manuscript and thoughtful suggestions. Heidi is a talented instructor in our PeopleSoft training program and assisted significantly in the development of the case study. Dawn is a senior manager in our PeopleSoft consulting service and provided valuable insights in our discussion of globalization.

We know that there are many people at McGraw-Hill Computing who contributed to the publication of this work. Special thanks to our editor, Simon Yates, for his support and feedback throughout the project. We thank Patricia Wallenburg for her skillful typesetting, page layout, graphics, and attention to the details.

Finally, our heartfelt thanks to our teachers and students. In particular we thank Eric Zucco, Master Technical Instructor at PeopleSoft, for enthusiastically sharing his deep expertise on this subject. We thank the hundreds of students in our PeopleSoft technical classes at our firm for challenging us to learn something new from every class that we teach.

—*Jami Clott and Stephen Raff*

Contents

Part 2
Understanding the Data   55

Part 4
Incorporating Code into Your Application   165

Part 5
Completing the Application   219

Part 1

Getting Started

Introduction

Our objective in writing this book is to provide information systems professionals with a clear and concise introduction to PeopleSoft applications development. PeopleSoft is one of the leading providers of Enterprise Resource Planning (ERP) applications. The popularity of the PeopleSoft applications is due at least in part to the flexibility and adaptability of the software. This quality permits the organization implementing the PeopleSoft applications to modify or customize the application software more fully to suit their particular business requirements.

This book is intended to provide applications developers with the "how to" skills necessary to customize PeopleSoft applications. These same skills can be used to develop new applications utilizing the PeopleSoft applications development tool set. Previous knowledge or familiarity with PeopleSoft applications or the PeopleSoft applications development tool set is not assumed.

The contents of the book begin with *Getting Started* to introduce the reader to key concepts, the look and feel of the PeopleSoft applications, and preview the new PeopleSoft integrated development environment—the Application Designer. This section is concluded with a discussion of planning the application development effort, including gathering the business requirements and designing the application. The book then moves directly into the PeopleSoft applications development methods. *Understanding the Data* leads the reader through the design and definition of the data objects required for PeopleSoft applications. The next part, *Developing the User Interface*, instructs the reader in all of the techniques for the design and development of the interactive PeopleSoft application. *Incorporating Code into your Application* provides the reader with an introduction to the PeopleCode programming language. Finally, *Completing the Application* covers the many steps necessary to complete and implement the PeopleSoft application. The *Case Study* follows and provides the reader with an opportunity to use and practice these skills.

Our approach to this book is based on our experience teaching PeopleSoft application development skills to literally hundreds of information systems and consulting professionals. Throughout the book we have tried to present the topics in a clear, concise and accessible format. We hope that our approach will prove to be useful to our readers and assist in the successful design, development, and implementation of PeopleSoft applications in your organization.

Please consider that the implementation of a (large-scale) Enterprise Resource Planning application system such as PeopleSoft can be a major project for an organization. The application software implementation may be accompanied by changes to business processes and changes to staff members' job functions. For the PeopleSoft client organization, this book is *not* a substitute for thorough training of information systems professionals nor for skilled professionals with experience gained from previous PeopleSoft implementation efforts. This book is devoted to PeopleSoft application development tools and skills.

Using this Book

To assist the reader in the use of this book, specific typographical conventions have been followed. Throughout the book we will use **Bold** typeface to indicate a PeopleSoft command or menu navigation path. These commands or navigation paths are separated by use of slashes (/). For example, the statement **Go/PeopleTools/Application Designer** should be understood as:

1. select the **Go** command from the menu,
2. select the **PeopleTools** choice from that menu, and
3. select the **Application Designer** choice from the next menu.

Please refer to Figure 1.1 below for a screen image of this menu navigation example.

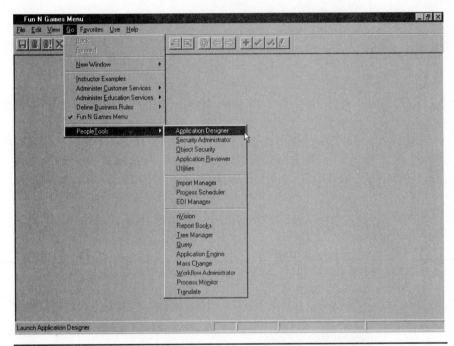

Figure 1.1 *Screen image of Go/PeopleTools/Application Designer*

This book has been written using PeopleSoft version 7.5, the most current version of the software as of Summer 1999. The features and tools discussed in this book and all screen images are taken from version 7.5. The changes to PeopleTools introduced in version 7.5 compared to version 7.0 are relatively minor. Therefore, if you are working in either of these versions of PeopleTools, this book should be an equally valuable resource. However, the changes in PeopleTools from version 6.0 to 7.0 were very significant. Most notable is the introduction of the Application Designer, completely replacing several prior PeopleSoft application development tools.

The Case Study Approach

Throughout the writing of this book we have remained neutral with respect to any specific PeopleSoft application (e.g. Human Resources, Payroll, General Ledger, Accounts Payable), hoping to make the book useful to developers working on any application. Therefore, rather than utilize examples taken from any one of the many PeopleSoft applications, we have developed our own case study application system.

The case study will be the design and development of a new time and expense (T&E) application for a fictional company. Throughout the book we will use this case study application to demonstrate various PeopleTools and PeopleCode application development skills. Please bear in mind that the development of a new application is somewhat different from the modification of an existing application. However, the same PeopleTools and PeopleCode skills that we illustrate in the development of our case study application are the skills required for the customization of the licensed PeopleSoft applications. We think that even the smallest customization effort can be considered a small application development effort, with a fixed starting point (the current or delivered application) and a desired ending point in terms of new application functions and performance.

Throughout the book, numerous examples and screen images will be taken from the case study application. We will progressively develop that application, with a full discussion in Part 6 of the book including:

▲ Requirements and design
▲ Data fields, records, and tables
▲ Online interface (panels, menus)
▲ Security and testing
▲ PeopleCode development
▲ Globalization.

For readers with access to a PeopleSoft application development environment, we strongly suggest joining us in the development of the case study application. The case study reinforces the concepts introduced in each of the chapters and provides the opportunity to practice the skills learned. Alternatively, the book can be read without developing the case study application or even reviewing the case study chapters. The book can also be used as a reference for the application developer needing to refresh knowledge of a particular PeopleTools or PeopleCode topic.

Introduction to PeopleSoft

The PeopleSoft company is one of the largest vendors of Enterprise Resource Planning (ERP) application software in the world, with 1998 revenues in excess of $1.3 billion. The company has an interesting and colorful background, marked by extraordinary growth since its founding in 1987. PeopleSoft offers a broad range of application software products, including Human Resource Management systems, Financial and Accounting systems, Manufacturing and Distribution systems, and Higher Education and Government systems. PeopleSoft also offers a number of specialized industry solutions. In recent versions of PeopleSoft, the applications have been significantly "globalized" to support the language, currency, and special requirements of international and multinational organizations. Currently, PeopleSoft counts over 2900 client organizations worldwide using its software. However, it is *not* our intention here to provide an introduction to the PeopleSoft company and its many product and service offerings. We suggest a visit to the **www.PeopleSoft.com** corporate Website for the most up-to-date information on the company and its culture.

In addition to the many important business processes supported by the PeopleSoft applications, the PeopleSoft technical architecture is another important factor in the success of the application software products. The PeopleSoft application software is based on a client/server technical architecture. The software may be implemented on a wide variety of hardware platforms, utilizing various operating systems. It can also be used with any of the leading relational database management systems. This flexibility to run on different platforms and scales to support different-sized implementations is another reason for the popularity of the PeopleSoft applications.

Of particular interest to the authors is the unique PeopleSoft application development environment. The PeopleSoft application development tools permit the client organization that is implementing PeopleSoft applications to modify the software better to meet their specific business requirements. The PeopleSoft licensed applications are delivered to the client with what is essentially complete application "source code" developed in the proprietary

PeopleSoft application development tools and programming language—namely, PeopleTools and PeopleCode. Of course, the applications may be installed without change or may be customized by the PeopleSoft client organization.

To perform customization of the delivered applications requires staff with skill and experience in the PeopleSoft development process and tool kit. Before proceeding with any customization, organizations implementing PeopleSoft applications should understand the costs and risks associated with customization of the licensed applications as well as the many benefits. The primary benefit of customization is the implementation of an application system that more fully meets the business requirements of the organization. The associated costs and risks include (but are not limited to) the initial cost of customization design and development, the potentially increased cost of ongoing support and periodic application upgrades, and the risk of introducing errors in the customized application.

Naturally, the capability to customize the delivered applications enables the flexible and adaptable nature of the PeopleSoft product line that is attractive to so many client organizations. The "we work in your world"™ slogan of PeopleSoft really is their trademark and best expresses the widespread appeal of the PeopleSoft application software.

02

Understand the Application User Perspective

Before starting the design and development of a new PeopleSoft application or, more likely the customization of an existing PeopleSoft application, it is necessary to understand the basic "look and feel" of all PeopleSoft applications. In this chapter we will introduce the basic usage and navigation of PeopleSoft online applications. Our case study application will be used to demonstrate a PeopleSoft application from the end-user perspective. We will illustrate the signon process for starting the application, basic navigation to menus and panels, the use of application actions and toolbar icons, the use of the search dialog box to select data, and the enforcement of data integrity rules through data validation and the important concept of effective dating.

Signon to the Application

An application user, referred to technically as an *operator*, can start a PeopleSoft application in the Windows® client (Windows 95 or Windows NT) by finding and clicking on a PeopleTools program entry from the Windows Start button. The name of the program group and program entry can vary from installation to installation. The signon process for PeopleTools application developers is the same as the process for application users. But, in addition to executing PeopleSoft applications, the developers will have the ability to use the PeopleSoft development tools (see Chapter 16, Administer Security). The result of clicking the PeopleTools program is the display of the PeopleSoft Signon screen, as seen in Figure 2.1.

Figure 2.1   *PeopleSoft signon screen*

Initially visible in the PeopleSoft Signon screen are defaults for the workstation that are set in the Configuration Manager (this tool will be introduced in Chapter 3). Optionally, some fields in the PeopleSoft Signon screen may be changed by the application user before proceeding to signon, as follows:

▲ **Connection Type:** May be reset by some operators depending on their own security. Select your Database Management system for (two-tier) database connection or Application Server for three-tier execution.

▲ **Application Server Name:** Must be selected if the Connection Type is Application Server. Select the appropriate Application Server to sign onto.

▲ **Database Name:** Must be selected if the Connection Type is a Database system. Enter the name of the specific database to sign onto. At many sites, there will be different databases for purposes of application development, test, and production (live data) application systems.

▲ **Operator ID:** Enter the operator ID that was assigned for your individual use. This identifies you to the PeopleSoft system.

▲ **Password:** Enter the password assigned to you to verify your identity. If no password is entered the password will default to the operator ID.

If all information entered is valid and the operator has been provided with security access, the PeopleSoft application signon will be successful. If some piece of information entered (e.g. password) is *not* valid then a PeopleSoft Signon error will be displayed, as in Figure 2.2, and the PeopleSoft application will not be started.

Figure 2.2   *Invalid access message*

You may attempt the PeopleSoft Signon process again with correct signon information. The initial PeopleSoft window displayed after successful signon is another default set in the Configuration Manager.

You may notice that you are able to sign on successfully to multiple PeopleSoft applications *concurrently* using different database names and even using different Operator IDs. This enables you to have several applications open for work at the same time. For an application developer this can be extremely helpful, allowing you to view the current application in one window, while developing a new or changed application in another window. Similarly, for a single signon to a given database there may be several PeopleSoft application windows open concurrently (see instructions below). If there is ever a question of what database or operator is active for any PeopleTools application window, simply click **Help/About PeopleTools** to get a display of this information for the active window. See Figure 2.3 for an example of the About PeopleTools display.

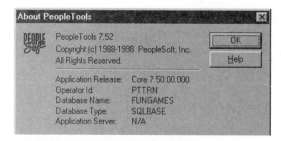

Figure 2.3   *Help/About PeopleTools*

Finally, we do not suggest keeping more than a few PeopleSoft application windows active at a time as this can become confusing and can lead to workstation errors.

Menu Navigation

Any PeopleTools application to which an operator has been given security access can be accessed from one of the many application menus. There are four alternative forms of navigation in the PeopleSoft application system. Each of the alternatives provides a navigation path to the execution of the *same* application panels. An individual operator may set the preferred navigation mode by selecting from the menu bar **View/Navigator Display** from any PeopleSoft application window, as seen in Figure 2.4.

In this book we will discuss and illustrate the **Menus Only** navigation display. Briefly, selecting the **Business Process** navigation mode places the application user in the Business Process display and allows the user to navigate through the application graphically by clicking on steps in a predefined business process map. This mode also supports the concept of PeopleSoft workflow, showing the steps in a defined business process that may go "outside" the PeopleSoft application (such as sending an e-mail). Likewise, the **Worklist** navigation mode can be used when PeopleSoft workflow is implemented. This allows an application user to see the work items directed to his or her attention. The **Query** navigation mode shows the Operator a list of available queries and will allow the user to run queries from within the online application (and export the results to Excel or Crystal™ Reports). Recall that each of these navigation alternatives with the exception of **Query** provides a path to the ultimate execution of the same application panels. The development of application menus and panels will be the subject of this book; no matter which navigation mode is selected the application menus and panels must be developed.

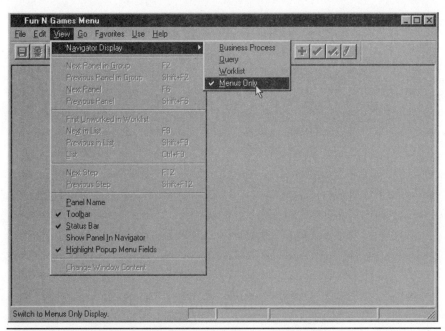

Figure 2.4   *View/Navigator Display*

The structure of each PeopleTools application menu is basically the same, and should be largely familiar to users of other Windows applications. Please see Figure 2.5 for a sample taken from our case study Fun-N-Games application.

On the menu bar there are several items that are PeopleSoft provided and will be found on all menus. These PeopleSoft menu bar items *cannot* be changed or customized by the developer. These include the following menu bars: **File**, **Edit**, **View**, **Go**, **Favorites**, **Language**, and **Help**. Each of these will be discussed in more detail. Other menu bar items are application specific and can be changed or customized by the application developer. Typically, these include menu bar items with names such as: **Use**, **Setup**, **Inquire**, **Process**, and **Report**. Notice that under a menu bar those menu items not available to the application user at a particular time will be displayed in gray, while the available choices will be dark.

The display of the toolbar near the top of the menu and the status bar at the bottom of the menu window are optional. Select menu bar **View/Toolbar** to toggle the toolbar display on and off and select **View/Status Bar** to toggle the status bar on and off. As with menu items, toolbar icons that are not available at a particular time will be displayed in gray, while the toolbar icons that are available will be dark.

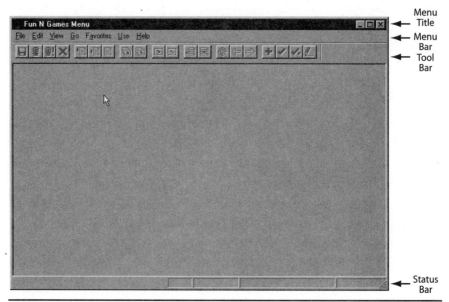

Figure 2.5   *Labeled sample application menu*

All of the PeopleTools application menus to which an Operator has security access can be found under a Menu Group. This is a term for a collection of somewhat related application menus. From any PeopleTools application window, select the **Go** menu bar to display the complete list of available Menu Groups. Please see Figure 2.6 for a example of the menus found under the **Go** menu bar.

This is a cascading display of menu groups, with a small dark triangle indicating that there is more than one menu within a particular group. Positioning the cursor over a menu group will display the individual menus in that group. Clicking on the name of a particular menu will start the display of that menu. This is the basic form of menu navigation within PeopleTools applications. Returning to the **Go** menu bar will *always* provide the application user with a display of available menu groups and allow selection and access of a particular menu from within a group.

Typically, the newly selected menu is displayed in place of the current open menu window. However, to keep the current menu window active, the application user may select **New Window** from within the **Go** menu bar and then select the desired application menu. The new selected menu window will be opened and made active, while the previous menu window will remain open but not active. The previous menu window may be made active by selecting it from the Windows taskbar. As mentioned before, this allows the application user to keep several windows open for work at the same time.

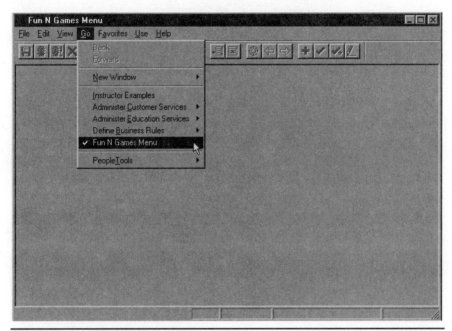

Figure 2.6 *Go list of Menu Groups*

Upon selection and display of a particular menu from within a menu group, the application user may make a selection from one of the menu bar items. When an application-specific menu bar item (e.g. **Use**) is selected a cascading list of menu items, panel group items and actions is displayed. See Figure 2.7 for an illustration of a cascading menu.

As before, the presence of a dark triangle indicates that there are additional choices for the application user to make. Under the menu bar item selected, each menu item corresponds to a panel group, or a collection of one or more related panels. For a panel there may be one or more available actions. Finally, the selection of a panel and an action starts the execution of a PeopleTools application. Each action and the various panel options will be discussed in turn.

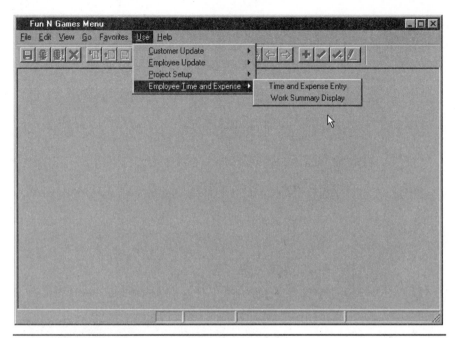

Figure 2.7   *Menu bar item—cascading to menu items, panel group items, actions*

Panel Actions

Selection of the **Update/Display** action provides the application user with the ability to browse application data and make updates if necessary. This action is almost always available to the application user. Selection of the **Update/Display All** and the **Correction** actions are similar to the **Update/Display** action but are only appropriate for effective dated tables and the related panels. Effective dated tables and the difference in the actions will be discussed more fully later in this chapter. If available, the **Add** action enables the application user to add a new high-level key value and corresponding row of application data. If available, the **Data Entry** action provides a panel for repetitive entry of new rows of data. Each of these actions is discussed in more detail, from the application developer's perspective, in Chapter 10 (Define Panel Groups).

Search Dialog Box

Selection of the **Update/Display** action, or **Update/Display All** or **Correction** actions for effective dated tables (later), will result in the display of a PeopleSoft Search dialog box like the one seen in Figure 2.8.

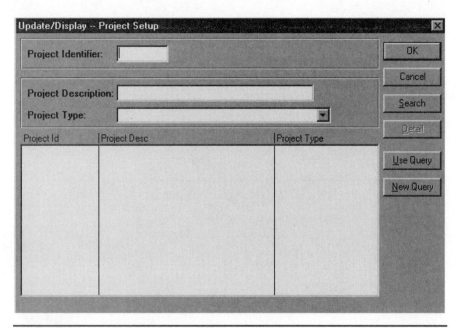

Figure 2.8 *Search dialog box for sample application*

The Search dialog box always has the same structure. The top frame includes fields referred to as the *search keys*. The second frame includes fields referred to as the *alternate search keys*. These search keys and alternate search keys allow the application user to enter a value or values and perform a search for rows in the database that meet the search criteria. The value entered may be a full or partial key value. Wild card characters ("%") may be used in the value entered to substitute for any unknown characters. One or more of the search and alternate search key fields may have a prompt available. Clicking the prompt button (the down arrow or hitting **F4**) will provide the application user with a list of the valid values for that key field and allow the user to select a value for use in the search. Notice in Figure 2.9 that the valid values for Project Type are displayed.

If the search key or alternate search key value entered uniquely identifies one row in the database, then the application panel will be immediately displayed to the user with that selected row of data.

If the application user does not enter a search key or alternate search key value, or if the value(s) that are entered do not uniquely identify a particular row in database, then the bottom of the Search dialog box (we refer to this as the "list box" area) will be populated with rows of data for the user to choose from. If no search key or alternate search key values were entered, then the first

300 rows of data will be presented to the application user in search key order. If some search key or alternate search key values were entered, then the first 300 rows of data that match the search criteria will be displayed to the user (potentially in alternate search key order). See Figure 2.10 for a sample Search dialog box with a list of rows retrieved.

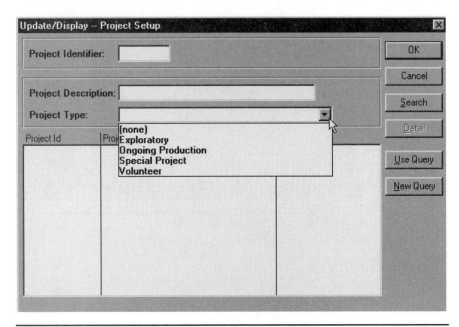

Figure 2.9   *Prompt for a value in an alternate search key field*

If the application user does not find the desired row of data, the search or alternate search key field values may be changed by the user and another search initiated by hitting **Enter** again. Highlighting a particular row of data from the list box area and clicking **OK** will bring the application user to the desired application panel (described in next section) with the selected row of data displayed.

Selection of the **Add** action from the cascading menu of panels and actions will result in the display of the PeopleSoft Add dialog box as shown in Figure 2.11 taken from our sample application.

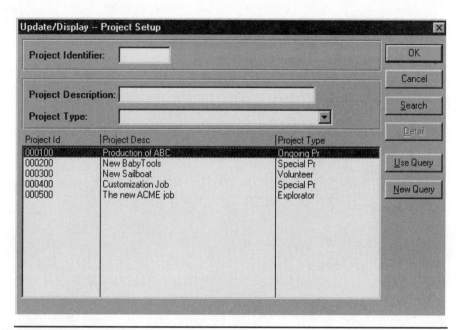

Figure 2.10   *Search/List box with rows of data*

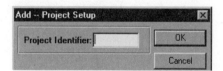

Figure 2.11   *Add dialog box for sample application*

The Add dialog box always has a very simple structure. The only fields included are the high-level key fields that must be entered for unique identification of the new row of data to be added. If the key is a composite or concatenated key, some of the key fields may have edits defined to ensure that the value(s) entered are valid (on other reference tables). Once all value(s) have been entered the selected panel is opened with the high-level key fields populated from these values entered in the dialog box.

Panel Operations

Once the application panel is displayed, the user has several navigation choices available. First, of course, the user may hit the **Tab** key or use the mouse to move between fields on the panel. Fields shown in *white* boxes are available to *write* data on this panel, while those shown in *gray* are for *display* only on this panel. At the top of the panel (below the tool bar) the panel folder tab is displayed. If there is more than one panel within the panel group, the user can move from panel to panel within the group by clicking on the folder tab. See Figure 2.12 for a display of several panels in a panel group.

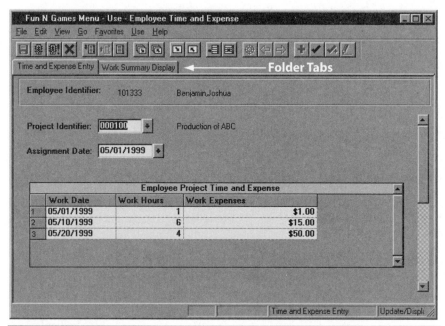

Figure 2.12   *Several panels in a panel group (showing folder tabs)*

There are a number of useful toolbar icons that become active when a panel is displayed. Each of these represents a command that can also be performed from the menu bar. Figure 2.13 contains the toolbar icons, with short labels indicating functions.

The first icon is for the **Save** command. This becomes active if the application user changes any data on the panel. Clicking the **Save** icon or selecting the **File/Save** command saves all of the data from the panel, and from all panels in the panel group, to the database. Related to this icon is the **Cancel** icon. **Cancel** allows an application user to exit the panel without saving any changes. Please note, the **Cancel** command does *not* warn the user that the changes made will be lost, the panel group is simply closed with no changes saved to the application database.

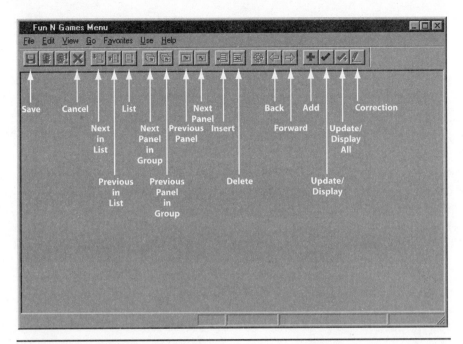

Figure 2.13   *Labeled toolbar icons*

The next group of three icons represent the **Next in List, Previous in List**, and **List** commands. These icons are only active if the display of the panel follows the display of a list of values within a search dialog box. Essentially, the **Next** and **Previous in List** commands allow the application to redisplay the same panel for either the next or previous row of data from this list box. The **List** command returns the user from the panel to the search/list box itself.

The next two icons represent the **Next Panel in Group** and the **Previous Panel in Group** commands. These commands provide the application user with another form of navigation between the various panels within the current panel group, and allow the user to cycle through all the panels in the panel group (at the last panel in the group, cycle back to the first panel in the group). By contrast, the two icons representing the **Next Panel** and **Previous Panel** commands provide the application user with (yet another) form of navigation to the next and previous panels, not within the panel group but within the menu. It should be noted that if the application user selects the **Next Panel** or **Previous Panel** (not within group) and has made changes on the panel currently active, there will be a prompt to save or cancel the panel (group).

If a panel has one or more scroll bars, then the icons representing the **Insert** command (**F7**) and the **Delete** command (**F8**) are active. These commands allow the application user to position the cursor within the scroll bar and either insert or delete a row of data. With inserting, a new set of fields with default values will be opened up on the panel in the scroll bar. If deleting, the user will be asked to confirm the decision to delete the selected row in the scroll bar. An insert or delete within a scroll area will only insert or delete rows within the high-order key that was selected when entering the panel.

The next two icons represent the **Back** and **Forward** navigation commands, taking the user back and forward among the last panels visited (like a browser). These commands operate on the same list of panels as the **Go/Recent** menu command.

The last few toolbar icons represent the **Add, Update/Display, Update/Display All,** and **Correction** commands. These are simply shortcuts to the respective action for the last panel that the application user has selected.

Data Validation

Data validation features or edits can be found on many PeopleSoft application panels. These are intended to ensure the selection of a valid value by the application user for certain data fields on the panel. One data validation feature is the use of a Prompt Table edit, most commonly found on the panel as an edit box with a Prompt button next to it as seen in the example in Figure 2.14.

This provides the application user with the ability to click the **Prompt** button (or press **F4**) and see another search dialog box—this time to search for a valid value and return that value into the panel. The application user may choose a value from the displayed values list or the user may perform a partial key search using the Search dialog box functionality shown in Figure 2.15.

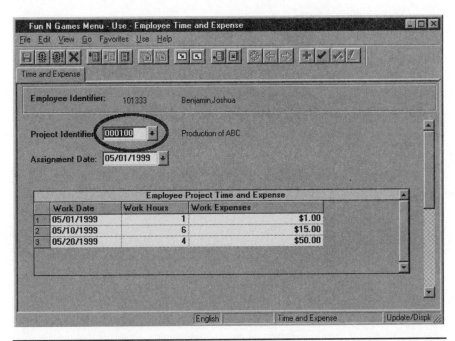

Figure 2.14 *Panel field with Prompt Table edit*

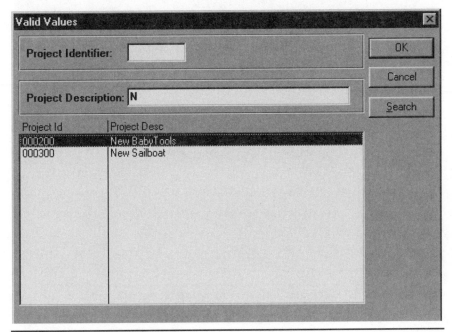

Figure 2.15 *Search dialog box with partial key search*

Similar to the Prompt Table edit is the Translate Table edit. This feature also provides the user with a list of valid values. The Translate Table edit does not make use of the Search Dialog Box, but typically displays the valid values in the form of a drop-down list as seen in Figure 2.16. Note the limitation of only 300 values that will be displayed in the drop-down list. While the Search dialog box has the same 300-row limit, use of partial key searches provides a convenient solution to this limitation.

Again, the application user may select one value and return it to the panel field. Alternatively, the Translate Table edit may be presented on the panel as a series of radio buttons. Only one button on the panel may be selected by the user at any time. Each button represents a different valid value. Lastly, some data fields may be defined to take only an On or Off value, typically Yes or No. These edits are generally represented on the panel as a check box.

The implementation of Prompt Table edits, Translate Table edits, and Yes/No edits will be discussed from the application developer's perspective in significant detail in Chapter 5 (Define Fields) and Chapter 6 (Define Records).

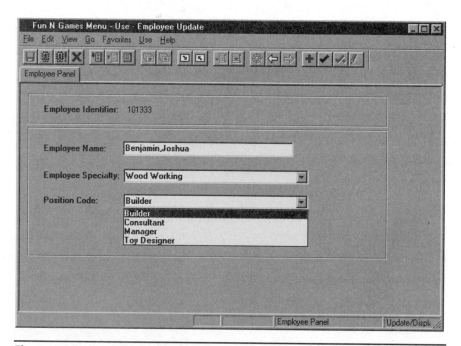

Figure 2.16   *Panel field with Translate Table values in drop-down list*

Effective Dating

Effective dating is another important PeopleTools technique to support the integrity of the application data. From the application user's perspective, effective dating provides the ability to maintain a history of different values of application data on different dates for a particular unique key value. For example, effective dating can provide the capability to maintain a history of a customer name as of different dates while keeping the same unique key (e.g. customer identifier). This is different from keeping an audit of changes to the database tables in that effective dated panels display to the application user the various data values over a range of different dates. Specific application data tables and their associated panels may be made effective dated by the application developer. This is discussed in more detail in Chapter 6 (Define Records).

There are two additional actions valid for effective dated tables, namely the **Update/Display All** and the **Correction** action. There are two important differences in their logic compared to the **Update/Display** action. To understand the differences we need to define the terms used in effective dating. All effective dated tables make use of an effective date field to distinguish between the data values on different dates. All rows of data on the effective dated table are termed history, current, or future rows based on their effective date field value, as follows:

▲ **History**—Row(s) with an effective date less than the effective date of the current row

▲ **Current**—Single row with the effective date *closest to and less than or equal to* today's date

▲ **Future**—Row(s) with an effective date greater than today's date.

This is a frequent source of confusion for new application users and application developers alike. We explain the current effective dated row as being like the winner in the game of blackjack, where the winner is the player with cards that have a total value *closest to and less than or equal to* a total of 21 points. Unlike casino blackjack where several players can win a game, there is only one Current row for a single high-level key value on an effective dated table.

With this understanding of effective date terminology, we can distinguish between the two new actions, based on what rows of data are available for display and for update, as follows:

Table 2.1   *Comparison of effective dated panel actions*

Action	Retrieves Rows	Updates Rows
Update/Display	Current and Future	Insert a row with date greater than current row effective date, or update any future rows.
Update/Display All	History, Current, and Future	Same as Update/Display
Correction	History, Current, and Future	Insert or update all rows, with any effective date.

Since the Correction action permits the user to go back and change rows of history data, this action in particular is to be used sparingly and provided only to experienced and trusted application users. Inappropriate usage of the Correction action can destroy the history of the data values in the table, the very reason that effective dating was implemented. Fortunately, using Security Administrator we can easily limit access to this panel and action combination (see Chapter 16).

Summary

In this chapter we have tried to present some of the basic concepts and generic usage of PeopleSoft online applications. Of course, there is much more to learn regarding the correct usage of any one of the specific PeopleSoft applications. Again, while remaining neutral to a specific PeopleSoft application, we have presented the basic understanding required of any PeopleTools application developer regardless of the specific application.

03

Preview the Development Tools

Now that we have an understanding of the basic navigation and "look and feel" of a sample PeopleSoft application from the end-user perspective it is time to begin to discuss and learn the PeopleSoft application development tool kit. Of course, the PeopleSoft application development process and tool kit is our main subject for the book. In this chapter we will simply introduce the concepts and preview the major elements of the development tool kit. More detailed discussions will follow in the subsequent chapters, especially on the new integrated PeopleSoft development environment known as the Application Designer.

PeopleSoft Technical Architecture

Before beginning to develop a PeopleSoft application it is useful to have at least a basic understanding of the PeopleSoft technical architecture. Here we will introduce the PeopleSoft client/server architecture. We will also discuss the logical database structures, referred to as the PeopleTools tables, that support the integrated development environment.

Prior to version 7, the PeopleSoft technical architecture could be described as a traditional client/server model, with a client workstation running an application connected to a database server over a network to retrieve data from a shared database. This is referred to as a two-tier model. Starting with version 7, PeopleSoft introduced a new three-tier technical architecture. The significant change in the new architecture is the implementation of a new application server. As seen in Figure 3.1, in the three-tier architecture the client workstation running the application is connected to an application server instead of being connected to a database server. The application server generates all of the SQL statements to retrieve data from the database server. The new three-tier architecture also enables the support of a new PeopleSoft web client, connected to the application server through a Web server.

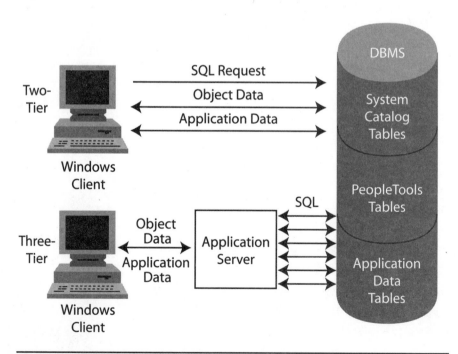

Figure 3.1   *Two-tier and three-tier architecture diagram*

In the three-tier architecture, significant portions of the application transaction processing are moved to the application server, resulting in a "thinner" client application. This architecture has numerous advantages, but perhaps the greatest benefit is the reduced network traffic and corresponding improved system performance over a Wide Area Network. The other important advantage is the improved ability to scale the PeopleSoft system to meet increased requirements by implementing additional application servers. PeopleSoft still supports the relatively simpler two-tier architecture. In this instance, no application server is configured and the client workstation is connected directly to the database server.

Within a single installation some client workstations may connect to the database directly (two-tier) while others can connect to an application server (three-tier). An individual operator may specify the connection type for a session right from the initial PeopleSoft Sign on window. We will point out three-tier processing options that are significant for the application developer later in the book (Chapter 10, Define Panel Groups).

Database Architecture

PeopleTools applications are developed to work with any one of a number of different Relational Database Management Systems (RDBMS). Some of the most popular commercial RDBMS platforms that PeopleTools applications will run on include: ORACLE from Oracle Corporation, DB2 from International Business Machines, Microsoft SQL/Server, and others. Regardless of the particular RDBMS, the data that is important to the user of the PeopleTools application is stored in a collection of relational database tables.

In both the two-tier and three-tier architecture, the database server is the ultimate source of all PeopleSoft applications and data. In the two-tier architecture, operators will be asked to sign on to a particular PeopleSoft database by name. In the three-tier architecture, operators will sign on to an application server that is in turn connected to a single database. You may hear developers refer to a specific PeopleSoft system by its database name. One or more PeopleSoft applications may reside in a single database.

Understanding the design of the PeopleSoft database is important to developing a full understanding of the PeopleTools application. Each PeopleSoft database can be divided into three logical groups of tables, as follows:

1. *Application data tables* contain data of interest to the user of the application.
2. *PeopleTools tables* contain application development objects.
3. *Catalog tables* are maintained by the RDBMS.

The tables that contain the data required for the application (e.g. Employee Salary data) are referred to as the PeopleSoft application data tables. The number of application data tables required for a single application can be quite large. The PeopleSoft applications such as Payroll or General Ledger modules are delivered with literally hundreds of different application data tables as part of the application. The design of the application data tables is dictated by the application data requirements and good database design principles. In the database management system the application data tables are named "PS_RecordName" (by default).

The second group of tables, the PeopleTools tables, are used to store the PeopleTools application objects created by the developer within the Application Designer tool (discussed next). These application objects include Fields, Records, Panels, etc. It is useful for the application developer to have some familiarity with the PeopleTools tables. For the curious application developer, the contents of these tables may be queried directly using the appropriate interactive SQL tool. The naming convention for these tables begins with "PS", but with no underscore. There are over 200 such PeopleTools tables.

Since all application objects are stored in PeopleTools tables, moving a PeopleTools application from one application environment (e.g. Test system) to another environment (e.g. Production system) requires the migration of application objects from one set of PeopleTools tables to another. This migration of PeopleTools application objects is *not* typically the responsibility of the application developer. The application developer may not be permitted to perform this function, as it may be considered to be the responsibility of a system administrator or database administrator to maintain application change control. PeopleSoft provides tools for data migration, however these will not be discussed within the scope of this text.

The third logical group of tables are the RDBMS system catalog tables. Although slightly different in structure among the different supported RDBMS platforms, the system catalog tables store information necessary for the RDBMS itself to keep track of the physical characteristics of relational tables, columns, indexes, etc. The names of the catalog tables are dependent on the actual RDBMS being used in the installation.

Application Designer

The Application Designer is the PeopleSoft integrated development environment (IDE). The Application Designer tool was new to PeopleSoft version 7.0, replacing the Data Designer, Panel Designer, and Menu Designer tools used in prior versions. The Application Designer is now the primary interface used to develop PeopleTools application objects and PeopleCode programs. By PeopleTools application objects we mean the different components that make up a PeopleTools application, including menus, panel groups, panels, records, and fields. Application objects are created and have all their properties defined within the Application Designer tool. We think of the PeopleTools application development process as really being an application object definition process, as compared to a more traditional procedural programming exercise.

The developer can access the Application Designer tool from any PeopleTools application window by selecting **Go/PeopleTools/Application Designer**. The Application Designer tool is divided into three windows: 1) Object Workspace, 2) Project Workspace, and 3) Output Window. Please see Figure 3.2 for an illustration of the Application Designer windows.

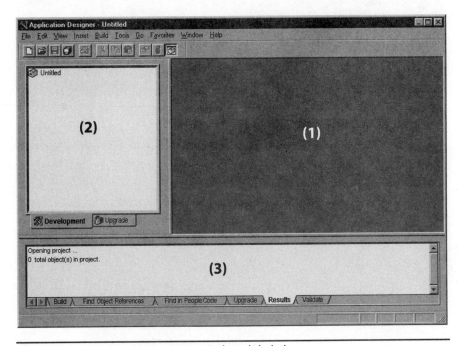

Figure 3.2   *Application Designer windows labeled*

The Object Workspace is where the current application objects are defined, modified, and saved. The contents of a **Project** (defined below) are listed in the Project Workspace, using the metaphor of a filing cabinet. The Output Window is where messages and output from development processes are displayed to the developer. Display of the Project Workspace and the Output Window can be selected or deselected from the **View** menu in the Application Designer.

An application object may be opened by choosing **File/Open** from the Application Designer menu, or by clicking on the **Open** icon on the tool bar. The developer will then be presented with the Open Object box as shown in Figure 3.3.

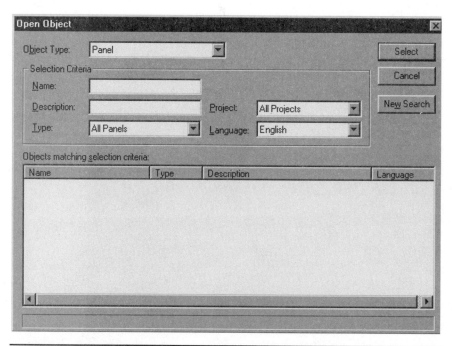

Figure 3.3   *Open Object box*

First the developer should select the application object type of interest (e.g. panel, record, field) from the drop-down list box. Selection criteria can then be entered to identify the specific application object. Typically a partial name is used to search for the desired application object. Note that the "%" character can be used as a wild card in the selection criteria to represent any string of characters before or after a known string of characters (e.g. entering name

"%quote%" will retrieve the "Curr_Quote_Tbl" record). For some object types (menu, panel, record) the selection of a specific object subtype (e.g. popup menu, secondary panel, query view record) is also available. If no selection criteria are entered by the developer, an unqualified list of all objects of the selected type is displayed—but avoid doing this as it will likely be a slow process. From the list of objects the developer can highlight one object and use the **Select** pushbutton to open the desired application object, or simply double-click on the application object name itself. Either way, the selected object will be opened in the Object Workspace.

Once an application object is open in the Object Workspace it may be modified and then saved by the developer. Depending on the object type (e.g. field, record, panel) there are many different choices that will be made by the developer while creating or defining that object. The various options will be discussed in detail in the chapter of the book describing that step of the application development process. One of the great benefits of the new PeopleSoft integrated development environment is the ability to open more than one object at a time. This allows the developer to view and work with several related objects in the Object Workspace. To switch between open objects (making one current in the foreground) select the **Window/Cascade** or **Window/Tile** command from the Application Designer menu. When several application objects are open in the Object Workspace, the **Window/Close All** command is also useful. When closing an object that has been changed, the Application Designer will prompt the developer to save the object. From our experience with new developers, we suggest keeping only a few application objects open at one time. This helps avoid confusion and reduces the chance of errors.

A new application object can be created by selecting **File/New** or selecting the **New** icon from the tool bar. The developer will be presented with the New dialog box and will be prompted to specify an application object type, as seen in Figure 3.4.

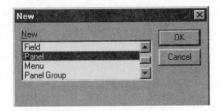

Figure 3.4 *New Object box*

After the object type is selected and **OK** is clicked, a blank occurrence of that object type will be placed in the Object Workspace. For field and menu objects the developer will be prompted for a field type or menu type before the blank object is displayed. The new object can now be modified, properties defined, and saved by the developer. During the save process, the developer will be prompted to name the object. Please note, these object names are internal to PeopleTools. They will be shown in all uppercase and blank characters are not acceptable. These names will *not* be displayed to our application users. Each object has text label(s) defined as an object property. These labels will be displayed to the application users during execution of our application.

Before we leave this introduction to the Object Workspace, there are several other useful commands for all object types that are worth mentioning. The **Edit/Find Object References** command will search the PeopleTools database and find all objects that have a direct relationship to the current open object and produce a list in the Output Window. This command has been enhanced for PeopleTools version 7.5; in version 7.0 this command was only available for field objects. The Find Object References command is a valuable tool for researching the impact of a change to the definition of an object—and should *always* be performed *in advance* of making a change to an existing object. Please see Figure 3.5 for an illustration of the messages in the Output Window in response to a Find Object Reference command issued for a field in our case study application.

By the way, clicking on an object name from the list displayed in the Output Window will also open up that object in the Object Workspace for the developer. This is very useful for directly finding and opening related application objects.

Another useful command is the **Insert/Current Object into Project** or **F7** key. This will place the current open object into the current Project (see below). Finally, the **File/Print** command or tool bar icon provides the developer with a printout of the properties of the open object. This is very useful for application development documentation.

Within the Application Designer, all work on application objects can be organized into one or more Projects. A Project is simply a useful collection of application objects, perhaps all related to a particular application module update, or related to a particular application development or customization project. The Project is a list of application objects, it does not actually keep a copy of the object. Please see Figure 3.6 for an illustration of the Project Workspace with our case study Fun-N-Games Project open.

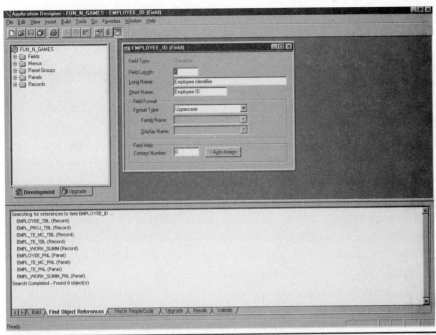

Figure 3.5 *Output Window showing results of Find Object References*

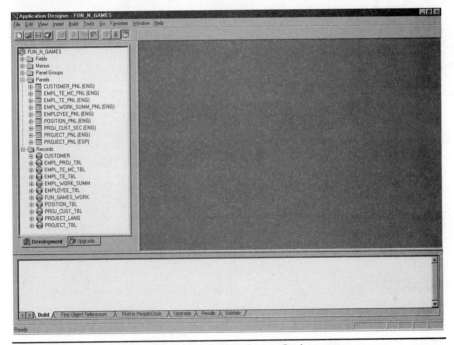

Figure 3.6 *Project Workspace with Fun-N-Games Project open*

Notice that for each of the application object types in the project there is a file folder with a plus (+) sign to the left of the file folder. Clicking on the plus sign expands the list of all objects of that type in the project. Clicking on an object within the Project Workspace list opens that object and makes that object current in the Object Workspace.

The Project entry is simply a reference to the application object. A particular application object may be included in one or more Projects, or may not be included in any Project. An application object exists only once in the PeopleTools database, no matter how many Projects that object is included in. If an application object is changed and saved by a developer working in one Project, that object is changed for all developers regardless of the Project being used.

A new Project can be created by selecting **File/New** and choosing the object type **Project**. An empty and untitled Project will be opened in the Project Workspace. The **File/Save Project As** command will prompt the developer to enter a Project name. After saving, that Project name will be displayed next to the file cabinet at the top of the Project Workspace. It is a good practice to set Project Options at this point. Select the **Tools/Options** command to display the Options dialog box–Project tab, as seen in Figure 3.7.

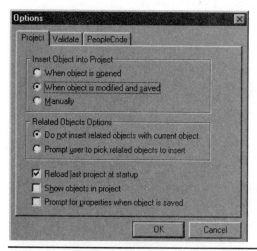

Figure 3.7   *Project Options box—Project tab*

For the Insert Object into Project, we use the **When Object is Modified and Saved** option. This option automatically places all new application objects that we create and all existing objects that we modify into our current Project when we **Save** or **Save All**. The default option for Insert Object into Project,

Manually, requires the application developer to use the **Insert Object (F7)** command for each object to be included in the Project. We also check off the **Reload Last Project at Startup** to immediately open the last Project that we were working on when we enter the Application Designer.

Security Administrator

Our PeopleTools application will be created using objects defined by the developer working in the Application Designer tool. Upon completion of a new menu or panel, the application developer will need to gain security access to the newly created application. Simply being the developer of an application does not give security access to execute the application. Hence the application developer will need to become familiar with PeopleSoft application security and the Security Administrator tool.

The basic concept behind PeopleSoft application security is that an individual application user is defined to the PeopleSoft system as an *Operator*. Numerous operators with similar security attributes may be assigned to a *Class*. In fact, since version 7.0 an operator may be assigned to more than one class. Application security profiles are defined for either the class or the operator. The profile includes General attributes, Menu Items, Signon Times, Process Groups, and Classes (only for Operators). The most interesting profile option is Menu Items. This provides access to an application menus, panels, and actions to allow the developer to begin to test the new application.

The definition of classes and operators in a new PeopleSoft implementation can be a large effort, requiring consideration of how an organization wants to divide the application functions. This can be the responsibility of an Information Security group, working closely with the business "owners" of the application. We will discuss use of the Security Administrator tool and the various security profile options in Chapter 16 (Administer Security).

Configuration Manager

The Configuration Manager is a PeopleTools utility designed to simplify client workstation administration. There are numerous workstation options that can be set during client installation. The Configuration Manager provides a simple, consistent interface to maintain these options. You may access the Configuration Manager tool either through the PeopleSoft program group directly, or from any PeopleTools application window by selecting **Edit/Preferences/Configuration**. We will discuss several of the more useful tabs in the Configuration Manager tool.

From the **Startup** tab the developer may set several useful defaults for the PeopleSoft Sign on, including the Database Type, Database Name, Operator ID and the Initial Window to be displayed after signon to PeopleTools. Please see Figure 3.8 for the Startup tab of the Configuration Manager tool.

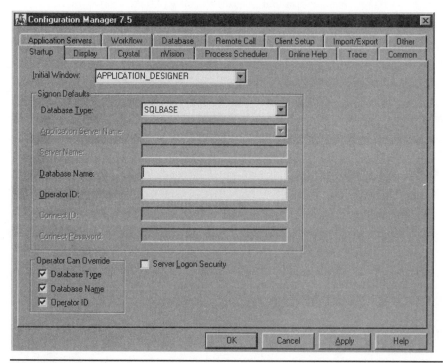

Figure 3.8   *Configuration Manager—Startup tab*

From the Common settings tab the developer can specify the language preference for the workstation operator (more discussion in Chapter 18, Globalization). Also on the Common tab, the developer can indicate the directory for PeopleTools Cache Files. Please see Figure 3.9 for the Common tab of the Configuration Manager tool.

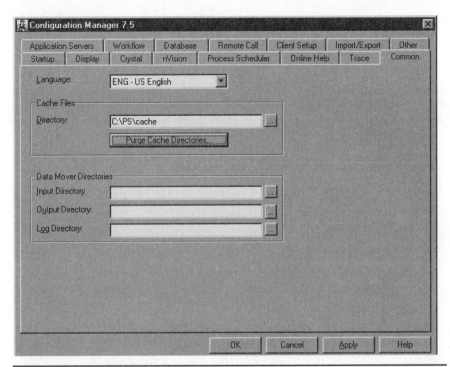

Figure 3.9 *Configuration Manager—Common tab*

The cache files are stored in a directory on the client workstation that will be built systematically and used during the execution of PeopleTools applications. The cache files contain PeopleTools application objects required for execution of the application. During the first access of a particular application (panel) each application object will be retrieved from the PeopleTools tables on the database server and placed in a cache file. As long as that application object does not change, subsequent executions of the same application from the same workstation will use the object found in the cache file of the workstation. Notice the pushbutton labeled **Purge Cache Directories** on the Common tab. It may be necessary to use this to purge the cache files from the client workstation (while PeopleTools is not executing) if cache files become full or if there is a workstation error. Cache files will be gradually rebuilt as required during the next execution of PeopleTools applications.

From the **Import/Export** tab the developer can choose to export to a file all of the current settings in the Configuration Manager that are in effect for this workstation. The file can subsequently be used for an Import to overwrite the Configuration Manager settings for one or more other workstations. Use of the

Export and Import functions allows for relatively simple, consistent configuration of many client workstations. Please see Figure 3.10 for the Import/Export tab of the Configuration Manager tool

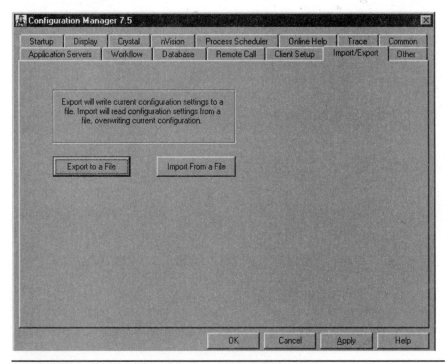

Figure 3.10   *Configuration Manager—Import/Export tab*

PeopleBooks

PeopleBooks is the complete online source for all PeopleSoft technical and application reference documentation. For the PeopleTools application developer, PeopleBooks is a valuable resource. PeopleBooks can be accessed from any PeopleTools application window by selecting **Help/PeopleTools PeopleBooks** to start the online documentation system. For each of the various PeopleSoft application modules there is also **Help/Application PeopleBooks** available. We consider the PeopleTools PeopleBooks an excellent reference and research tool.

All of the PeopleBooks documents are accessed through use of a software product known as Folio Views (delivered with the PeopleSoft install). This tool provides many powerful features, including document links and searching capabilities. We suggest reading the Folio Views help files for assistance with the usage of this tool.

Utilities

Certain PeopleTools application development functions that are performed outside the Application Designer tool are found in the PeopleTools utilities menu. To access the PeopleTools utilities menu shown in Figure 3.11, select **Go/PeopleTools/Utilities** from the Application Designer or from any PeopleTools application window.

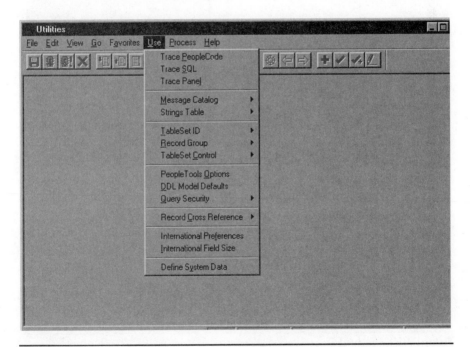

Figure 3.11   *Utilities menu —Use bar menu items*

In this section we will introduce some of the more useful PeopleTools utility functions. Several of the utility functions will be discussed in more detail in later chapters of the book.

Function	Description
Trace SQL	To initiate SQL Trace for debugging and performance analysis. Discussed further in Testing, Chapter 17.
Message Catalog	To update and display Messages in PeopleCode. Discussed further in PeopleCode, Chapter 12.
International Preferences	To set (non-base) language preferences for an Operator. Discussed further in Globalization, Chapter 18.
Record Cross Reference	To produce useful reports showing usage of a record.

The Record Cross Reference in particular is a very valuable tool for performing impact analysis prior to customization to a PeopleSoft delivered application object. Please see Figure 3.12 for a sample report, showing all uses of a record from our case study application.

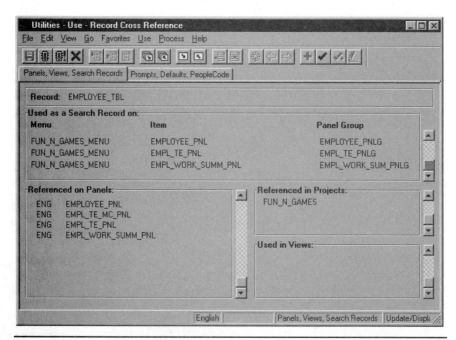

Figure 3.12   *Record Cross Reference report*

Globalization

PeopleSoft applications can be implemented to support operators with different language requirements and different national currency requirements. PeopleSoft application modules can be licensed and installed in nine different international languages, including: Canadian French, Dutch, English (U.S.), French, German, International English, Japanese, Portuguese, and Spanish. Translated versions of the applications display all application text, including menu text, panel text, message text, and even much of the application data itself (some character data values) in one of the translated languages. This supports numerous concurrent users with different language preferences, all working in a single PeopleSoft database with translated versions of essentially the same functioning application.

The process of implementing and potentially customizing the applications to support different languages and currencies is termed the "globalization" process. In Chapter 18 we will discuss the concepts of globalization and present the steps that the application developer will take to customize a global application or build a new global application. If an organization has a "base" language application and wants to translate it to make it global, this can be performed at any (later) point in time. While we present this topic in detail at the end of this book, a large globalization effort should not be considered as an afterthought but should be planned for at the start of the implementation project.

04

Design the Application

The application development or customization effort must begin with the analyst or programmer gaining an understanding of the business requirements for the application in question. Undoubtedly, this step is one of the most difficult and has the potential for misunderstandings that may be very difficult to resolve later in the application development or customization project. While there are numerous formal approaches to business requirements analysis, this is the phase of the application development process that seems the least "systematic" (to us) and most dependent on the experience and insights of the developer.

45

We offer here a *very* general discussion of basic techniques that may be used to gather business requirements. We also suggest formats for documenting these requirements to share with other developers and for review with the business sponsors of the application project. We encourage the reader to utilize any requirements analysis techniques that are familiar and to produce a reasonably detailed requirements document.

The requirements document should serve as a useful reference throughout the application project, providing input for the design phase, reminders during the development phase, and even a basis for test case development. The requirements document should serve as a useful introduction for the many developers who will follow the original developers and will be asked to support and maintain this application system. At a minimum, the design document should include a data model of the data required for the application and a process description of the required application functions. The data model will ultimately be the basis for the development of data fields and records in our PeopleTools application. The process description will be the basis for the development of application menus and screens. However, there is no specific PeopleSoft application design tool or technique for producing the data model or process description.

Requirements Analysis

From discussion with business people familiar with the business functions that are the subject of the new information system, we may obtain a general understanding of the functions. Another valuable source of information may be standard operating procedure guides, employee handbooks, training manuals, or any other documentation that describes the existing business functions. The analyst may also wish to observe these business functions as they are currently performed. Through examination of these functions (using any sources available) the analyst will break apart or *decompose* the functions into an organized set of relatively short, simple business processes. Each of these business processes may be thought of as a single step in the larger business function. Each is likely to be developed as an online screen or background program in our new information system. One method to document the business processes is development of an indented and numbered list as a representation of a business process decomposition. Of course, this document should be thoroughly reviewed and approved by the business people and managers knowledgeable about the business functions.

From discussions with individuals familiar with the business functions, the analyst will begin to develop an understanding of the data required to support the business processes. Other sources of information that may be available include existing business forms, transaction reports, and activity logs. We will define a "data entity" to be some thing of lasting interest in the performance of the subject business functions (e.g. a person, place, thing). The analyst must identify and describe the significant data entities within the scope of the new information system. Collecting a list of the attributes for each data entity (e.g. full name for a person) is also required. These data entities and attributes will be the building blocks for our application database. We think of the data entities as the nouns in our discussion of the application area, while we think of the processes as the verbs.

Gap Analysis

In designing a modification or customization to an existing PeopleSoft application, the most direct requirements analysis technique may be to perform a *gap analysis*. In this approach the business requirements are defined, and then the existing application functions are examined. Each meaningful difference between the defined business requirements and the existing (available) application functions is noted as a potential *gap*. Gaps may be noted but may be determined to be insignificant to the business. For each significant gap, a data model and process description should be developed. Alternatively, revisions should be made to the current data model and process descriptions if they are available.

Context Diagram

For some new development or customization design efforts, it may be helpful to create a context diagram illustrating the significant flows of information in and out of the business function being examined (flows may be from/to various other internal or external organizations). This serves several purposes. First, it may help the developer to discover business processes not previously considered or to identify data entities not previously considered. At a minimum, the context diagram will help to identify data interfaces (e.g. input/output files) that may be required in the information system. Perhaps most important, the context diagram may help the developer discuss the scope of the proposed new information system with the business managers.

Data Model

As discussed in Chapter 3, the data that are important to the users of any PeopleTools application are stored in a collection of relational database tables called the application data tables. The design of these relational tables is critical to the functioning of the PeopleTools application. Development or update of the application data model is the formal process for understanding and documenting the basic application data structures. We will describe the development of a type of data model known as an entity-relationship model and then the use of a technique known as data normalization.

Entity Relationship Model

We have defined a data entity to be something of lasting interest to the business function (e.g. a person, place, thing). Each data entity is typically implemented in our database as a single table. We will further define the relationships between data entities. These will be supported through the selection of keys to our tables.

From discussion with business people familiar with the business function, examination of business forms, review of sample data, and even observation of the business functions that are the subject of the new information system, the analyst has identified a set of required data entities and required attributes of each entity. At this point the analyst should attempt to select the key to each data entity. The key to a data entity is the data attribute or combination of several data attributes that uniquely identifies an occurrence of the data entity. Keys are typically codes or numbers that identify something (for example, a Part Number in a PARTS table).

The next step in the development of the data model is to examine the inherent relationships that exist between the various data entities. Understanding the relationships between the data entities, and the discovery of new data entities, leads to the drawing of the Entity–Relationship Diagram (ERD). The relationship between two data entities may be a one-to-one, a one-to-many, or a many-to-many relationship. Each type of relationship is discussed below.

One-to-one relationships are generally rare, often indicating that the two data entities can be combined into a single entity. The two data entities will have the same unique key. An example might be the relationship between a PERSON and a SPOUSE. Presumably a PERSON may only have one SPOUSE at a time. However, if the relationship may become a one-to-many (over time) it is best to define two different data entities in the entity relationship model.

One-to-many relationships between data entities are much more common. An example might be the relationship between one SUPPLIER and its many PRODUCTS. In the one-to-many type relationship the "Many" data entity in the relationship has a key that includes the key of the "One" data entity in the relationship, plus at least one additional field. For our example, the key to the SUPPLIER data entity might be the Supplier ID while the key to the PROD-UCT data entity might be the Supplier ID plus a specific Product Code. Please refer to Figure 4.1 for our first illustration of an entity–relationship diagram. We will use a simple ERD convention, with a rectangular box representing each data entity, and a line with an arrow representing each relationship. The end of the line with the arrow will indicate the data entity with many occurrences in the one-to-many relationship.

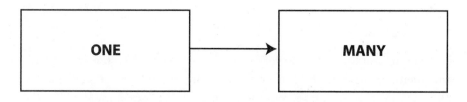

Figure 4.1   *Simple ERD convention showing a one-to-many relationship*

Many-to-many relationships are also very common. However these must be resolved into a pair of one-to-many relationships to be stored in the relational database. The resolution is accomplished by finding a new intersection data entity between the two data entities in the many-to-many relationship. For example, there may be many ORDERS for a particular PRODUCT and many PRODUCTS included in a single ORDER. However we find that one ORDER contains many lines of detail referred to as ORDER-ITEMS, and that one PRODUCT is included on many ORDER-ITEMS. In this example, the newly considered ORDER-ITEM data entity is the intersection of the ORDER and PRODUCT entities. Please see Figure 4.2 for a simple ERD showing the resolution of this many-to-many relationship.

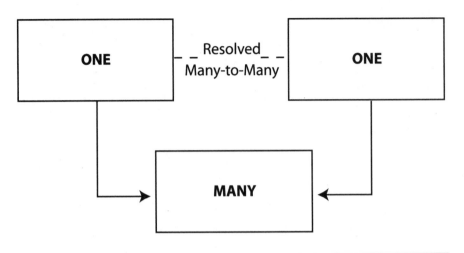

Figure 4.2   *Simple ERD showing the resolution of a many-to-many relationship*

Normalization

Data normalization is another very powerful technique that should be applied along with creation of the Entity–Relationship model. In simple (intuitive) terms a data entity is in normal form if that entity has a primary key and all of the other non-key attributes are dependent on the key, the whole key, and nothing but the key. If a data entity is found *not* to be in normal form, the usual solution is to break out some of the non-key attributes and define a new data entity with those attributes. The key of this new data entity will generally be one of the attributes that remains on the original table (to relate the new entity back to the original entity). For an example of data normalization, please consider the following data entity ORDER-ITEM. The key is Order Number and Product Code to identify uniquely the ordered items (or line items).

Table 4.1   *ORDER-ITEM data entity and attributes,*
              illustrating need for normalization

Order Number	Product Code	Product Name	Quantity Ordered
1000	123	Glove	10
1000	456	Bat	5
2000	123	Glove	20

In this example the Product Name attribute does not depend on the *whole* key, but rather just depends on the Product Code. Therefore this attribute would be removed from this data entity as part of the normalization process. In this example, the Product Name would be found on the PRODUCT data entity.

Notes on Data Modeling

An excellent reference on the subject of relational database management systems, with thorough treatment of the normalization process, is found in *An Introduction to Database Systems*, (Third edition) by C. J. Date (Addison-Wesley). There are many specialized tools and techniques available for the development of sophisticated data models. While there are several ERD conventions and data modeling tools that support the different conventions, we have utilized a simple and common form. Please refer to the case study design Chapter 19 for an example of an ERD for our sample application.

Again, we encourage the reader to use those data analysis methods and design tools that are familiar and available. There is no requirement for PeopleTools to use a specific method or tool, only the requirement to produce a data model that will be the basis for the definition of fields and records in the Application Designer tool. The development of the field and record definitions and the eventual implementation of relational database table views will be the subject of the next part of the book, Understanding the Data.

Process Design

In addition to the data model for the application database, the business processes must be defined. Understanding the business processes will provide direction in design of the application panels and navigation. Process design begins with examination of the process decomposition by the application developer. For each significant process, a reasonably detailed description should be prepared and should include the business rules for performance of the process (e.g. frequency, data edits, calculations, etc.). Each of the described business processes that is to be performed by a user of the application is likely to be designed as one or more screens or programs in the application. From development of the process descriptions and approval by the business managers, we shift our attention to the design of the user interface (the "window" into the application).

The activities performed in developing the user interface are perhaps the most fun and creative step in an application development process, and in this area

PeopleTools is no exception. Naturally, the development process begins with the design of the user interface. Perhaps the most important and certainly the most apparent to the users of our application will be the design of the application panels, including the arrangement of fields of data on the panel. Additionally, the design of the user interface includes decisions about the navigation to the actual panel through menus, the appearance of the PeopleSoft Search dialog boxes, and the selection of appropriate user actions. Finally, the design of the user interface may include consideration of the application security constraints.

Panel Design

A panel is the PeopleTools term for an application screen or window. Referring to the data model, the developer will recall the data entities and attributes required to support the business process. By now, these data entities and attributes will have been defined as PeopleTools records and fields, and the resulting database tables have now been created. Hence, in the design of the new panels, the fields of data required on the panels will typically be taken directly from these records.

The application developer now has the enviable position of approaching the design of the panel with an understanding of the information requirements (the blank canvas is not nearly so intimidating with this as a starting point). A developer will typically begin to draw out the panel design using paper and pencil, or perhaps a group of developers and the users will meet to discuss the panels and draw them out on a large whiteboard with markers. Alternatively, using the PeopleTools Application Designer tool, the developer may draw sample panels relatively quickly (Chapter 9). Regardless of how the panel design is drawn, these illustrations must be carefully reviewed with the end-users of the new application. The review is intended to ensure that the panels are complete from the perspective of the application user and that they are a fair and accurate representation of the required business functions.

Beyond the panel image, attention must be given to definition of the rules relating to the business function. For example, certain fields of data may be required—meaning a user must enter a value into the field. Likewise, there may be data validation rules for certain data elements—meaning the value must come from a set of valid values. Some of these business rules will be established within PeopleTools in the record definition (Chapter 6). There may be other business rules, such as field calculations or cross-validation of values, that will be implemented within PeopleCode (Chapters 12–15). All business rules that are relevant for a particular panel should be noted on the panel design document. Again, these should be reviewed with the application user to ensure that the panels and the related business rules are complete and accurate. Incidentally, the panel design and other design documents will be extremely useful as the developer prepares to test the application. The application should function as designed.

Navigation Design

Recall from our introduction to the end-user view of PeopleSoft applications that navigation within the application from panel to panel is fairly standard. User actions are defined within PeopleTools as are many of the application menu bars and the icons in the menu tool bar. The application developer controls the placement of newly created panels into panel groups and then into menus (Chapter 11). This is another consideration for the design of the user interface. The developer should consider grouping panels in a menu based on panel usage patterns. Panels that are expected to be used together should be placed together on a menu.

Application security considerations may lead the developer to separate panels onto different menus. In fact, security requirements may force the developer to split a single "logically" designed panel into two distinct panels. For example, if certain data fields appearing on a panel are very sensitive and only for a very limited user audience, they should be placed on a separate panel. This is because it is simplest to restrict users to specific functions based on panel and action combinations (Chapter 16).

Once a menu item is selected by the application user, access to the data on a particular panel is (generally) limited through use of a Search dialog box. The selection of the appropriate Search dialog box and the appearance of the Search dialog box is another set of design decisions for the application developer. The appearance and function of the Search dialog box is based on the Search record selected and the record field properties of the selected record. Any number of panels may utilize the same Search record—the access to each of these panels will be preceded by the display of the same Search dialog box.

Summary

All aspects of the requirements analysis and design are important to the development of the application. The design should be well understood and well documented prior to moving onto the development stages of the application. Insufficient understanding of the business requirements or incomplete agreement on the design will lead to increased questions and difficulties later in the application development project.

Part 2

Understanding the Data

05

Define Fields

A field is the first and smallest component object created for a PeopleSoft application. It should be considered the "building block" of your application. In relational database terms, a field generally becomes a column on a relational table.

One of the most critical things to understand about a field is that it has global attributes. A field may be used in multiple places in the application. If the attributes of a field are changed, those changes will immediately take effect throughout the application. Therefore, when making a change to a field, it is important to understand where and how that field is being used throughout the application. It is not recommended that field changes be made to any PeopleSoft provided fields in their delivered applications. Later in this chapter, we will review how to check where fields are being used throughout the application if a change is necessary.

A question often asked by developers is: When should a new field be created versus using an existing field? There is no clearcut answer to this question. When the data requirements have been determined, there might be an existing field that seems appropriate to use for the application customization. The field must be evaluated to determine if all of the attributes associated with the field meet the new data requirements. If they do, then it would be appropriate to use the existing field. It is appropriate to create a new field if the requirements are different.

Field Attributes

A field has attributes which describe it. Some attributes are common to all field types and others vary depending on the type of field. This section will address the attributes common to all fields. The field-specific attributes will be covered in the field type section which follows.

The field length must be determined for all field types (with the exception of date and time field types). The length should be based upon the expectations for the data. When the appropriate field length is considered, both current and future requirements should be taken into account. It would be difficult to change the field length in the future if it is determined that the field was not created with a large enough length.

The long name and short name are the names that the user will see in the application. By default, these are field labels that will be used on the panels. Therefore, it is important to make these names meaningful and clear. Abbreviations should be avoided unless it is very clear what they mean. The long name will allow 50 characters while the short name will allow 30 characters. One reason for having long and short names is that on different panels you may want to refer to the same field by different names. Another reason would be to save space on a panel; a panel may have a lot going on and there may not be enough room on the panel for the long name; in that case, the short name would be used.

Again, because field attributes are global, if the long or short name is changed, the change will immediately carry through the entire application. This may be a desired effect. Perhaps the business manager decides after a year that he wants to change what a field is called on all panels. If the long and short names have been used throughout the application, then the change only has to be made in one place, the field definition. Application maintenance is therefore much easier. In contrast, if the developer had used static text throughout the application, the change requested by the business manager would have been much more difficult because the changes would have to be made on each and every panel. This approach is especially true when translating applications into non-base languages; it is much simpler to translate fields once and have all panels updated at once. (Refer to Chapter 18 for additional discussion on translating applications.)

Field Types

The first requirement that must be identified when creating a new field is what type of field should be created. Determining the answer to this question depends on how the field will be used and what type of data will be captured. After having completed the requirements analysis and the data model, this information should be clear to you as a developer. If a field is going to be used to capture cost, then a numeric field type would be appropriate. But if a field is going to be used to capture a contact name, then a character field would be appropriate.

It is important to note that once a field is created with a specific type identified, the field type cannot be changed. The only way to change the field type at that time would be to create a new field with the desired field type and resave this field with the already existing field name; the result will be that the new field will "overwrite" the field of the same name. Note that PeopleSoft does not allow multiple fields to have the same name even if they are different types. Field names must be distinct across all field types.

A *character* field type should be used to capture text based information. Figure 5.1 presents a field definition for a character field type. Character fields have very few attributes aside from the common attributes. The only other attribute that can be specified for a character field is the field format.

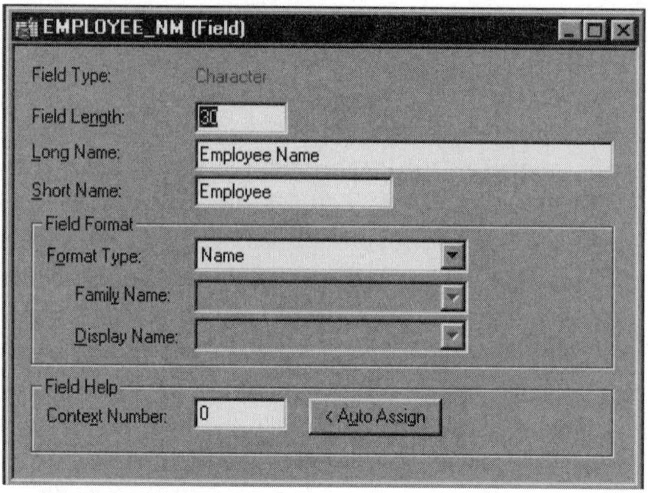

Figure 5.1   *Character field*

The field format arranges the information the user enters into the field so that it is displayed and stored to the database in a particular format. There is also an option to create custom field formats. The PeopleSoft-provided formats include: uppercase, mixed case, social security number (SSN), social identifier number (SIN), numbers only, raw binary, name, zip/postal code North American, zip/postal code International, phone number North American, and phone number International. For example, the name format uses the lastname,firstname (no spaces) as the format. This is the pattern the user must enter into the field and the pattern which gets stored to the database. The user must enter a name with the format of lastname,firstname into the field or it will not be possible to continue on and save the panel.

A *long character* field type, shown in Figure 5.2, should also be used to capture text-based information. Long character fields are typically used to capture comments when it is not certain how much text will be entered. The long character field can be a variable length field. It is recommended that the field length be set to zero. With a length of zero, the field will inherit the maximum length possible as provided by the database management system being used with PeopleSoft. PeopleSoft delivers a field called DESCRLONG with its applications. This field is defined as a long character field. For comments and long text, this field is typically used.

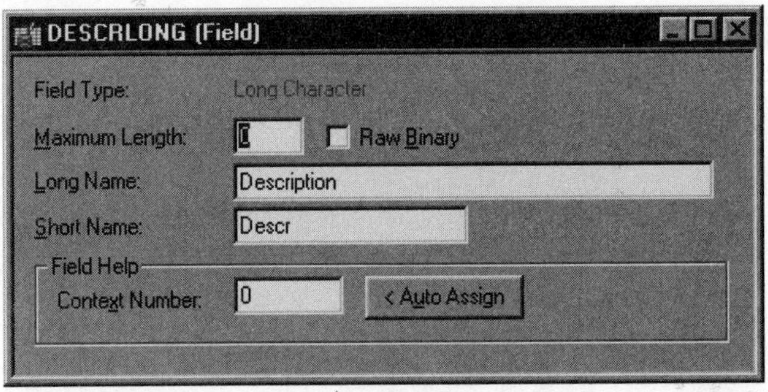

Figure 5.2   *Long Character field*

A *numeric* field type should be used to capture numeric information that will be used for calculations. An example of a numeric field is shown in Figure 5.3. The attributes of the numeric field that must be determined are: how long the field is going to be and how many decimal positions it will carry. The integer position indicates how many positions to the left of the decimal and the decimal positions indicate the number of positions to the right of the decimal.

A *signed number* field type is exactly the same as the numeric field type except that it allows the value captured to be negative or positive. Notice that in Figure 5.4 there is a check box for signed number; uncheck it and the field type will change to the field type number. This is the only exception to the rule that all field types must be determined when the field is created.

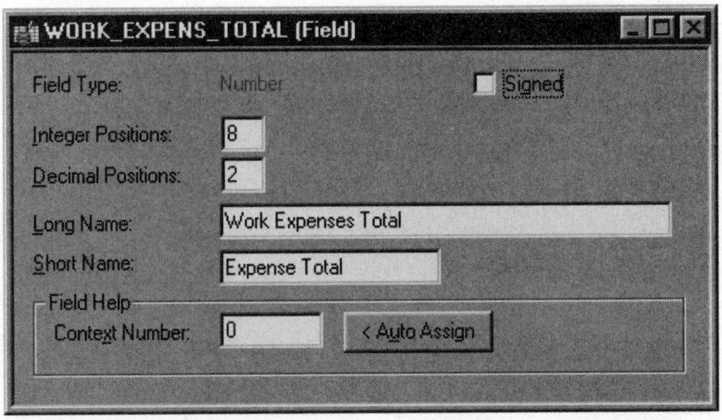

Figure 5.3   *Numeric field*

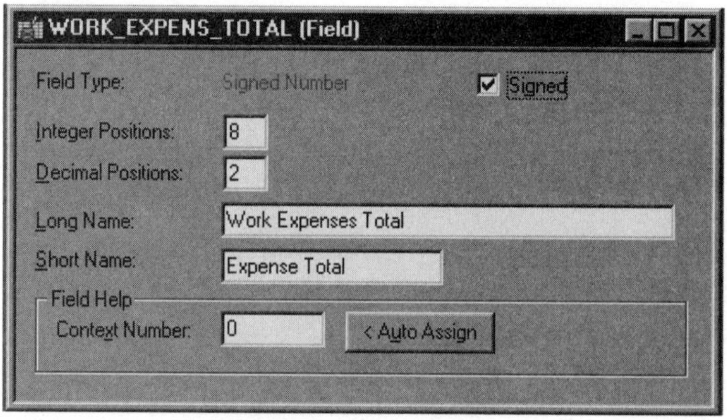

Figure 5.4 *Signed number field*

The *date* type field captures dates. A date field is shown in Figure 5.5.

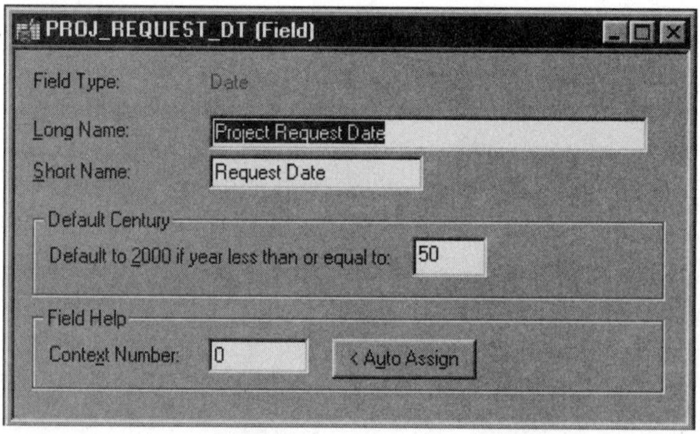

Figure 5.5 *Date field*

The important attribute that must be set for a date field is the default century. PeopleSoft will always write a four-digit year to the underlying database. The default century feature is to assist the user when entering a date. If a user enters a date using only a *two-digit year*, the application will determine what century to default to based on the attribute set in the field definition. If a user enters a four-digit date, the default century will have no impact; the system does not need to determine what century the user intended. The default century should be thought of as the threshold point. All two-digit years less than or equal to the default century value will be stored with the century 2000; all two-digit years greater than the default century value will be stored with the century 1900. For example, if a user enters the date 10/01/99 and the default century value is 50, the system will interpret the date as 10/01/1999. If a user enters the date 09/07/45 and the default century value is 50, the system will interpret the date as 09/07/2045. If a user enters the date 10/01/1999, the system will not use the default century because there is no need to set for date entered.

When a new date field is created, note that the default value for the default century is 50. This is the default century that PeopleSoft delivers with all the date fields provided with its applications. It is recommended the default century of 50 be used. The rationale behind this recommendation is that within an application, a user will become accustomed to the default being used. If on every date field, there is a different default, this will become confusing to the user. The only exception to this might be birthdate. On a birthdate field, it is recommended that the default century value be set to 0. This will be interpreted by PeopleSoft so that every date entered into this field will be interpreted as the year 1900.

The *time* field captures time. The attribute that must be selected for a time field is the format of the time. The time can be formatted in hours and minutes (HH:MI); hours, minutes and seconds (HH:MM:SS); and, hours, minutes, seconds and milliseconds (HH:MI:SS:999999).

The *datetime* field is a combination of a date field and a time field. It has all of the attributes of both those field types. This type of field is most typically used for a date/time stamp for system processes. This field is typically not used for data entry by the user.

The *image* type field allows an image to be stored in the database. The type of image file must be specified as part of the field attributes. Image fields tend to require a great deal of memory so they should be used cautiously.

Translate Values

With every PeopleSoft application, a translate table (named XLATTABLE) is delivered. The translate table is a table used to store lists of valid values. The translate table is used for validation purposes. The table is delivered with a specific format and must not be modified. The table can be opened in Application Designer to view the fields that are used to build the table. The translate table has the following columns: FIELDNAME, LANGUAGE_CD, FIELDVALUE, EFFDT, VERSION, EFF_STATUS, XLATLONGNAME,

XLATSHORTNAME, LASTUPDDTTM, and LASTUPDOPRID. For example, the EFF_STATUS field is setup in the translate table with two values, active and inactive. Therefore, within the translate table, there will be two separate rows, as shown in Table 5.1.

Table 5.1   *Entries in translate table*

COLUMN NAME	ROW 1	ROW 2
FIELDNAME	EFF_STATUS	EFF_STATUS
LANGUAGE_CD	ENG	ENG
FIELDVALUE	**A**	**I**
EFFDT	1/1/1900	1/1/1900
EFF_STATUS	A	A
XLATLONGNAME	ACTIVE	INACTIVE
XLATSHORTNAME	ACTIVE	INACTIVE

Why are we introducing the concept of translate table in the fields chapter? Translate values are associated with a particular field. Translate values can only be assigned to a field which is a character type field and has a field length less than or equal to 4. Translate values should be used for a field that has a short list of valid values which are static and relatively stable. One reason for these rules is that the translate values are maintained through Application Designer and therefore developers rather than users, have the responsibility to update these values. Another reason is that the translate table is used throughout the application for all fields that have translate values. For every value of every field, a new entry is made to the translate table; in order to maintain the table at a manageable level, the list of values for each field should be short. PeopleSoft recommends that the number of values for a field not exceed 30. The reason to keep the list relatively short is that the list of values is stored in cache on the client machine.

To add translate values for a particular field, refer to the field properties either from the Toolbar or from the menu, **File/Object Properties**. When a field has been defined as a character field with a length of no more than four, in addition to the General tab, there will be another tab for Translate Values, as shown in Figure 5.6. From this tab, translate values can be added.

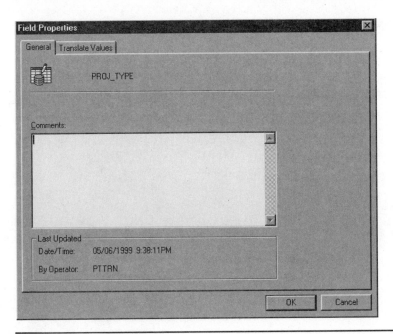

Figure 5.6 *Translate tab*

Figure 5.7 shows a field with translate values. Note that translate values are effective dated. Later in the book, the concept of effective dating will be covered in more detail. For now, it is important to understand that the effective date of the translate value will determine when the value becomes available for a user to see. PeopleSoft recommends that all translate values be set with an effective date of 1/1/1900. This is the effective date that the delivered applications will have for all the translate values. The rationale for this date is that the values will be available to the user from the year 1900 forward. There will certainly be exceptions to this recommendation. There may be a business rule that requires some translate values not to be dated as early as that because it does not make sense. For example, if a company introduces an additional color for a product it sells and the color is only available as of 8/01/1999, it is likely that the company would not want this translate value to be available as of 1/1/1900. The rule of thumb is to use 1/1/1900 except where the business rule mandates otherwise. Also note that translate values have an effective status; typically, translate values have an effective status of active, 'A.'

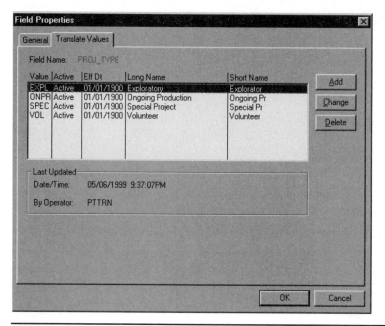

Figure 5.7   *Translate values*

Also recommended when establishing translate values is that the field length always be set to four characters. Although it can be argued that this may require unnecessary space at the database level, this will have minor impact on the performance of the application. The reason for recommending always using the length of four is so that if the number of values required increases over time, it is not limited by the length of the field.

Object References

We have mentioned that fields have global attributes and before making any changes to a field, one *must* understand where this field is being used throughout the application. PeopleSoft provides a utility to help make this determination. Within Application Designer, under the Edit menu, there is an option called Find Object References (shown in Figure 5.8). This option will be available if the field is open in the object workspace. This utility will list all records and panels where the field is being used. The output will appear in the output window.

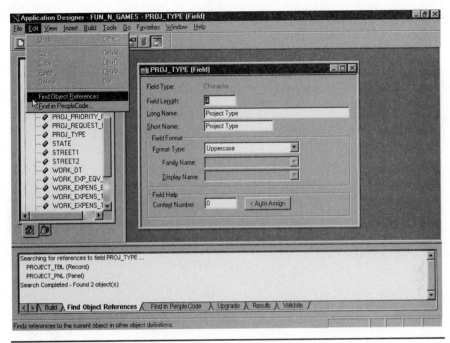

Figure 5.8 *Object references*

06

Define Record

A record definition is the combination of fields that will be used to capture information in the application. The record definition should be thought of as the instructions to the underlying database as to how the relational table should be built. Therefore, it is common to think of the record definition as the table definition, although PeopleSoft refrains from using this terminology.

To create a record definition, a new object can be created from either the
File/New menu or from the Toolbar. When a new record is created, a record
definition will be opened in the object workspace, as shown in Figure 6.1.

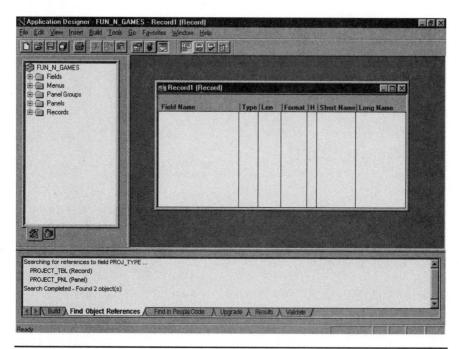

Figure 6.1   *New record definition*

The building blocks for a record definition are fields, which can be placed into
the record definition in two ways. Fields can either be "dragged and dropped"
from the project workspace or the **Insert/Field** menu can be used. The "drag
and drop" functionality was introduced in PeopleSoft's version 7 tool and can
ease the development process. To move fields around in the record definition,
"cut and paste" functionality is available. To move a field, right click on the
field and choose **Cut** from the popup menu or the short-cut keys
<CTRL><X>; then, highlight the field after which you want to position your
field and right click and choose **Paste** or **<CTRL><V>**. Once all the fields
required have been placed in the record definition in the desired sequence, the
record field properties must be defined.

Record Field Properties

The record field properties set the attributes of each field within the record. These properties are only relevant for the *field* within the current *record*. This field can exist in another record definition with very different record field properties. Recall that properties of fields, discussed in Chapter 5, are global. In contrast, the properties of record fields apply only to the field on that specific record. For example, in Record1, FieldA could be defined as a key field; in Record2, FieldA (the same field) may or may not be defined as a key.

There are three means of accessing the record field properties. The developer can either: double click on the field within the record definition, use the menu **Edit/Record Field Properties**, or right click on the field within the record definition and choose **Record Field Properties** from the pop-up menu. Once the Record Field Properties window is open, there are two Properties tabs that must be reviewed and set for each record field, Use Attributes and Edit Attributes. Figure 6.2 shows the first of these two tabs.

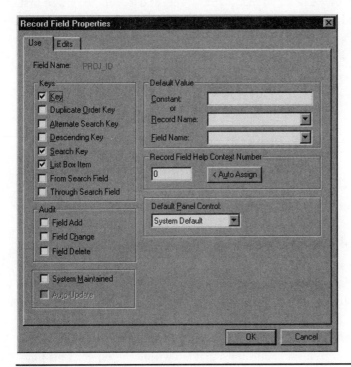

Figure 6.2   *Use Attributes tab*

Use Attributes define how the field will be "used" within the record. The significant properties that are set include whether the field is a key, whether any audits are performed, and any default values applied. We will review each of the Use attributes to be considered.

Every record must have one or more *key field*(s) defined. Key field(s) identify a unique row of data on a relational table. Keys must be placed at the top of the record definition and should always be marked "required" on the Edits tab.

A *duplicate order key* is also a key to the relational table but it will allow duplicate values to be entered into the field. Duplicate order keys are typically used as part of a concatenated key (a key made up of multiple fields). Duplicate order keys should be placed at the top of the record definition and should also be marked "required" on the Edits tab.

By default, all fields that are marked as keys will be sorted in ascending order (e.g., A–Z or 1/1/1999-12/31/1999). The *descending key* attribute allows the sort order to be marked as descending (e.g., Z–A, 12/31/1999-1/1/1999). This attribute will be disabled unless the field is marked as a key. Descending keys are typically used for date fields so that the most recent date can be viewed first.

A field is marked as a *search key* if the record will be used as a Search record for the application and this specific field will be used to assist the user in selecting a row of data. (Refer to Search record section later in this chapter.) A field cannot be marked as a search key unless it is a physical key to the record.

A field is marked as an *alternate search key* if the record will be used as a Search record and this field will be used as an Alternate Search field. A field cannot be marked as an alternate search key and a search key; these are mutually exclusive. Also, an alternate search cannot be a (physical) key on the record.

A *list box item* serves multiple purposes. A field will be marked as a list box item if the record is to be used as a Search record and the developer wants this field to show in a list of values for the user to view. This field may also be set as a list box item when the record will *not* be used as a search record; but when the record will be used as a prompt table on another record and the developer would like the field to show in the list box presented to the user. By default, when the search or alternate search key attributes are selected, the list box item will also be selected.

The *From Search* field and *Through Search* field functionality is new to PeopleTools version 7.5. It allows a user to set a range when using the Search dialog box and only search for valid values that fall within the range. This functionality will be covered in more detail in the Search record section later in this chapter.

A default value is the value automatically populated when a new row is inserted by the user. A default value is only the initial value populated into the field; this value can be changed by the user. If a default value is desired, it should be placed in the default values section of the record field properties. A *constant default* will populate the field with a constant value. This value does not need to be specified in quotation marks. If the value is a valid value from a translate table, the value must be specified in the same format and case as it is stored in the translate table. Current system date and current system time can also be used as default values using %date and %time, respectively. An alternative to using a constant value is to use a *record/field value*. In this case, the default value is populated based upon the value that is stored in the specified record and field. A good example of when this might be used is in the COUNTRY field in the application. Each application is installed with an INSTALLATION table which stores an INSTALLATION.COUNTRY field. Any time the COUNTRY field is used on a panel, it would be helpful to the user that the INSTALLATION.COUNTRY field be used as the record/field default value. Therefore, if the application is installed in USA, any time a user needs to enter the country, the default value will be populated with USA. Again, default values can be overwritten by the application user.

The *Edit Attributes* tab (shown in Figure 6.3) specifies the validations that will be performed on the field. If the *required* edit box is checked, the user will be forced to enter a value into the field before the panel can be successfully saved. Key fields should always be marked as required. Other fields that should also be marked as required are alternate search keys, DESCR, EFFDT, EFF_STATUS, check box items, and radio buttons. Alternate search keys and DESCR should be marked as required because they will help the application users to search against the table, and therefore the field needs to be populated. Check box items and radio buttons should also be marked as required so that the user is forced to enter a value and a null value is not stored (it is recommended that both of these field types also have default values defined).

Reasonable date edit is a PeopleSoft-provided edit available for date type fields. It will test the date entered by the user to determine if it is either 30 days greater or 30 days less than the current system date. A warning will be issued to the user but the user will be able to accept the date and continue. An example of when this edit would typically be used is in enrollment date field; when a user is enrolling an individual into a benefits program or into a training class, the enrollment date should be close to the system date.

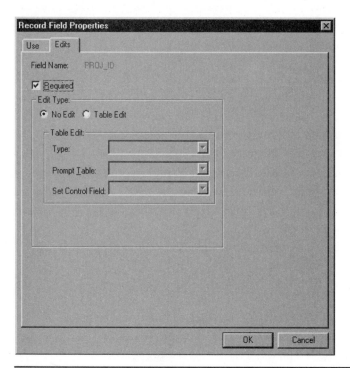

Figure 6.3   *Edit Attributes tab*

While the required edit and reasonable date edit do not demand that any additional information be specified, table edits are much more specific to the field on which the edit is being performed. Table edits will force the field to be edited against another table. There are four different types of table edits that will be discussed: prompt table edit, prompt table with no edit, translate table and yes/no edit. A *prompt table edit* has two functions. First, it provides a list of valid values to the user from the table that is being prompted against. Second, it validates the value entered by the user against the valid values that exist in the prompt table. If a user enters a value that does not exist on the prompt table, an error message will appear and the user will be forced to choose an existing value from the list. A *prompt table with no edit* is similar to the prompt table edit but does not perform the second function. It does not validate the value entered by the user. The prompt table with no edit will allow the user to choose a valid value from the list but will also allow entry of a value that does not exist on the list. The value entered by the user will not be added to the prompt table and therefore will not be automatically available to other users who might want to enter the same value. This type of edit is used very infrequently.

The *translate table edit* is used for fields that have values established in the translate table; it will only allow users to select valid values that exist in the translate table for the field. If a field has values created in the translate table and then the field is placed in the record definition, this edit will be set by default. If the field is placed in the record definition before the translate values are created, this edit will not be set and must be selected manually.

The *Yes/No edit* is used for fields that will have either an on or an off value. The Yes/No values do not have to be set up in the translate table, but are provided by PeopleSoft. Fields that utilize a Yes/No edit must be set up as character field with a length of 1. These field types will typically be displayed on the panel as a check box.

Display Icons

When a record is open in the object workspace, new buttons become available on the toolbar (refer to Figure 6.4). These icons allow the developer to view the record field properties in a summary view.

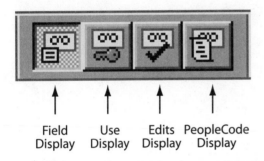

Field   Use   Edits PeopleCode
Display Display Display   Display

Figure 6.4 *Display icons*

The *field display* icon shows the record with the global field characteristics of field name, type, length, format, and the short and long names. The *use display* icon shows the use attributes for each record field on the record including the keys, search and alternate search keys, list box items, defaults, and audits. The *edits display* icon shows the edit attributes for each record field on the record including the edits performed, the prompt table (if applicable), reasonableness date, and if PeopleCode exists for the fields. The *PeopleCode display* icon shows the PeopleCode events and indicates a Yes when there is code available for a particular field in the record. PeopleCode will be discussed in detail in Chapters 12, 13, 14, and 15.

Record Properties

In addition to record field properties which are specific to the fields on a record, the record itself has properties. To access the record properties, the record should be open in the object workspace. The properties can be accessed from the menu using **File/Object Properties**, using the icon for object properties, or by using the hotkeys **<Alt><Enter>**.

The record properties box has three tabs, General, Use and Type. The General tab is used for documentation. It provides a place for a record description and an area for additional comments. This would be the appropriate section to include the purpose of the record, when it was created, who created it, or if this was an existing record, what modifications were made, when and why. For purposes of change control, when a record is changed, documentation can be added here so that other developers understand why changes were made.

The Use tab, shown in Figure 6.5, establishes many of the relationships that exist between the record and other records.

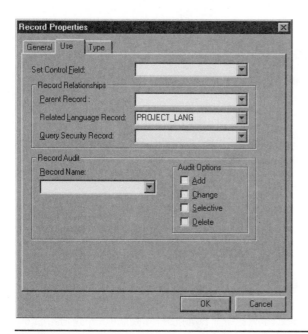

Figure 6.5   *Record Use tab*

The *set control field* is used in applications when taking advantage of the SetID or table sharing functionality that PeopleSoft delivers. It will define what field will control the rows that are shared on this record. (This is an advanced topic which is outside the scope of this book.)

The *parent record* is also defined in the Use tab. A child record is defined as a record that has the same keys as the parent, in the same sort order, plus at least one additional key. It is important to note that the parent relationship specified here is *only* used by the query tool. The parent record can be specified here but there is no validation performed to ensure that a valid parent-child relationship exists.

The *related language record* is the associated record used when taking advantage of a multi-language installation. The related language record contains information specific to the language that would be used by the operator. This will be discussed further in the Globalization chapter.

The *query security record* specified here limits access to the record based on a security view. Therefore, if the operator's rights should be limited based on a view, then the view record should be specified.

The Type tab defines the type of record. Figure 6.6 presents the Type tab. Generally, a record may be a table, view, subrecord or derived/work record. Our discussion thus far has assumed an SQL table or a physical table that will exist in the underlying relational database. Views and derived/work records will be discussed in Chapters 7 and 15, respectively. A discussion of subrecords follows.

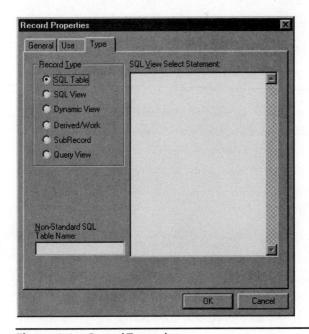

Figure 6.6   *Record Type tab*

Subrecords

The *subrecord* is used to save a group of related fields together that are often used repeatedly on records. This is a convenience for the developer because it allows fields to be grouped together into an object and then that object can be used over and over again. The benefit of using a subrecord is that it makes maintenance much easier. Once fields are grouped together as one object, any changes to that group of fields will only have to be made at the subrecord level. For example the street, city, state, and zip code fields of a mailing address could be saved together as a subrecord. A subrecord is defined in much the same way as other "ordinary" records are defined. Fields are either dragged and dropped into the record from the current project workspace field list or inserted from the Application Designer menu bar. All record field properties found on the Use and Edits tab can be assigned. The record is identified by the developer as a subrecord by clicking record type of Subrecord on the Record Properties and then saving the record. The PeopleSoft naming convention for subrecords is the suffix "_SBR" on the record name to indicate that it is a subrecord.

The subrecord by itself is not very useful. However, the application developer may now include this subrecord in one or more other records—wherever this particular group of record fields is needed. The subrecord is included in another record by opening a record in the object workspace, selecting **Insert/Subrecord** from the Application Designer menu, and then choosing the desired subrecord. A subrecord cannot be dragged and dropped from the project workspace; the insert menu must be used. Notice in Figure 6.7 that the subrecord comes into the "main" record as a single line.

The subrecord fields are not visible and the subrecord field properties cannot be changed from within the main record definition. To view the field list or make subrecord field changes the developer must return to the subrecord definition. If the main record is type SQL table (typically) then the application developer must still perform the SQL build on the main record definition (the build process will be discussed in Chapter 8). It is *not* possible to perform the SQL build process on a subrecord. When the SQL build of the main record is completed, the new SQL table will have columns for all record fields and expanded subrecord fields (as expected); this will not be visible within the Application Designer but the underlying database table will show this. From the perspective of the underlying RDMS, there is no knowledge of a sub-record. Since any changes to the subrecord will affect all records that use the subrecord, it may be necessary to rebuild all the "main" records that use the subrecord when a change is made. (For discussion on Building Objects, refer to Chapter 8.)

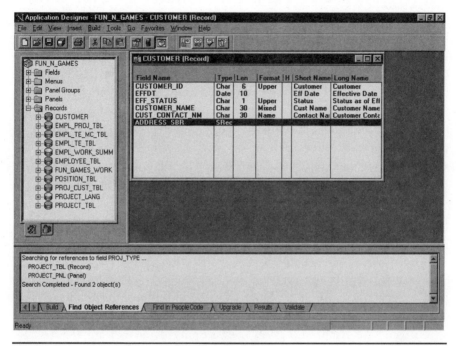

Figure 6.7 *Record definition with Subrecord line*

Effective Dated Records

Perhaps one of the most important concepts to be understood when working with a PeopleSoft application is the concept of effective dating. Stated in its simplest terms, effective dating allows historical data to be maintained in a table. This section will define how an effective dated record is created, how it is used online and what actions are available to the user based on the fact that the record is effective dated.

A record that is effective dated must have the reserved field EFFDT included as part of its concatenated key and must also include EFF_STATUS as a required field. In addition, the field EFFSEQ may be included as part of the concatenated key. The effective date field permits multiple rows at the same high-level key to be maintained. This allows historical, current, and future rows to be maintained in the database. The reason to use effective dated functionality is business driven. If there is no interest in maintaining historical information, i.e., the information can be overwritten, effective dating does not need to be included. If a business requirement is to be able to maintain, for example, a history of product retail prices over time, effective dating should be employed.

Effective-dated rows on a table are categorized into three types of rows: history, current, and future. There is no flag on the record which indicates the type of row. The row category is determined based upon the effective date and its relative position to both the system date and the current row date. It is important to understand the definitions of these categories. The *current* row is the row of data where the effective date is closest to today's date (usually the system date) without exceeding today's date. There is only one current row per high-level key on a table. *Historical* rows are all rows with effective dates less than the effective date of the current row. There can be multiple historical rows per high level-key. *Future* rows are all rows where the effective dates are greater than the system date. There can be multiple future rows per high-level key.

We should walk through an example to further explain this concept. Continue with the assumption that our business rule requires us to maintain the product retail prices over time. Table 6.1 shows a section of the product pricing table. The PRODUCT_ID and EFFDT are keys to the table. Assume that the system date is September 12, 1999. The far right column indicates the row category of history (H), current (C), and future (F).

Table 6.1 *Product pricing table*

PRODUCT_ID	EFFDT	EFF_STATUS	PRICE	H/C/F
PR01	01/01/1997	A	5.00	H
PR01	06/03/1997	A	5.25	H
PR01	12/31/1997	A	5.35	H
PR01	09/08/1998	A	5.40	H
PR01	09/10/1999	A	5.95	C
PR01	09/13/1999	A	6.00	F
PR01	12/31/1999	A	6.10	F
XY05	05/05/1998	A	25.28	H
XY05	05/15/1998	A	25.30	H
XY05	08/07/1998	A	25.45	C
XY05	12/31/1999	A	26.05	F

This section of the table represents rows for two different products, PR01 and XY05. The key learning points from this example include:

▲ For both products PR01 and XY05, there are current, history and future rows
▲ There can be multiple history and future rows
▲ The current row for product PR01 is the row with the effective date of 9/10/1999 even though this date is further from the current system date than the next dated row of 9/13/1999; but the 9/13/1999 row is greater than the current system date and therefore does not meet the rule(s) for definition of the current row
▲ The current row for product XY05 is the row with effective date of 8/7/1998 even though this row is over a year prior to the current system date; again, the next row available does not meet the rule(s) for definition of the current row.

In Chapter 2, we discussed user actions. Two of these apply only to effective-dated records; these are the actions of Update/Display All and Correction. These two actions make sense only for effective dated records. They should never be issued if the record is not effective dated. It is important to understand what records the user will have the rights to view or update based on the user action selected. See Table 6.2 below.

Table 6.2   *User access to rows*

	Access to View Rows	**Access to Update Rows**
Update/Display	current and future	future
Update/Display All	history, current and future	future
Correction	history, current and future	history, current and future

It is clear from Table 6.2 that the Correction mode allows users access to view and modify all records. The reason to have effective-dated records is to maintain history. A user who has access to modify history records may change data that should otherwise be unchanged. This is a powerful action and should be provided to users with caution.

Search Records

The purpose of a search record is to create the Search dialog box. A record should only have Search and Alternate Search keys defined if the record will be used as a search record. Not all records are Search records. Search records can be SQL tables or views. A view will often be used as a Search record to limit the rows of data the user will have access to on the panel. This will be discussed further in Chapter 7.

A record is defined as a Search record by specifying Search keys and Alternate Search keys. As mentioned earlier, the Search keys must be physical keys to the record whereas Alternate Search keys are not physical keys. Search keys will be displayed to the user in the top frame of the Search dialog box, as shown in Figure 6.8.

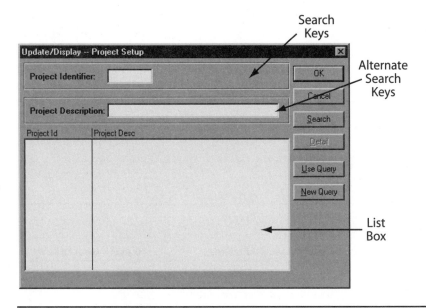

Figure 6.8   *Search dialog box*

The Alternate Search keys will be displayed in the bottom frame. The order in which the Search keys will be displayed is based on the order the fields appear in the record definition. Therefore, it is important for the developer to think about how the user will be searching against the data so the fields are ordered correctly.

The bottom section of the Search dialog box is referred to as the *List Box*. When the user does not enter the full key or unique information to identify a row of data, the List Box will display the Search and Alternate Search keys and possibly additional information. The List Box is used to assist the user in selecting the appropriate record. The List Box fields are also defined in the record definition. By default, Search and Alternate Search keys will be defined as List Box items; it is recommended that the default be accepted. Any other fields the developer thinks will be useful to the user in determining the appropriate row of data should also be included as List Box item. Note that List Box items will cause additional indexes to be built for those fields.

The screen shots below demonstrate how the Search and Alternate Search keys defined in the record definition (Figure 6.9) will produce the desired Search dialog box (Figure 6.10).

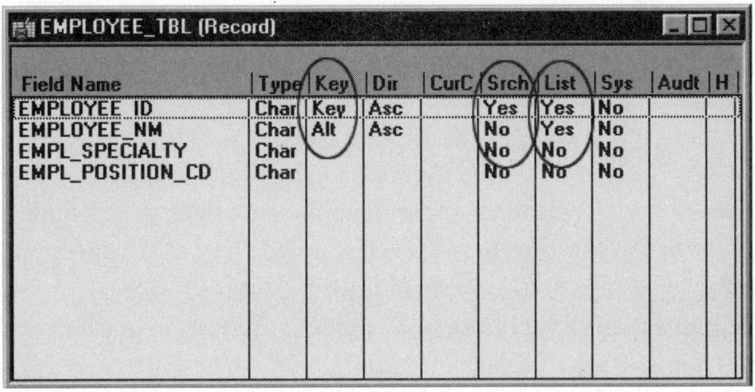

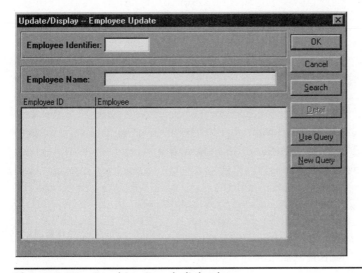

Figure 6.9 *Record definition with Search and Alternate Search keys*

Figure 6.10 *Resulting Search dialog box*

New to version 7.5 is a feature referred to as *from and through search keys*. This is a powerful function that can ease a user's ability to narrow the search. It allows a user to specify a range of values within which to search. Because this feature requires the use of an SQL view, this topic will be reviewed in more detail in Chapter 7.

Data Auditing

Two types of data audits can be performed in the application: field-level audits and record-level audits. The primary consideration when using either of these is performance. The purpose of audits is to track, by operator ID and date/time stamp, what additions, changes, or deletions were made to fields on a record. Transparent to the user, each time a user makes changes to the record, entries are being written to other tables to record what was done. As one might imagine, this would have an impact on the performance of the application. It is strongly suggested that this be discussed with application users to explain that the requirement to use auditing will cause deterioration in the application's performance.

Field-level audits require very little work to set up. In fact, for a developer, the only steps necessary are to check the Field Add, Field Change or Field Delete checkboxes on the Use tab of the Record Field properties window. Field-level audits are used specifically to capture information about changes to that field on that particular record. The audit information is stored in the PeopleTools table, PSAUDIT. The PSAUDIT table will capture the operator ID, the date/time stamp, the audit action (A, C, D), the record and field names, and the old and new values.

Record-level audits are used when there is a need to capture audit information at the record level. They require additional setup. For each record on which the developer wants to conduct audits, there must be a corresponding audit record created. The recommendation for creating an audit record is to clone the record for which the audit functionality is desired. Audit records should be named with the AUDIT_ prefix and should not have any key fields. To capture audit information, typically the audit fields found on the PSAUDIT table will be added to the audit record. For example, the fields AUDIT_OPRID, AUDIT_STAMP, and AUDIT_ACTN are added to the top of the new record definition (refer to Figure 6.11).

```
┌─────────────────────────────────────────────────────────────────┐
│ 🖳 AUDIT_EMPLOYEE (Record)                          _ □ ✕         │
├─────────────────────────────────────────────────────────────────┤
│ Field Name      |Type|Key |Dir  |CurC |Srch |List |Sys |Audt |H |│
│ AUDIT_OPRID     Char                    No    No    No           │
│ AUDIT_STAMP     DtTm                    No    No    No           │
│ AUDIT_ACTN      Char                    No    No    No           │
│ EMPLOYEE_ID     Char                    No    No    No           │
│ EMPLOYEE_NM     Char                    No    No    No           │
│ EMPL_SPECIALTY  Char                    No    No    No           │
│                                                                   │
│                                                                   │
└─────────────────────────────────────────────────────────────────┘
```

Figure 6.11   *Audit record*

The AUDIT_STAMP field should be marked as auto-update in the Record Field properties Use tab on the record. This will indicate to the application processor that this field should be updated with the system date and time. Once the audit record is created, the main record or the record that is being audited must have certain properties set. In the Record properties, in the Use tab, the Record Audit name must be specified. In addition, the type of audit to be performed must be indicated by the checkbox items of Add, Change, Selective, and Delete. Each of these actions will determine what is written to the audit record. The Add action will write a row to the audit table when a new row of data is added to the main table; the Change action will write a row to the audit table whenever a row of data is changed on the main table; the Selective action will write a row to the audit table when a change is made to the main table for a specific field included on the audit record; and the Delete action will write a row to the audit table when a new row of data is deleted from the main table.

In summary, the steps necessary to perform record level audits are:

1. Create audit record (by cloning existing record).
2. Include audit fields such as fields AUDIT_OPRID, AUDIT_STAMP. and AUDIT_ACTN.
3. Mark the AUDIT_STAMP field as autoupdate in the Record Field properties.
4. On the main record, name the audit record and set the audit actions.

07

Define Views

In Chapter 6, we discussed creating the record definition for an SQL table (a physical table defined to
the underlying database). In comparison, a view is a
logical representation of a database table; it is like a
snapshot of the table(s). Because a view is a logical
representation of tables, it does not physically store
any data. It is typically used to limit the rows or
columns of data a user can access. A view may also
be used to join tables together so that the joined
information is available for use. To define a view in
PeopleTools, the same record definition is used that
was used to define for the SQL table. However,
there are some differences in the definition and the
properties of a view.

PeopleSoft recognizes that a record will be used as a view by the attribute set on the record properties. The Type tab on the Record Properties window has a list of radio buttons which indicate the type of record (refer to Figure 7.1). Views can be of various types: SQL, Dynamic, and Query. The most common view types are SQL and Query. Both of these types can be used to create the same view. The only difference is the method by which the view is created. Later in the chapter, we will discuss SQL views and Query views in more detail.

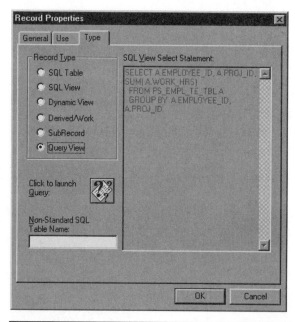

Figure 7.1   *Record Type tab*

Uses of Views

Views are most often used in PeopleSoft applications as search records or on summary panels.

Recall that a search record is used to create the Search dialog box which is presented to the user prior to launching the panel. Often there is a need to present information in the Search dialog box that is stored in multiple tables. To accomplish this, a view is created and then used as the search record. Probably the most common reason for using a view as a search record is to limit the list of values a particular user will see. Therefore, a view can actually be used as a means of security for the application. A view can be created that will join security tables which select the operator ID and will join to other tables which store the application data. With criteria in the SQL statement, the list of values accessible to the user will be limited based upon that user's operator ID. This is a common use of views in the PeopleSoft delivered modules and is sometimes referred to as row-level security.

Summary panels present information stored in the database to the user; they do not allow the user to enter information. They can be thought of as online reports. Views play an important role on summary panels for two reasons. First, views allow information stored in the database tables to be presented to the user in a new sort order. For example, the Project_Cust table stores projects and the customers who have requested these projects (Table 7.1).

Table 7.1 *Project_Cust table*

FIELD	TYPE	LENGTH	SHORT NAME	LONG NAME
PROJ_ID	CHAR	6	Project ID	Project ID
CUST_ID	CHAR	4	Customer	Customer ID
REQUEST_DT	DATE	10	Request Date	Request Date
DEADLINE_DT	DATE	10	Deadline Date	Deadline Date
DESCRLONG	LONG	0	Descr	Description

However, a sales manager might want to look at all customers and the projects they have requested. Because this information is already available in the SQL table, the data would just need to be reordered to provide the manager the required "view." The information would be reordered by selecting the data from the table in a view. The SQL below represents the syntax that would be used to create the view.

```
Create View PS_EXAMPLE (CUST_ID, PROJ_ID) as
Select CUST_ID, PROJ_ID from PS_PROJECT_CUST
```

The second reason views are useful on summary panels is because they allow information stored in multiple database tables to be combined and presented to the user. A single SQL table may not have all the information that would be useful to the user; by creating a view, two or more tables could be combined and then the view could be used as the basis for developing the panel.

SQL Views

SQL views are view definitions created by the developer by writing an SQL statement in the record definition. The steps for creating an SQL view are:

1. Identify the requirements for the view including the base tables, fields, and criteria. Consider how the view will be used and the key fields needed to identify a unique row.

2. Create a new record definition. Drag or insert the fields into the record definition based on the requirements. Enter a record description in the Record Properties General tab. Save the record definition. The standard naming conventions for view records are the recordname_VW or recordname_SRCH (if the view record will be used as a search record).

3. Open the Record Properties and change the record type to SQL View. When this is done, the SQL View Select Statement window is enabled, as shown in Figure 7.2. The developer should then type the SQL that will be used to create the view. When the SQL view is created, the fields must be selected in the SQL statement in the same order in which they appear in the View Record definition. This will keep the PeopleTools record definition in sync with the underlying relational table. Also, when the SQL statement is written for the SQL view, all PeopleSoft application tables must be referred to by the full table name, PS_ prefix.

4. Save the record. Note that there is no validation done on the SQL statement—if the SQL is incorrect, the record definition will still save successfully.

Dynamic views are similar to SQL views. However, they are never stored in the underlying database. The SQL statement is stored and is executed when the application is run. In contrast to other view record definitions, there is no need to build the dynamic view. The views are dynamically created at the time they are used on the panel or in PeopleCode. A dynamic view can sometimes provide better performance than an SQL view. The dynamic view is created the same way the SQL view is created.

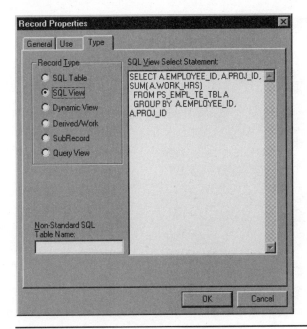

Figure 7.2 *SQL View Select statement*

Query Views

Query views are record definitions created using PeopleSoft's Query tool. The advantage to using the Query view is that the developer does not have to write an SQL statement; the Query tool will generate the SQL based on the fields and criteria selected in the tool. The steps for creating a query view are:

1. Identify the requirements for the view including the base tables, fields and criteria. Consider how the view will be used and the key fields needed to identify a unique row.

2. Create a new record definition. Enter a record description in the Record Properties General tab. Save the record definition. The Query view cannot be created until the record definition is saved. The standard naming convention for view records is recordname_VW. Do *not* drag and drop or insert fields into the record. The fields will be "automatically" brought into the record *after* the query is created.

3. Open the record properties and change the record type to Query View. When the type is changed to Query View, the Query button will appear, as shown in Figure 7.3.

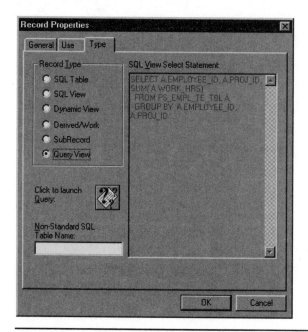

Figure 7.3   *Record Properties box with Query button*

4. Click on the **Query** button and the Query tool will open. Within the
   Query tool, there are six tabs: Dictionary, Fields, Criteria, Having
   Criteria, SQL, and Results.

The Dictionary tab is where the tables used to create the view will be selected.
The tab displays the database dictionary on the left side and the query dictionary on the right side, as shown in Figure 7.4.

The database dictionary is a listing of tables within the application. The
query dictionary will display the tables included in the view. The key point to
remember is that the database dictionary is used to select the "main" record for
the query. The "main" record is typically the record where the majority of the
data for the view is stored and is also the record from which other records can
be joined. Once the "main" record is selected, other records can be selected
from the database dictionary (depending on security access) but it is recommended that other records be selected by joining through the main record. To
select the main record, highlight the record and then either double click on the
record name or use the button between the database dictionary and the query
dictionary to move the record over. Once a record is selected, the tool automatically brings the developer into the Fields tab; we recommend that you go back

to the Database tab and continue the selection of the tables before moving on to selecting the fields from the table(s).

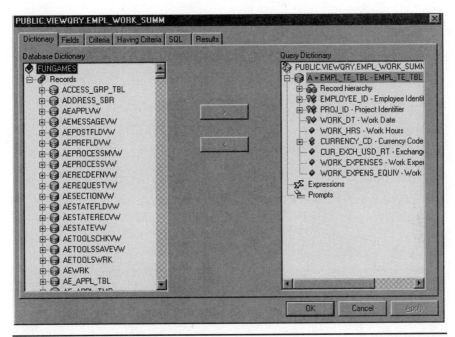

Figure 7.4   *Query tool—Dictionary tab*

Joining records in the query can be accomplished through the record hierarchy or the related record hierarchy or by selecting another record from the database dictionary. The record hierarchy and the related record hierarchy are established through record relationships.

To access the record hierarchy, click the plus sign next to the record selected in the query dictionary. Expanding this will list the record hierarchy plus all the fields that exist within that record. The record hierarchy also has a plus sign which can be expanded. When this is done the record hierarchy will show all children and grandchildren records but will not display sibling records. In order for the children and grandchildren records to be displayed, the parent record must be specified in the Use tab of Record Properties on the child record. Figure 7.5 shows the Record Use tab.

To join to a record through the record hierarchy (shown in Figure 7.6), either double click on the record or right click and choose **New Join**. Either of these methods will create a join and add the record into the query dictionary. Note that PeopleSoft automatically assigns aliases to records when joining them.

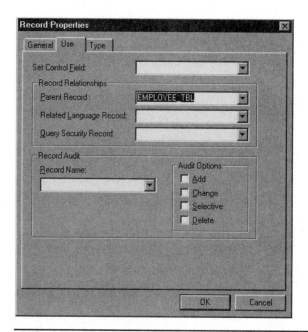

Figure 7.5   *Record Use tab*

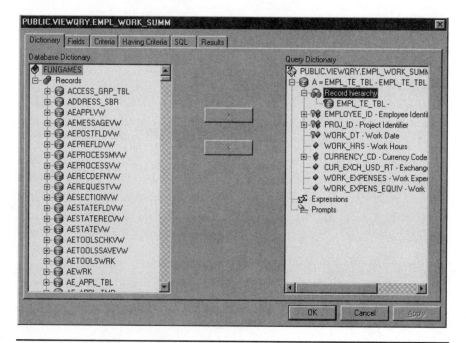

Figure 7.6   *Record hierarchy (in Query tool)*

The related record hierarchy is accessed through a specific field that exists on a record in the query. When expanding on the plus sign for a record, observe that when the fields are listed, some of the fields may have plus signs next to them. Expanding on a plus sign will cause the related record hierarchy to be displayed. The related record hierarchy exists because on this particular record, this field has a Prompt Table edit to another record. When the related record hierarchy is expanded, the Prompt Table record will be displayed and its children/grandchildren records will also be accessible.

Joining a record through the related record hierarchy (shown in Figure 7.7) is done the same way as through the record hierarchy; either double click on the record or right click and choose **New Join**. Either of these methods will create a join and add the record into the query dictionary.

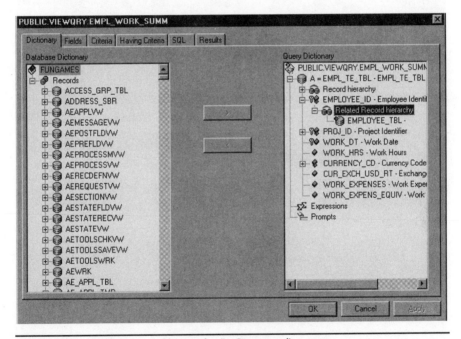

Figure 7.7 *Related Record hierarchy (in Query tool)*

Additional records can also be added to the query dictionary from the database dictionary. When this approach is used, PeopleSoft will look for common fields between the record that is being added and the existing records in the query dictionary. Based on the common fields, it will propose the joins that can be created between the records. A dialog box will be presented (Figure 7.8) which will show the joins selected; these joins can then be modified.

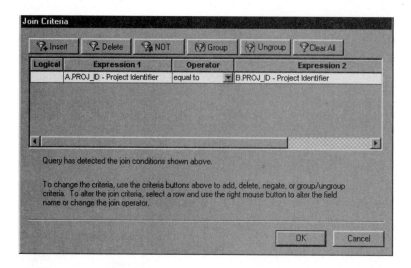

Figure 7.8   *Join dialog box*

If a record is selected which has no relationship to the existing records in the query dictionary, the tool will present a message box (Figure 7.9) indicating that there is no relationship. The record will still be included in the query.

Figure 7.9   *Message box for "Invalid" join*

This situation can be "dangerous" because there will be no way actually to join the records selected. We recommend that when records are joined, the record hierarchy or related record hierarchy methods be used. Note that when PeopleSoft creates a join using the database dictionary, the join will be explicitly stated on the Criteria tab; this is not the case for joins created through the record hierarchy or related record hierarchy.

Once all the records to be joined are selected, the fields to be displayed from these records must be selected. In the Dictionary tab, highlight the record in the query dictionary from which you want to select fields. Then, move into the Fields tab as shown in Figure 7.10. Listed in the Fields tab will be all the fields that exist in that record. To select a field, double click in the column or right click and choose **Select**. The sequence of the column will be the sequence of the fields in your query view.

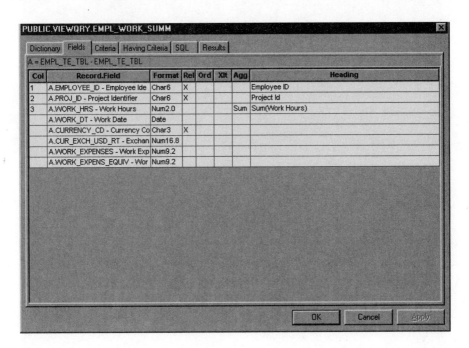

Figure 7.10   *Query tool—Fields tab*

Once you choose fields, if you want rearrange the sequence, right click and choose **Column** and then enter the column number you want (PeopleSoft will then renumber the remaining columns selected). To include fields from another record, go back to the Dictionary tab, highlight that record, and then return to the Fields tab.

The Criteria tab, shown in Figure 7.11, is where the conditional statements for the query are assigned. To include additional criteria, choose the Insert button and a new line will be added to the criteria. Note that it will be added, by default, with the Boolean operator AND. If these criteria should use OR, double click and the operator will change to an OR.

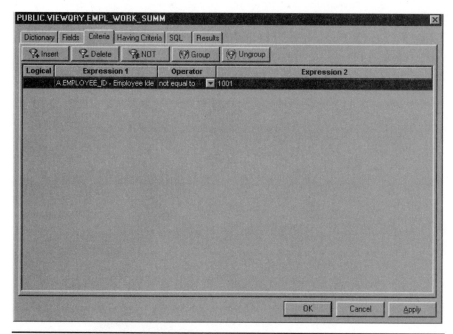

Figure 7.11   *Query tool—Criteria tab*

Once a new criteria line is inserted, the Expression 1 must be selected. Right click and you will be prompted to select either a field or an expression. Selecting a field will provide access to any field on any record included in the query. A condition may be established on a field even if that field is not selected as part of the data set for the query results.

After the field or expression is selected, the comparison operator must be chosen. The operators available include all those one would use when writing a SQL statement such as:

equal to	not between
not equal to	exists
greater than	does not exist
not greater than	like
less than	not like
not less than	is null
in list	is not null
not in list	in tree
between	not in tree

To complete the criteria statement, the second expression must be selected. Again, right click on the expression. The list of choices available will depend on the comparison operator selected. Table 7.2 shows a selected list of operators available.

Table 7.2 *Operators for use in Criteria statement*

Expression	Definition
Field	Allows for any field within the records selected for the query to be used as comparison
Expression	Allows any valid SQL expression
Constant	Allows a constant value
Subquery	Allows another query to be used; subquery option will allow a query within a query
Prompt	Creates a prompt so that when the query is run, the user is prompted to enter a value
In List	Allows a list of values to be entered; typically used with the In List or Not in List operators
Current Date	Current system date
Tree Option	Allows a tree to be selected and then allows a list of valid values that exist within that tree

The Having Criteria tab is also used for conditional statements. This tab should be used when query results have been grouped and a condition is placed on the grouped results.

The SQL tab displays the SQL that will be generated to create the Query view. The SQL cannot be changed in the SQL tab. It is a good idea to copy (**<CTRL><C>**) the SQL statement so it can be pasted (**<CTRL><V>**) into the General tab of the record definition for documentation purposes. Those developers proficient in SQL may be interested in reviewing the SQL generated.

The Results tab will display the data that will be returned when the query view is executed. The Results tab is useful for two reasons. It permits the developer to test whether the data expected to be returned is the correct set of data. It also indicates how long it will take for the query results to be returned; if the query takes a while to return the data set, it should be considered that this is also how long the user will wait for the data. If the query is created and then some changes are made, clicking on the Results tab will result in a dialog box

(Figure 7.12) that asks if the query result set should be refreshed. Clicking **Yes** will display the new set of data.

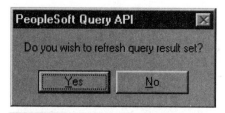

Figure 7.12   *Refresh dialog box*

Once the query is created, press **OK**. This will bring you back to the Record Properties. The SQL will get populated in the SQL View Select statement. In contrast to the SQL view, this SQL cannot be edited. To make any changes to the query view, launch back into the tool and make the appropriate changes. We recommend pasting the SQL copied from the SQL tab in the query tool into the General tab, in the comments section.

If OK is hit again, the fields selected in the Query view will populate the Query record definition. At this point, the record definition appears like any other record. For a Query view, Use and Edit attributes can be set. We recommend that any default values be removed from the view because the view will just be looking through to the underlying relational table. If default values remain on the view definition, ghost rows on a panel could result. The ghost row appears to be a row of data, though in fact no row exists. An example is presented in Figure 7.13.

Additionally, fields should *not* be reordered once in the record definition; if it is determined that the fields should be in a different sequence, the Query tool must be relaunched and the fields must be reordered from there. This will ensure that the Query view definition and the SQL view generated are in sync with one another.

After a change is made to the view by relaunching the Query tool, PeopleTools will present a dialog box which will confirm that the changes should overwrite the existing view record. If the changes are needed, click **OK**. Note that any defaults removed will now need to be removed again and any other record field properties will also have to be reselected.

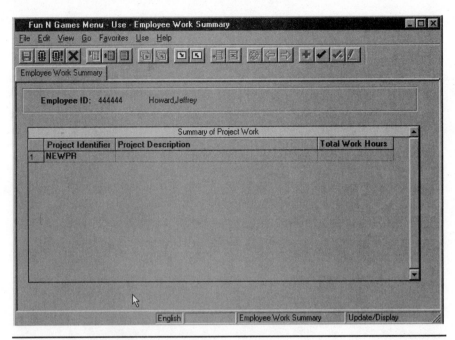

Figure 7.13   *Ghost Rows on a panel*

From and Through Search Keys

In Chapter 6, a new feature of PeopleTools 7.5, From and Through search keys were introduced. Recall that From and Through search keys allow the user to select a range of key values in the Search dialog box as shown in Figure 7.14. To take advantage of this feature, an SQL view must be created. The From and Through search keys *cannot* be developed using a query view. To accomplish this, use the following steps:

1. An SQL record must be defined.
2. In the SQL statement, the field for which a range of values will be entered should be entered twice in the Select statement. Any other fields used as part of the search view should also be selected.
3. In the record definition, the first field listed should be the key field for which the range will exist. The second field listed should be a new field created to act as the Through key field. By convention, this field is named THRU_fieldname.

4. Set the Record Field properties for the first key field. The field should be marked as a key field, Search key, List Box item and as a *From search field*.
5. Set the Record Field properties for the second key field, i.e., the through search field. This field should be marked as key field, search key, and as a *Through search field*. Note that the this second field should not be marked as a List Box item. If it is, the values will be listed twice in the list box (recall that in your SQL, you selected the same field twice).
6. Save the view record and build the view.

It is possible to have multiple From and Through search keys in a single view record. Remember that this feature provides additional flexibility to the user for using the Search dialog box. Although multiple From and Through search keys can be used, the developer should use judgment because the Search dialog box can become overly complicated and difficult to manage.

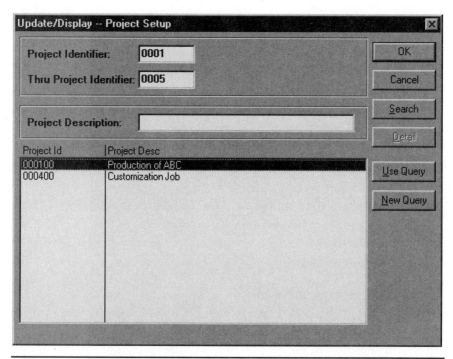

Figure 7.14   *Search dialog box with From and Through search keys*

08

Build SQL Objects

The final step in the process of understanding your application data is to build the SQL objects that will be required for your application. Up to this point the developer has created field definitions and record definitions working within the Application Designer. The result has been the update of PeopleTools tables with entries for new fields and new records, but no new physical database tables, views, or indexes have yet been created. The PeopleTools developer can proceed into the design and development of the user interface (e.g. panels) without stopping to build the SQL objects, but the physical database objects will be required to test the execution of the new PeopleTools application.

103

For the PeopleTools application developer, the build SQL object step is fairly simple to perform in the Application Designer tool. However, it is important to understand what is happening "behind the scenes" in the creation of the actual database objects. Remember that PeopleSoft applications will execute on any one of several RDBMSs such as ORACLE, DB2, SQL/Server, etc. Regardless of the RDBMS, the approach to the build SQL object step is the same. Based on the record definitions in the PeopleTools tables and on the build options selected by the developer in the Application Designer, PeopleTools will generate (and will optionally execute) appropriate SQL syntax to create the tables in the relational database.

The build SQL object step can be performed to create database tables or database views, to alter database tables, and to create database indexes. Each of these operations will be discussed in this chapter. In many projects it will be advisable or even required for the developer to review the SQL objects and build syntax with an experienced database administrator (DBA) on the project team. Particularly in a "production" database, the application developer will typically *not* execute the SQL directly but will provide the SQL scripts to a DBA for review prior to execution.

Build Table

The build table operation is based on a selected PeopleTools record definition. This record must have the record type of SQL Table set within record properties (Chapter 6). The result of the build table operation will be the creation of a relational database table named "PS_recordname". For example, the build table operation for the "Product_Tbl" record will result in the creation of the "PS_Product_Tbl" relational database table.

The actual build operation can be initiated in one of several ways. Open the record that is the subject of the build in the Object Workspace, and select **Build/Current Object** from the Application Designer menu, or click on the **Build** ("building blocks") icon from the toolbar. Alternatively, right click on the record of interest in the Project Workspace list of records and select **Build**. Any of these three methods will bring the application developer to the Build dialog box. Please refer to Figure 8.1 for the Build dialog box for the PROJECT_TBL record from our case application.

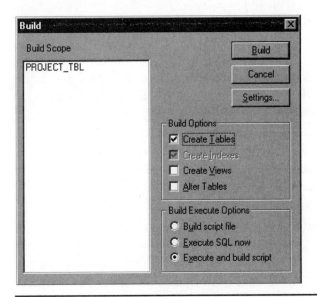

Figure 8.1 *Sample Build dialog box for Create table*

Within the Build dialog box, the developer should immediately note the names of the record(s) within the Build Scope, and ensure that the intended record(s) has been selected. Next, the developer should check the **Create Tables** box within the Build Options frame. Notice that selecting the Create Tables checkbox automatically also checks the Create Indexes box and the Create Indexes box cannot be deselected by the developer. We will discuss the Create Index, Create Views, and Alter Table choices later in this chapter. The final decision for the developer to make in the Build dialog box is the selection of one of the Build Execute Options, as follows in Table 8.1.

Table 8.1 *Description of Build Execute Options*

Build Execute Options	Description of Option
Build Script File	Generate the appropriate SQL statements required to create the relational database table and save the SQL syntax in a script file. The table will not be created until this SQL syntax is actually executed.
Execute SQL Now	Generate the appropriate SQL statements and execute the SQL commands, but do *not* save the syntax to a script file.
Execute and Build Script	Generate the appropriate SQL statements, execute the SQL commands, *and* save the syntax to a script file.

Certainly the Execute and Build Script is the most useful option for the developer, as it builds the table immediately and also saves the SQL statements for subsequent review.

Regardless of the Build Execute Option selected, the actual SQL statements generated are identical. The first SQL statement is a "Drop table PS_Record." Note that dropping a table completely deletes the table, its data contents, any views defined on that table, and any access rights (grants) to that table. Therefore, executing the Build for a record that has already been built and has an existing relational table can be dangerous! Build settings discussed in detail later in this chapter, can prevent the processing of a table that already exists. Of course, for a newly created record, the Drop statement is harmless. The next SQL statement generated by the Build process is the Create table PS_Record command that creates a relational table with columns corresponding to the record fields. By default, PeopleTools makes character and number fields Not Null in the database (putting the value of spaces in character and zero in number fields). Following the Create Table command, the next SQL statement(s) is one or more Create Index commands depending on the keys, Search keys, Alternate Search keys, List box items, and custom indexes defined on the record. Please refer to the following example of SQL syntax generated by the Build process for the PROJECT_TBL record.

```
DROP TABLE PS_PROJECT_TBL
CREATE TABLE PS_PROJECT_TBL (PROJ_ID CHAR(6) NOT NULL,
   PROJ_DESC CHAR(30) NOT NULL,
   PROJ_TYPE CHAR(4) NOT NULL,
   PROJ_PRIORITY_RT CHAR(1) NOT NULL,
   PROJ_ESTIM_HRS SMALLINT NOT NULL,
   PROJ_ACTUAL_HRS SMALLINT NOT NULL)
COMMIT
CREATE UNIQUE INDEX PS_PROJECT_TBL ON PS_PROJECT_TBL (PROJ_ID)
CREATE INDEX PS#PROJECT_TBL ON PS_PROJECT_TBL (PROJ_ID,
      PROJ_DESC)
CREATE INDEX PSOPROJECT_TBL ON PS_PROJECT_TBL (PROJ_DESC,
      PROJ_ID)
COMMIT
```

Build Views

Similar to the Build of a relational database table, the Build of a relational database view is based on a PeopleTools record definition. To build a view, set the record type to either SQL View or Query View in the Record Properties (see Chapter 7 for details). For the record type of Dynamic View the Build is not available or required; these select statements are executed at run time. The Build View operation is initiated from within the Application Designer tool just as for the Build Table operation, either by selecting the **Build/Current object** item from the menu while the subject record is current within the object workspace or clicking on the **Build** blocks icon in the Application Designer toolbar. The same Build dialog box will be displayed. Again, the developer should immediately note the names of the record(s) within Build Scope, and ensure that the intended view record(s) has been selected. Next, the developer should check the **Create View** box within the Build Options frame. The Build Execute Options are the same as for the Build table, and again the Execute and Build Script is the recommended choice. Please see Figure 8.2 for the Build dialog box for the EMPL_WORK_SUMM view record from our case.

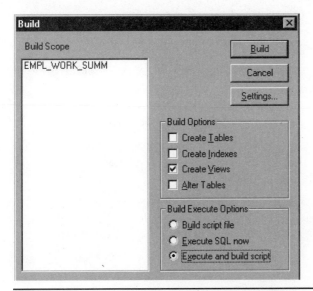

Figure 8.2   *Sample Build dialog box for Create View*

The result of the Build View operation is a set of SQL statements that will be executed to create the database view. The main SQL statement generated by the Build process is the Create View PS_Record... As Select... command that creates a relational view with columns corresponding to the record fields and with the embedded Select statement. The embedded Select statement, whether entered by the developer in a SQL view or generated by the Query tool in a Query view, is used to select the columns from the database tables that the view references. See the following example of SQL syntax generated by the Build View process for the EMPL_WORK_SUMM record.

```
CREATE VIEW PS_EMPL_WORK_SUMM (EMPLOYEE_ID, PROJ_ID, WORK_HRS)
     AS
  SELECT A.EMPLOYEE_ID, A.PROJ_ID, SUM( A.WORK_HRS) FROM
  PS_EMPL_TE_TBL A GROUP BY A.EMPLOYEE_ID, A.PROJ_ID
COMMIT
```

Alter Table

When an application developer changes the definition of a record of type SQL Table and the corresponding relational database table for that record already exists, it *may* be desirable to perform an *Alter Table* operation. Modifications to the record definition that change the physical structure of the relational database table require the developer to either build or alter that table. The specific types of record definition changes that will require the developer to build or alter the table include the following: adding or deleting a field, changing a field name, changing a field length, or changing a field data type.

Recall that the Build Table process will include SQL Drop Table and Create Table. The advantage of the Alter Table process, compared to the Build Table, is that the Alter Table will preserve the database table contents (rows of data). Naturally, if the database table is significant and contains business information that must be preserved an Alter Table will be required.

The Alter table process will be based on a revised PeopleTools record definition. The Alter Table operation is initiated from within the Application Designer tools just as for the Build Table or Build View operations. The same Build dialog box will be displayed. Again, the developer should immediately note the names of the record(s) within Build Scope, and ensure that the intended view record(s) has been selected. Next, the developer should check the Alter Tables box within the Build Options frame. Notice that selecting the Alter Tables checkbox automatically also checks the Create Indexes box,

although the Create Indexes box can now be deselected by the developer. The
Build Execute options are the same as for the Build Table and Build View. See
Figure 8.3 for the Build dialog box for an alteration of the PROJECT_TBL
record.

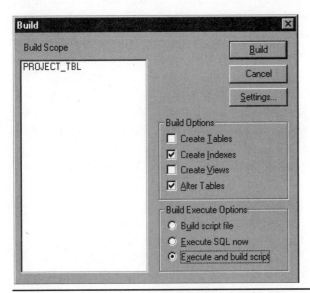

Figure 8.3   *Sample Build dialog box for Alter Table*

The result of the Alter Table operation is a set of SQL statements that will
be executed to modify the database table. The actual SQL statements generated will vary based on the nature of the change to the record structure. If
for example, the change is the addition of a field to the record, the first statement will be Alter Table PS_Record to add the new field. The next SQL
statement generated by the alter process will be an Update PS_Record command that will set the new field equal to default field values (if any). Please
refer to the following example of SQL syntax generated by the Alter Table
process, in this case adding the Project Manager field to the
PROJECT_TBL record.

```
ALTER TABLE PS_PROJECT_TBL ADD PROJ_MANAGER CHAR(30)
UPDATE PS_PROJECT_TBL SET PROJ_MANAGER = ' '
ALTER TABLE PS_PROJECT_TBL MODIFY PROJ_MANAGER NOT NULL
COMMIT
```

Indexes

PeopleTools will generate Create Index syntax to build one or more indexes on all new database tables. The standard indexes created by PeopleTools will be based on the keys, Alternate Search keys, and List Box items selected in the record definition that is the basis for the new table. As illustrated in the discussion of the Build Table process, these standard indexes are built by default when the underlying table is built. However, there may be occasion for the developer to change the designation of keys, Alternate Search keys, or List box items in a record after the database table is created. While the selection of a key is a structural change to the record that will require the developer to rebuild the base table and therefore rebuild the standard indexes, the designation of different Alternate Search keys or List box items will not require the developer to build the table. Rather, the developer may simply build the set of indexes on the base table.

The Build Index operation is initiated from within the Application Designer tool just as for the Build Table operation, either by selecting the **Build/Current object** item from the menu while the subject record is current within the object workspace or clicking on the building blocks icon in the Application Designer toolbar. The now familiar Build dialog box will be displayed. The developer should just check the Create Indexes box within the Build Options frame. Again, the Build Execute options remain the same as before. Please refer to the following example of SQL syntax generated by the Create Index process, again using the PROJECT_TBL record definition.

```
DROP INDEX PS_PROJECT_TBL
DROP INDEX PS#PROJECT_TBL
DROP INDEX PS0PROJECT_TBL
CREATE UNIQUE INDEX PS_PROJECT_TBL ON PS_PROJECT_TBL (PROJ_ID)
CREATE INDEX PS#PROJECT_TBL ON PS_PROJECT_TBL (PROJ_ID,
       PROJ_DESC)
CREATE INDEX PS0PROJECT_TBL ON PS_PROJECT_TBL (PROJ_DESC,
       PROJ_ID)
COMMIT
```

There may be reasons to create "custom" indexes in addition to these standard indexes created by the Build Table process. Within PeopleTools there is the capability to define additional database indexes. With the appropriate record open in the object workspace, the developer may select **Tools/Data Administration/Indexes** from the Application Designer menu bar to initiate the Change Record Indexes dialog box. Please see Figure 8.4 for the Change Record Indexes dialog box showing the standard indexes on the PROJECT_TBL record.

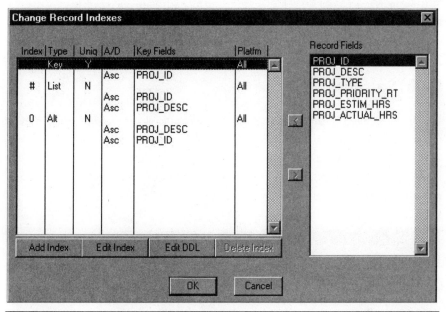

Figure 8.4   *Change Record Indexes dialog box*

In the Change Record Indexes dialog box, each of the standard indexes is found along with the Index Key fields. From this dialog box the developer may click **Add Index** and choose the desired fields for the new custom index from the base record definition. After completing the selection of indexes, the developer should (as above) choose **Build/Current Object** from the Application Designer menu and then check the **Create Indexes** box within the Build Options frame to initiate the Build Index process. The determination of whether additional indexes are needed will be based on the developer's knowledge of the database size and structure and the application use of the database table. Consultation with a project database administrator might be helpful. The PeopleSoft naming convention for the standard indexes as well as the custom indexes that may be defined in the Data Administration tool as follows in Table 8.2.

Table 8.2   *Naming convention for database indexes*

Index Name	Index Based on
PS _ Record Name	The keys (search keys) of the record
PS # Record Name	The list box items in the record
PS **0** Record Name (0– 9)	One for each alternate search key
PS **A** Record Name (A–Z)	One for each "custom" defined index

Build Settings

Execution of each of the various Build processes (Create Tables, Create Views, Create Indexes, Alter Tables) discussed here can be controlled by the application developer through use of the Build Settings dialog box. This is accessed by clicking the **Settings...** pushbutton from within the Build dialog box. Please refer to Figure 8.5 to see the first tab of the Build Settings dialog box.

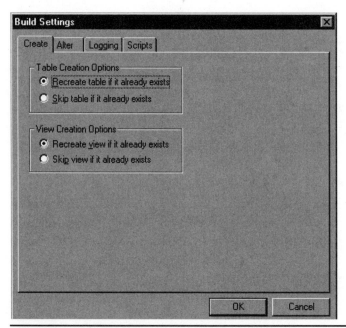

Figure 8.5   *Build Settings dialog box—Create tab*

On the Create tab of the Build Settings dialog box, Table Creation Options permit the developer to recreate a table if it already exists or, alternatively, skip the table if it already exists. As previously noted, to recreate an existing table will result in the loss of the table data contents. PeopleTools will display a warning to the developer of these consequences, as shown in Figure 8.6 below.

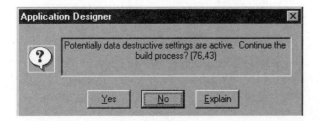

Figure 8.6   *Warning message generated by Recreate Table option*

Likewise, View Creation Options on the same tab in the Build Settings dialog box provides similar alternatives. The developer can choose to recreate or skip the Build of a view if it already exists. The skip settings may be useful if there are multiple records and views in the Build scope. These skip options will allow Build processing of records that have not yet been created, while not harming the existing tables and views.

On the Alter tab of the Build Settings dialog box, Drop Columns Options permits the developer to specify how to proceed in the case that a column has been removed from a table. The selection of Drop Column if Data Present will drop the column and write a warning to the log if data were present for that column. The selection of the Skip Record if Data Present option will cause the Alter process to fail and will write an error to the log if data were present for that column. Similarly, Change Column Length Options can prevent the inadvertent loss of data from a character field during an Alter process. Selection of Truncate Data if Field Too Short will simply truncate the column and write a warning to the log. Alternatively, selection of the Skip Record if Field Too Short option will cause the Alter process to fail and will write an error to the log. The Alter Any checkbox options allow for selective Alter processing of a change to a record definition. By default the Add, Change, Rename, and Delete of fields in a record definition will be processed. Please refer to Figure 8.7 for the Alter tab of theBuild Settings dialog box.

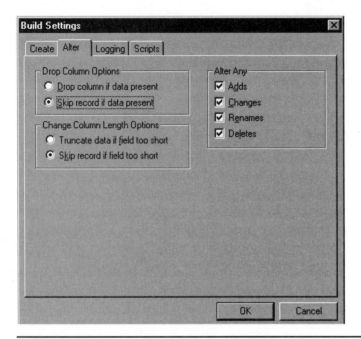

Figure 8.7   *Build Settings dialog box—Alter tab*

The Logging and Scripts tabs of the Build Settings dialog box enable the developer to set options for the output of Log and Script files created during any of the Build SQL Object functions. On the Logging tab the developer may specify the Logging Level and Logging Output options for error, warning, and informational messages generated during the Build process and the destination file name. See Figure 8.8.

On the Scripts tab the developer may specify the destination file(s) of the SQL syntax scripts generated during the Build process. See Figure 8.9.

All of the Build settings remain the same from one Build operation to the next. We strongly recommend that the application developer check or change the Build settings before clicking the Build pushbutton to initiate the Build process. In particular, the Skip options have been a source of confusion to new developers. It may appear that a rebuild operation has completed successfully (0 errors in the output) for an existing record—but the record has been skipped. This can be confirmed by review of the Log file.

Figure 8.8 *Build Settings dialog box—Logging tab*

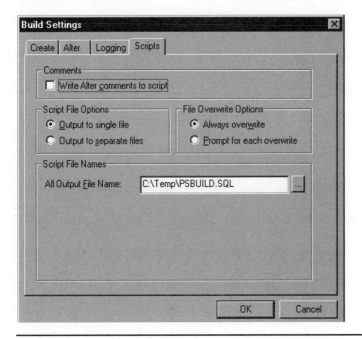

Figure 8.9 *Build Settings dialog box—Scripts tab*

Part 3

Developing the User Interface

09

Define Panels

Panel definition is the development of the application user interface. The panels will be of considerable interest to users of PeopleTools applications, and care should be given to their design and development. Taking the panel designs drawn in the requirements and design stage, we now move into construction of the panels themselves.

A new panel can be started either by selecting **File/New** from the Application Designer menu or by selecting the **New** icon from the toolbar and then choosing the panel object type. In either case, a new (blank) panel will be opened up in the Object Workspace. Just as fields are the building blocks in the definition of records, record fields are the building blocks in the definition of panels. You may consider the panel to be the user's interface to the data contained in the application database tables. In this case, the fields on the panel are taken from the records used to define the underlying application database tables.

Object Placement

There are two basic ways to place an object onto a panel. The first method is insert a panel control from the menu or toolbar. With a panel open in the Object Workspace, any object can be placed onto a panel by selecting the **Insert** bar from the Application Designer menu and then choosing a panel element from the long list of controls shown in Figure 9.1. Equivalent to this is the selection of a panel control icon from the Application Designer toolbar (also active when a panel is open and current in the Object Workspace).

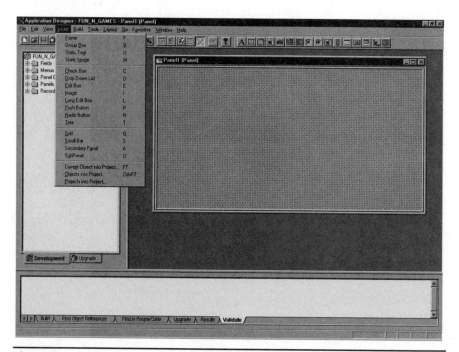

Figure 9.1   *With a panel open in the Object Workspace, the Insert menu bar*

The Frame, Group Box, Static Text, and Static Image objects are "cosmetic" elements that improve the appearance of the panel. The next group of panel controls available to be inserted onto a panel include the Check box, Dropdown list, Edit box, Long Edit box, and radio button. These panel controls are used to convey variable application data that the user may enter. The final group of panel controls that can be inserted are objects that control the processing of the panel, including: grid, scroll bar, secondary panel, and subpanel. Each of these various panel control types will be discussed later in this chapter. Please see Figure 9.2 for a mock panel with examples of each of the various panel control types.

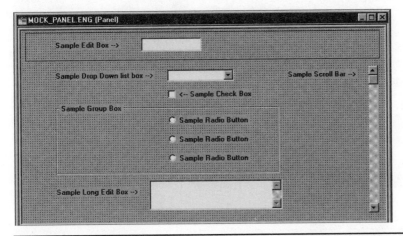

Figure 9.2   *Mock panel with various panel controls labeled*

The second way to place fields onto the panel is to use the drag and drop method. This is simpler and quicker than inserting from the Application Designer menu. To begin the drag and drop, go into the Project Workspace and expand the records that will be used in the panel definition, so that the complete list of record fields can be viewed as seen in Figure 9.3.

Select the field from the expanded record in Project Workspace, click on it and drag it to the spot on the new panel where you would like to place that field and then release it. You will find that the field is now represented on the panel with a type of panel control and a corresponding field label. The type of panel control the field takes depends upon the Record Field properties of that field or upon the (global) Field properties assigned. Table 9.1 indicates the default panel controls for fields placed onto the panels using the drag-and-drop method.

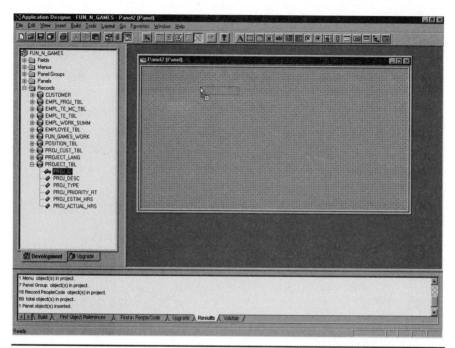

Figure 9.3   *Project Workspace with expanded record, ready for drag and drop to panel*

Table 9.1   *Default Panel Control corresponding to various record field or field properties*

Record Field or Field Property	Default Panel Control
Prompt table edit defined	Edit box with prompt (prompt for valid values)
Translate table edit defined	Drop-down List box
Yes/No edit defined	Check Box
Date Field	Edit box with prompt (prompt for calendar)
Long (variable) character	Long Edit box

If none of the above Record Field properties or field properties applies, then the default panel control will be an Edit box. Note that these are the default or "typical" panel controls used for fields with these characteristics. Other panel controls may be inserted from the Application Designer menu to override these default panel controls. For instance, an Edit box could be inserted for a field with a Translate Table edit defined—instead of the default Drop-down List box.

After a field or other control is placed on the panel the developer may find it necessary to move the object to another location on the panel, or perhaps to align a group of fields. For this purpose it is useful to show the **Object Inspector** tool, activated either by selecting it from the **View** menu bar or by clicking the **Toggle Inspector** icon from the toolbar. The resulting Object Inspector box as seen in Figure 9.4 can be very helpful for aligning fields on the panel, either horizontally (X axis) or vertically (Y axis).

Object Inspector	☒
Name	**Value**
X Coord	140
Y Coord	40
X Extent	65
Y Extent	19
Num	0
Lvl	0
Label	Project Identifier
Type	Edit Box
Field	PROJ_ID
Record	PROJECT_TBL

Figure 9.4   *Object Inspector on a panel*

Moving objects can be accomplished by clicking and dragging an object, or by selecting the object and moving it slowly with the arrow keys on the keyboard. If the data portion of a field is selected and moved, the corresponding label will follow in the default position (generally to the left). If the label itself is selected with the cursor it can be moved independent of the data field. The label can be returned to the typical spot by clicking the **Default Label Position** icon from the toolbar.

Another method for moving a field on a panel can be found on the popup menu for Panel Field definition. First right click the field to be moved and select **Cut**, then right click (again) and select **Paste**, move the cursor (cross-hairs) to the desired location and click once more. The selected field will now be placed in the new location. Using this popup menu in the Application Designer also permits the developer to **Copy** and **Paste** or just **Delete** a field or other panel control. A handy way to move a group of fields on a panel is to choose **Select Group** from the edit menu or the icon from the toolbar, draw a box around the set of fields to be moved, then click and drag the group to the desired location.

Panel Field Properties

Just as a field was assigned Record Field properties when included in a record definition, a field must be assigned Panel Field properties when inserted onto a panel. The Panel Field properties will establish the relation of the field to the underlying application data tables and will establish the display and usage of the field on the panel. After a field has been placed onto a panel, the Panel Field properties can be accessed by double clicking the field on the panel in the Object Workspace or by selecting **Panel Field Properties** from the popup menu on the Panel field. There are three tabs for Panel Field properties information, the Record, Label, and Use tabs. Each will be discussed in turn in the following sections.

Panel Field Properties–Record Tab

The Panel Field properties–Record tab options will vary somewhat depending on the type of panel control. We will begin with an illustration of the Record tab for a common panel control, the Edit box, as displayed in Figure 9.5.

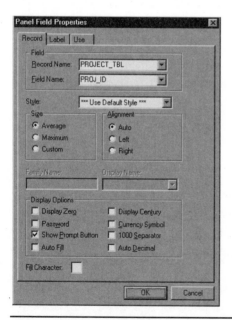

Figure 9.5   *Panel Field properties—Record tab for Edit box*

By far the most important of the Panel Field properties is the assignment of the Panel Field to the appropriate record and field. If the field was placed onto the panel by drag and drop from the expanded record in the Project Workspace, then the developer's job is relatively easy. The record name and field name in Panel Field properties will already be populated with both the name of the field "dragged" and the name of the record it was dragged from. However, if the field was placed onto the panel from the Insert menu, the record name and field names are unknown to the Application Designer tool (hence the Dummy Name label) and will need to be completed by the developer. In this case the developer must select the appropriate record name from a drop-down list of all records defined to PeopleTools and then select the intended field from a drop-down list of all fields in that record. As a hint to new developers, if a record and field are selected from the drop-down list and then it is determined that a different record should be selected, clear the field name first. Otherwise, the list of records will only include those records that include the field name shown.

Many of the remaining Panel Field properties on the Record tab will vary according to the type of panel control element. Our current illustration is of the Record tab for an Edit box. For this panel control, the remaining Panel Field properties on the Record tab relate to the size, alignment, and display of the field on the panel. Often the PeopleTools default properties will be acceptable for these properties and the developer can move on. Some of the more useful Panel Field properties for Edit boxes include:

Size: Size of the field on the panel
Average The default, and generally fine for character fields
Custom   Allows developer to size the field on the panel

Custom sizing can be very useful for large description or name fields on crowded panels. Sizing is performed by grabbing one edge of the field with the cursor and sliding the border to reduce the field size. Sizing can also be performed by depressing the shift key and pressing the arrow keys.

Alignment: Alignment of the data value within the panel field
Auto   The default, left aligned for characters, right aligned for numbers
Left   To force numbers to be left aligned
Right   To force characters to be right aligned

Display Options: Several of the more useful options include:

Display zero   To display a zero for a zero value (recommended)

Display century   To display the century digits in a date (strongly recom-
                      mended)

Currency symbol   To display a currency symbol, appropriate for monetary
                      amounts

1000 Separator   To display a separator character after every three digits
                      in the number

The Record tab of Panel Field properties for a drop-down list, seen in Figure
9.6, is somewhat different from the Record tab already discussed for the Edit
box.

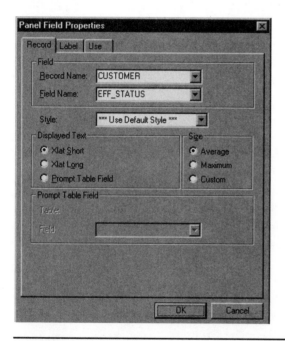

Figure 9.6   *Panel Field properties—Record tab for a drop-down list*

After selecting the record and field associated with the Drop-down List box, the
developer then selects the field of data that will be displayed within the Drop-
down List box on the panel. The field displayed may be *different* from the field
named in the top of the Record tab. The field displayed may be another field in

the same record, based on the value of the named field. This is remarkable! The choices for the developer are:

Displayed Text	Result
Xlat Short	Displays the short name for a field that has translate values
Xlat Long	Displays the long name for a field that has translate values
Prompt Table Field	Displays any list box field from a defined prompt table

Selecting this last option (if appropriate) will then activate the Prompt Table Field box found below on the Record tab and require the developer to select the actual field to display from the named prompt table. Again, the displayed text field is based on the value of the field named at the top of the Record tab. Please note, the Drop-down List box is really intended to be used with Translate values. Much as with a List box there is a limit of 300 rows or values displayed, therefore the use of a drop-down list for a field from a custom prompt table is not advisable unless the number of rows is known to be small.

The Record tab of Panel Field properties for a radio button, Check box, and Long Edit box are each a bit different from the Record tabs already seen for the Edit box and Drop-down List items. Please see Figure 9.7 for the Panel Field properties Record tab for a radio button.

For a radio button panel control the developer must enter the Translate value that the named field will take when the user depresses the radio button. The same field will occur several times on the same panel as a radio button, but for each occurrence a different Translate value will be assigned. Note, a radio button can only be used to represent a field that has Translate values assigned to it. It is easiest for the developer to insert the field onto the panel once, and then copy and paste the next occurrences. In a similar manner, the field values for a check box must be entered by the developer on the Record tab of Panel Field properties for that panel control type. Refer to Figure 9.8 for the Panel Field properties Record tab for a Check box.

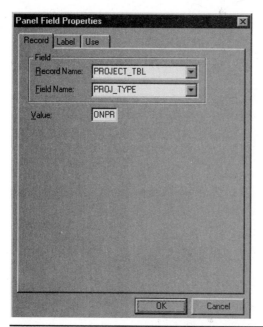

Figure 9.7 *Panel Field properties—Record tab for radio button*

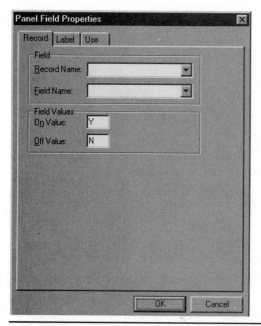

Figure 9.8 *Panel Field properties—Record tab for check box*

In this case, the On and Off values must be specified by the developer. Typically, the values are 'Y' and 'N' and a Yes/No Table edit has been indicated in the Record Field properties. Finally, the Record tab of Panel Field properties for a Long Edit box is the simplest yet, as it has no options aside from the naming of the corresponding record and field.

Panel Field Properties–Label Tab

The second of the three tabs of Panel Field properties information is the Label tab. Differences in the Label tab among the various panel control types are slight and fairly self-evident. For our discussion, we will select an Edit box to illustrate the label options. Please see Figure 9.9 for the Panel Field properties–Label tab for an Edit box.

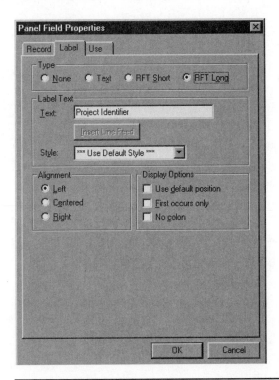

Figure 9.9   *Panel Field properties—Label tab for Edit box*

Here the label type and other characteristics are set by the developer. The PeopleTools default label type of RFT Long is preferred. This provides the field long name taken from the field definition as the Panel Field label.

Similarly, the RFT Short option takes the field short name from the field definition. The advantages of using label type RFT Long or RFT Short are clear—both save time for the developer and are automatically maintained on all panels if a developer changes the field long or short name (remember that the field names are global attributes of the field definition). Use of RFT Long or Short labels is particularly important if the application will be "globalized" as these labels can be translated into another language once and then displayed on many panels. This will prove to be much easier than translating text labels on many panels.

Occasionally it may be necessary for the developer to use a label other than the RFT Long or Short. By selecting the label type of *text* the developer may enter any desired label text and even insert line feed to create a label of more than one line of text. Finally, the label type of *none* permits the display of a field with no label at all. It is a good practice for the developer to enter a descriptive label in the Label Text box anyway as this will prove to be *very* useful to developers examining or debugging the panel later.

Other Panel Field properties set on this tab are the label alignment and display options. Generally the PeopleTools defaults (left alignment and default position) will be acceptable. The display option of First Occurs Only is very useful for a field that is shown repeatedly on a panel. This is commonly found on a panel with a scroll bar that displays multiple rows of data from a single record/table (find more on scroll bars later in this chapter). By using the First Occurs Only option the field label will be displayed only once, at the top of the column of field data within the scroll bar.

Panel Field Properties–Use Tab

The third tab of Panel Field properties information is the Use tab. Again, while there are slight differences in the Use tab among the various panel control types we will present an Edit box for our discussion. Please see Figure 9.10 for the Panel Field Properties–Use tab for an Edit box.

Here the field use options are set by the developer. The most significant field use option to discuss is the creation of a Display Control field and Related Display field combination. This is a very powerful and widely used PeopleTools feature that improves the appearance and meaning of a panel for an application user. Essentially, this feature allows the developer to bring a field of descriptive information onto the panel and automatically *relate* that field to a code field that appears on the same panel. The descriptive field is always found in a record other than the record that contains the code value. To illustrate this relationship, consider the following combinations of related code and descriptive fields:

Display Control Field	Related Display Field
Customer Code	Customer description (from customer record)
Product Code	Product description (from product record)

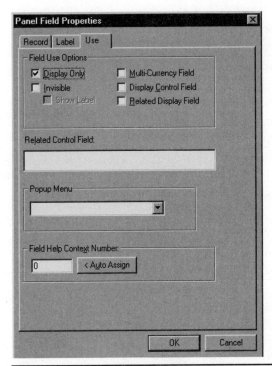

Figure 9.10 *Panel Field properties—Use tab for an Edit box*

To create a Display Control and Related Display field combination, the developer must first select the field that will be the Display Control and mark that field as such on the Use tab of Panel Field properties. It now becomes "eligible" to be a Control Field, that is, a field that will control the display of another field from another record at the same level on the panel (discussion of panel levels will be found later in this chapter). Next, the developer selects the Panel Field that will be the Related Display field and marks that field as such. For the

Related Display field, the developer must select the appropriate code field from the Related Control Field list. The Related Control Field list will show *all* Panel Fields that have been previously marked as Display Control. The Related Display field is marked as display only; this attribute cannot be changed by the developer. Note that typically the Related Display field is an Edit box that has been inserted from the Application Designer menu. Alternatively, the developer may have included the record that contains the Related Display field into the current project and dragged that field from the expanded record in the Project Workspace.

How does PeopleTools automatically and correctly relate the Display Control field to the Related Display field? The Display Control field must be a key field in the other record that contains the Related Display field. In one of our examples above, the customer code (Display Control) is the key to the Customer record, and customer name (Related Display) is another field in that record. Furthermore, if the (other) record that contains the Related Display field has a composite key, then values for each part of the key must be available from panel fields. Still, only one panel field will be marked as the Display Control — the last part of the composite key. PeopleTools does not provide any warnings if the developer establishes an incorrect or meaningless Display Control to Related Display combination. The panel will save in the Application Designer without warning, and the panel may even execute without error. However, at execution time the Related Display field will generally be blank as the SQL select statement will not return any value. For more information consider using the SQL Trace option (discussed in Chapter 17 on Testing). This error will only become obvious during testing of the panel with sample data.

Before leaving the Use tab of Panel Field properties, notice the field use options of Display Only and Invisible. In addition to Related Display fields, other fields on the panel may be marked as Display Only if the fields are retrieved from the database table and not intended for update by the application user on this panel. Marking a panel field Invisible may seem odd since the application user cannot see the field value, but it can be quite useful. Certainly there will be situations where the developer does not want the application user even to see a particular field value, but needs that field value as a Display Control in order to display the more meaningful descriptive Related Display field. Another reason to place a field on a panel but have it invisible is so that field can be used in a PeopleCode program (see Chapter 13).

Panel Design

Application panels should be designed in a manner appealing to the eye of the application user and presenting the information on the panel in a well-organized fashion. Conventionally, the information on a panel is presented from top to bottom, left to right. On a single panel, the information may include fields drawn from one or more records. Through proper arrangement of fields on a panel, the PeopleTools application processor will generate SQL statements to select and update data in the underlying database tables. The arrangement of data fields on a panel is governed by several important panel order rules as well as PeopleTools panel design conventions. Our discussion of panel order rules and panel design considerations follows.

Levels, Scroll Bars and Parent/Child Relationships

The following illustration of a panel introduces the very important concept of panel scroll levels. Basically, the panel scroll levels correspond to levels of detail in the application data itself.

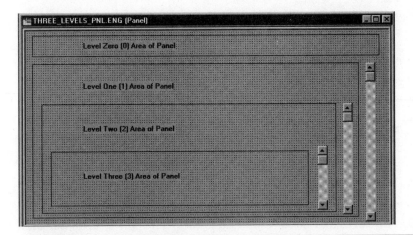

Figure 9.11   *Sample panel with levels 0 –3 labeled*

As seen in Figure 9.11, panel levels are incremented with the addition of scroll bars on the panel. Conventionally, as additional scroll bars are placed onto the panel by the developer they are nested to indicate increasing levels of detail in the data on the panel. This panel illustrates the greatest number of levels on a panel (level=3). In addition to nesting of scroll bars with increasing levels, there can be several scroll bars at the same level on a single panel. Therefore, although there is a limit to the number of levels on a panel, there is no theoretical limit to the number of scroll bars on a panel. Obviously, good panel design will dictate what is practical and appropriate. The level of a scroll bar is set by the developer at the time the scroll bar is inserted onto the panel. This is done by accessing the Panel Field properties Use tab for the scroll bar and setting the Occurs level to the desired level number as seen in Figure 9.12.

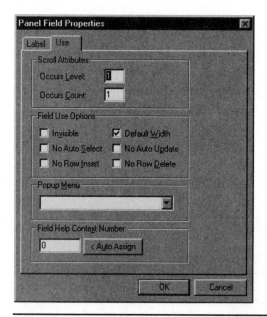

Figure 9.12   *Panel Field properties—Use tab for a scroll bar*

Another important Panel Field property for scroll bar found on the same Use tab is the Occurs count. This sets the number of rows of data that can be displayed at once within that scroll bar on the panel. Finally the developer should enter text on the Label tab of Panel Field properties for a scroll bar even though the text will not display on the panel itself. This text will be useful to the developer in understanding and perhaps fixing the panel later, as there may be several scroll bars on a panel and it will be impossible otherwise to distinguish between them.

There is a direct correspondence between the levels on a panel and the records/tables in the application database. First, the level zero information is largely taken from the search record (Chapter 6). There may also be Related Display data fields taken from any other record. While it is not required, it is a good practice to place the level zero key fields in the upper left-hand panel position. The level zero key fields should be set as Display Only on the panel. Once a particular row of level 0 data has been selected by the application user from the Search dialog box the key fields cannot be changed.

At level zero, the insertion of a scroll bar onto a panel establishes level one on the panel. Each increase in the level number on a panel corresponds to a lower level of detail in the database. We think of this as a way to permit the application user to take hold of a particular record of data and then scroll on multiple rows of subordinate data. In data modeling terms, we would say that there is a one-to-many relationship between the higher-level and the lower-level record on the panel. Often the lower-level data are coming from a record that is considered a "child" record to the higher-level or "parent" record. By definition, a child record must contain all the key fields of the parent record in the same sort order plus at least one additional key field. For example:

Panel Level	Database Record	Key Field(s)
0 (parent)	Customer	Customer code
1 (child)	Customer Orders	Customer code + Order number
2 (grandchild)	Customer Order Item	Customer code + Order number + Item number

Notice that each panel scroll level corresponds to *exactly* one database record. We will present more detail on the relationship between database records and panel scroll levels in the discussion of panel order rules (the next section of this chapter).

There are specific implications for effective-dated parent-child records placed on a panel. Notably, the user action to insert a new effective-dated entry (one row of data) for an existing parent key value will cause PeopleTools automatically to insert a complete set of rows into the child table—with all child rows taken from the previous effective date, but inserted with the new effective date. This logic preserves the relationship between the effective date of the parent table rows and the child table rows. This copy-down functionality when inserting a new effective-dated parent key value should be understood by the application developer as it can have significant implication for database table size and application performance. Use of PeopleCode can prevent this effective-dated logic.

Panel Order Rules

Given this understanding of panel levels, scroll bars, and corresponding database records, the developer can define a complex and powerful application panel with multiple levels accessing multiple records. However there are several very important panel order rules that must be well understood and observed by the panel developer:

1. A scroll bar must proceed all fields within a level, and all fields controlled by the scroll bar must be read from (be written to) a single database record *except* Related Display fields.
2. Place each Display Control field before the associated Related Display field in the panel order.
3. Group together in the panel order all radio buttons related to the same field.

A panel cannot be saved cleanly in Application Designer (without warnings or errors) unless these panel order rules are followed. These types of Panel Save warnings and errors are common and generally fairly simple to correct. Remember that the panel order dictates panel processing—*not* the panel appearance. Initial panel order is created by default as fields are placed onto the panel from top to bottom, left to right. Incidentally, the panel order also determines the tabbing order during execution of the panel by an application user.

To access the display of panel order and make any required changes, the developer can select **Layout/Order** from the Application Designer menu or click on the **Order** icon in the toolbar. The Order Panel dialog box then displays every panel field, indicating a panel field sequence number (Num), the very important panel field level (Lvl), the panel field label, the panel control type, and the corresponding database field and record. Refer to Figure 9.13 for an example of the order panel display.

To make a change to the panel order, the developer can **Select** a line in the Order Panel display causing that field line to disappear from the displayed list. The developer will then place the cursor on a line above the intended location/sequence for the selected field and click **Move**, causing the selected field to reappear in the new desired location/sequence. To correct any panel order rule violations it is usually necessary to move one or more fields, for example:

▲ **Rule 1 Violations:** The developer may need to select and move a scroll bar to the intended position ahead of the panel fields controlled by that

scroll bar. Moving the scroll bar ahead of a field will immediately increment the panel level for that field.

▲ **Rule 2 Violations:** The developer may need to select and move the
Related Display field after the associated Display Control field.

▲ **Rule 3 Violations:** The developer may need to select and move one or
more radio buttons associated with the same panel field to group them
together.

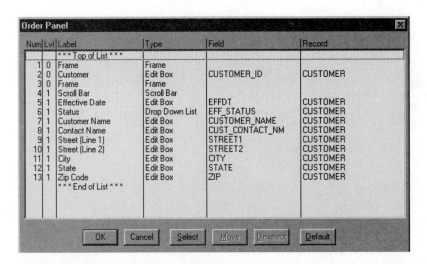

Num	Lvl	Label	Type	Field	Record
		* * * Top of List * * *			
1	0	Frame	Frame		
2	0	Customer	Edit Box	CUSTOMER_ID	CUSTOMER
3	0	Frame	Frame		
4	1	Scroll Bar	Scroll Bar		
5	1	Effective Date	Edit Box	EFFDT	CUSTOMER
6	1	Status	Drop Down List	EFF_STATUS	CUSTOMER
7	1	Customer Name	Edit Box	CUSTOMER_NAME	CUSTOMER
8	1	Contact Name	Edit Box	CUST_CONTACT_NM	CUSTOMER
9	1	Street (Line 1)	Edit Box	STREET1	CUSTOMER
10	1	Street (Line 2)	Edit Box	STREET2	CUSTOMER
11	1	City	Edit Box	CITY	CUSTOMER
12	1	State	Edit Box	STATE	CUSTOMER
13	1	Zip Code	Edit Box	ZIP	CUSTOMER
		* * * End of List * * *			

OK   Cancel   Select   Move   Unselect   Default

Figure 9.13   *Panel layout order example*

It is here in the Order Panel display that the developer will recognize and
appreciate the importance of meaningful field labels, even for fields that have
no label displayed on the panel and fields that are not displayed on the panel at
all. The field label is extremely important to the developer working to fix a
panel order rule violation (especially on an unfamiliar panel). Generally, we like
to look at the Order Panel display even after a clean save of a panel in the
Application Designer, just to ensure that we understand how that panel is working and to review the tabbing order.

Grid Properties

The grid panel control was introduced to PeopleTools in version 7.0 and is a
powerful new feature that can enhance the appearance and use of PeopleSoft

applications. The grid is essentially a package comprised of a scroll bar and a set of fields that appear on the panel in a tight grid/box pattern. Please see Figure 9.14 for a sample panel with a grid placed on it.

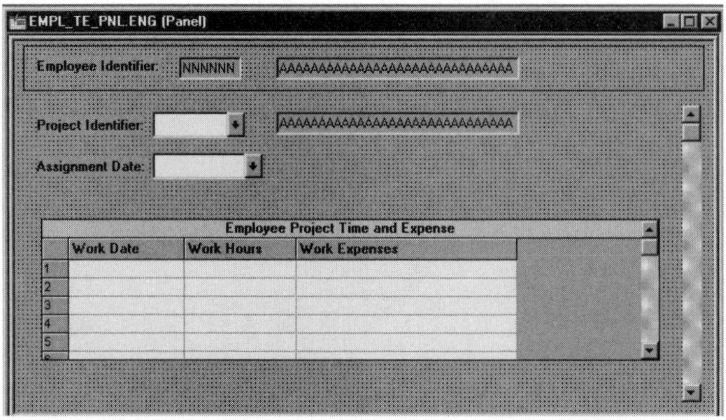

Figure 9.14   *Sample panel with a grid*

To place a grid onto a panel, first locate an appropriate area on the new panel. There may be only one grid on a panel and the grid must be the last panel control added to the panel, so be sure to complete the placement of all other panel fields before inserting the grid. The developer will find the grid panel control in the Insert menu of the Application Designer. Select that control type and place it in the desired position on the panel. The developer may initially click, drag and release to size the grid on the panel; or come back later and use the handles to size the grid like a frame or group box. Double clicking on the grid or right clicking and choosing **Panel Field** properties will bring the developer to the Grid properties dialog box. There are four tabs to Grid Properties, and we will discuss each in turn. The first is the General tab of Grid Properties, as seen in Figure 9.15.

First, the developer must name the Main record that will be the (default) source of the fields included in the grid as columns. The other general attribute is the Occurs level of the scroll bar. As with other scroll bars, all fields within this scroll bar (at this level) must come from one record, with the notable exception of Related Display fields. Panel order rules must be followed within the grid, although on the Panel Order display the grid will appear as a single line and the grid panel fields will *not* display. Note that since there may only be one grid on a panel, if the grid is to be nested within another scroll bar the Occurs count of the outer scroll bar must be set to one. The grid itself will not have an Occurs count, but rather will display as many rows of data as can fit within the size of the grid.

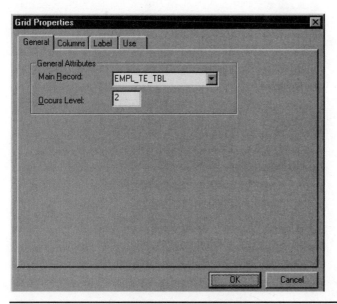

Figure 9.15 *Grid properties—General tab*

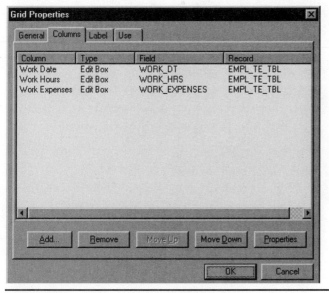

Figure 9.16 *Grid properties—Columns tab*

The second tab of Grid properties is the Columns tab, as seen in Figure 9.16 above. From here the developer can **Add, Remove, Move Up, Move Down** (to reorder) the set of columns that will be included in this grid. Clicking the **Add** button presents the developer with a choice of the column type (panel controls: Edit box, Drop-down list, Check box). Note, the selection of the column type cannot be changed. If the developer intended a different panel control type, the developer must **Remove** the column from the grid and **Add** it again with the desired panel control.

Once a new column has been added or the properties of an existing column are selected, the familiar Panel Field Properties dialog box is presented. This is to be completed by the developer with all the usual considerations. One additional and useful attribute is found on the Use tab of the Panel Field properties. The Freeze Grid Column option allows the developer to specify one or more contiguous left-hand columns to freeze in the grid while the application user scrolls to the right to see additional columns of data (freeze headings). The width of grid columns can be changed by the developer after leaving Grid properties by simply dragging on one of the column heading boundaries.

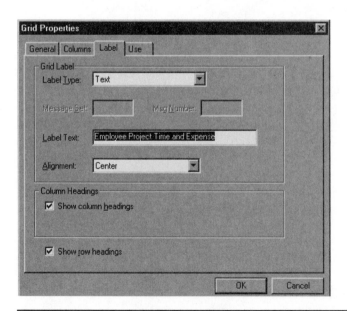

Figure 9.17   *Grid properties—Label tab*

The third tab of Grid properties is the Label tab, as seen in Figure 9.17. Here a Grid Label can be specified as either text or a Message Catalog entry. If text is specified, the label is typed in right below and the alignment is indicated. Also on this tab, the developer can specify whether column headings (set as field labels) and row headings (line numbers) will be shown. Changes made on the Label tab are reflected immediately in the grid as seen by the developer in the Application Designer. The final tab of Grid properties is the Use tab, shown in Figure 9.18.

The most commonly useful attribute on this tab is the Display Only option. This turns the entire contents of the grid to Display Only. The Data options of No Row Insert and No Row Delete can be selected to prevent the application user from inserting or deleting rows in the grid. The No Auto Select and No Auto Update attributes are more advanced options, to be used in combination with the PeopleCode ScrollSelect function.

The use of a grid provides several benefits to the application user at panel execution time, aside from the neat and compact presentation of the application data. First, the grid provides the application user the ability to sort the rows of data appearing on the panel by clicking on one of the column headings. The sort order can be reversed by clicking again on the same column heading. Additionally, the grid offers the user the ability to resize any column of data by dragging the column boundary and the ability to reorder the columns by dragging the column heading itself. These features combine to make the grid an even more convenient display option for the application user.

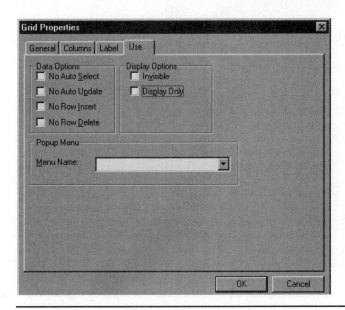

Figure 9.18 *Grid properties—Use tab*

Panel Properties

Like all PeopleTools objects created in Application Designer, the panel has properties. These are accessed from the menu **File/Object Properties** or the **Properties** icon on the toolbar while the panel is open in the Object Workspace. Refer to Figure 9.19 for an illustration of the Panel Properties dialog box.

The most significant choice in Panel properties is Panel type, which may be either standard panel, secondary panel, or subpanel. Our discussion thus far has been related to standard panels. Secondary panels and subpanels will be discussed later in this chapter. The other useful attribute on Panel properties is the Popup Menu option. This allows the developer to identify a popup menu that can be invoked by right clicking anywhere in the panel background during panel execution. Note, the Popup Menu option is also found in the Use tab of Panel Field properties. There it allows the developer to identify a popup menu that can be invoked by right clicking on that panel field. The creation of popup menus will be discussed in Chapter 11 (Menus).

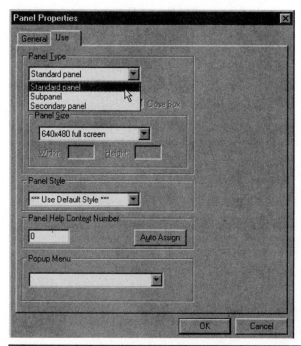

Figure 9.19   *Panel Properties dialog box*

Secondary Panels

A secondary panel provides the developer with a tool to create a panel of information that can be invoked by the application user from a standard panel by clicking a pushbutton. Typically this is done to provide additional or supplemental information that may be of occasional interest to the panel user, without further cluttering the main (or calling) panel with all of the additional fields of information. Please see Figure 9.20 for an illustration taken from our case study of a panel calling a secondary panel.

A secondary panel is defined in much the same way as a standard panel has been defined. A new panel is created, fields are dragged onto the panel or inserted from the menu, and all the same panel layout order rules apply. However, on the Use tab of the Panel properties (refer back to Figure 9.19), the developer will select the panel type of Secondary Panel. Two new attributes that will now become active are the OK and Cancel buttons, and the Close Box—to specify whether these controls should appear on the secondary panel. The other useful option found on the Use tab of Panel properties for secondary panels is the panel size Auto-Size. Selecting this option will immediately cause the panel boundaries to shrink around the panel controls on the panel.

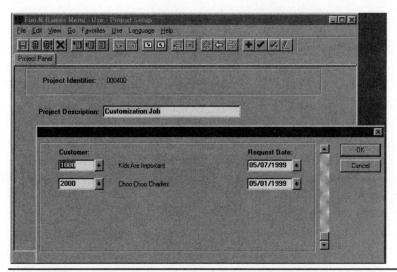

Figure 9.20   *Sample panel, with pushbutton calling a secondary panel*

Once the secondary panel has been defined and saved, the pushbutton that will invoke this secondary panel must be placed on the main (or calling) panel. The main panel must be opened in the Object Workspace of Application Designer. The pushbutton panel control can be found in the Insert menu and placed onto the main panel in the desired location. Like any panel control, the pushbutton has Panel Field properties that can be accessed by double clicking on the pushbutton itself. In this case, Panel Field properties has two tabs. The first is the Record tab, seen in Figure 9.21.

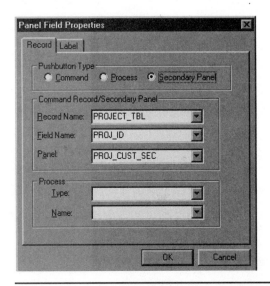

Figure 9.21 *Panel Field properties—pushbutton—Record tab*

The pushbutton type is Secondary Panel. The developer must then specify a record name and field name to associate with the pushbutton panel control. To observe panel order rules, a field within the record at this level must be specified. We suggest using a key field that is Display Only on the panel. Note that when the panel is saved there will be a warning message that the selected field occurs more than once on the panel—this is correct and expected. The most important choice is the name of the secondary panel to be invoked when this pushbutton is pushed. The intended secondary panel is named here.

The second tab of Panel Field properties for a pushbutton is the Label tab, seen in Figure 9.22. On the Label tab of Panel Field properties, the appearance of the pushbutton can be set. Label types include Image or Text. If the label will be text, the text can be entered directly below or taken from the record field label (using RFT short or RFT long). Even the size of the pushbutton on the panel can be specified.

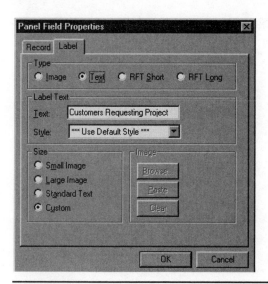

Figure 9.22   *Panel Field properties—pushbutton—Label tab*

An important consideration when defining secondary panels is the eventual scroll level of fields on the secondary panel. The scroll levels of the secondary panel shown in the Order Panel display must be added to the scroll level of the pushbutton on the main panel to determine the actual scroll levels within the secondary panel. In effect, the secondary panel is subordinate to the main panel. Please see Figure 9.23 for a simple illustration of this.

In this example, the pushbutton is at scroll level 0 on the main panel and the secondary panel has a scroll bar with an Occurs level of 1. The fields within the scroll bar in the secondary panel are at panel scroll level 1 (main panel pushbutton level 0 plus secondary panel scroll bar level 1). The maximum panel level number of 3 still applies to the eventual panel scroll level of the fields on the secondary panel.

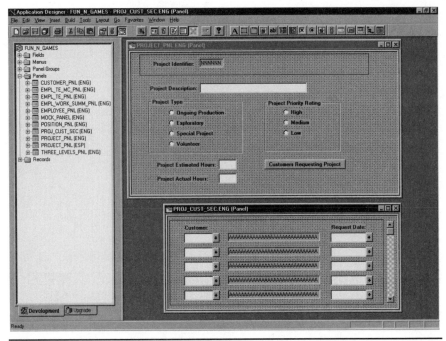

Figure 9.23   *Illustration of main panel with pushbutton, and secondary panel*

Subpanels

Subpanels are a convenience for the application developer, allowing a section of panel to be included on many different and even unrelated panels. While this is a convenience for the developer, the application user will not notice any difference in the behavior of the panel during execution. Subpanels are often found and used in combination with subrecords (discussed in Chapter 6).

A subpanel is initially defined by the application developer like any other panel. Panel fields and other panel controls are placed on the panel in the usual manner, and the Panel Field properties found on the Record, Use, and Label tabs are all defined. The panel is identified as a subpanel in the Panel Properties dialog box. Here the developer selects a panel type of Subpanel and saves the panel. It may also be useful to change the Panel Size option to Auto-Size to cause the panel boundaries to shrink around the panel controls on the panel (as in the secondary panel). The subpanel naming convention is to place the suffix "_SBP" on the panel name to indicate that this panel is a subpanel.

Like a subrecord, the subpanel is not useful by itself. However, this subpanel may now be placed on one or more other panels. The subpanel is placed onto a "main" panel by opening the panel in the Object Workspace and then choosing **Insert Subpanel** from the Application Designer menu.

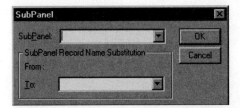

Figure 9.24   *Insert Subpanel dialog box*

The developer will be presented with the Subpanel dialog box (Figure 9.24) and be prompted to select the desired subpanel by name. After selecting the subpanel name, the developer may complete the subpanel record name substitution. The **From:** record name will be populated with the name of the ("generic") record or subrecord that is typically used as the source of the fields on the subpanel. The developer must specify a different **To:** record name in the substitution. Typically, this will be one of the main records on the panel that uses the subrecord referenced from within the subpanel. This allows the use of one subpanel on many panels, substituting the name of the specific record that is being read/written on that panel. The subpanel record name substitution nicely illustrates how the subpanel and subrecord are often used together.

Naturally, panel order rules must still be adhered to within the subpanel fields. However, on the panel layout order the subpanel fields will *not* be displayed. In the panel layout order the subpanel will be listed as a single line at a particular panel level. Therefore the substituted record name should be the record that is the current record at that panel scroll level.

The subpanel will be dropped onto the panel as a white box the size of the subpanel and can now be dragged by the developer into the desired location on the panel. Please see the sample in Figure 9.25.

The developer can click the **Test Panel** icon to display the panel with the subpanel fully expanded as it will appear at execution to ensure the correct placement of the subpanel fields and panel controls. Double clicking on the white box that represents the subpanel will open the Panel Field properties, though the only Panel Field properties that apply are the subpanel name and subpanel record substitution name (as discussed earlier).

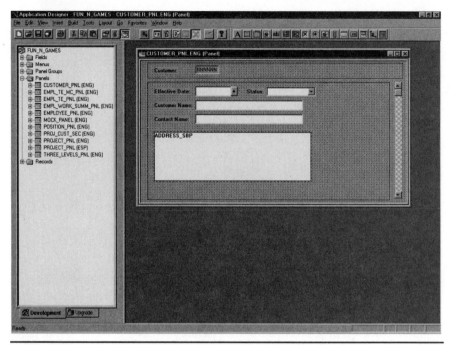

Figure 9.25   *Sample panel with subpanel in Application Designer*

To change any subpanel field or property the developer must open the subpanel in the Object Workspace and change its definition. Any changes made to subpanel definition have immediate impact on all other panels that include that subpanel. This is another good time to use the **Edit/Find Object References** command, in this case to identify and examine all panels that include a subpanel before making any changes.

10

Define Panel Groups

After completing the definition of one or more application panels the next step for the PeopleTools application developer is to place the panels into a Panel Group. The actual Panel Group definition step is relatively simple to perform, but does require careful consideration. Processing of application panels by PeopleTools is heavily dependent on several decisions made by the application developer in the Panel Group definition.

From the application user's perspective (Chapter 2) the panel group is accessed as a menu item selection. Basically, the panel group is nothing more than a group of one or more panels that have something in common and can usefully be grouped together. Please see the example in Figure 10.1.

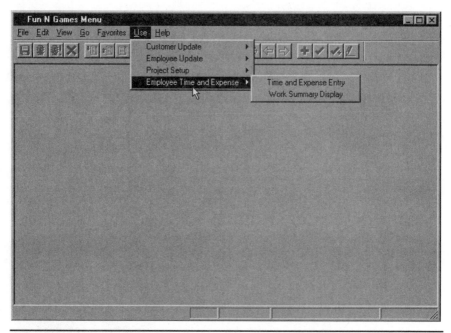

Figure 10.1   *Example of menu item selection of a panel group*

In particular, all panels in the panel group contain the same search record and therefore share the same high-level (level 0) key value. For example, two panels of information related to employees and some subordinate information also related to employees might be included in one panel group. Within the panel group, after any panel is opened for update/display by the application user all panels in the group are available for display for the same row of search record data. This is because all panels in the panel group share the same Search Key value. Additionally, the data on *all* panels in the panel group will be saved to the database when the user clicks on the Save button from *any* panel in the group.

Within the Application Designer, the construction of a panel group is relatively easy. From the **File/New** menu (or icon) the developer selects a **Panel Group** object to open a new blank panel group on the Object Workspace. The developer can simply drag a panel from the list in the Project Workspace and

drop that panel into the panel group. Please see Figure 10.2 for an example of a
Panel Group definition.

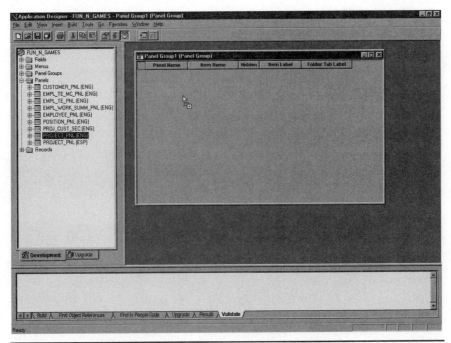

Figure 10.2   *Sample Panel Group definition in Object Workspace*

This is sufficient to associate that named panel with this specific panel group.
Alternatively, for panels not within the current project the developer may place a
panel into the panel group by selecting **Insert/Panel into Group** from the
Application Designer menu and picking the desired panel. Within the list of panels in a panel group, the developer may right click to bring up a popup menu that
provides the ability to **Cut, Copy, Paste**, or **Clear** a panel from the group. This
allows for reordering panels within the panel group, and therefore altering the
order of the panel display within that panel group at run time. These commands
even make it possible for the developer to **Cut** a panel from one panel group and
Paste it into another panel group that is open in the Object Workspace.

The first change the developer will probably want to make after dragging and
dropping or inserting the panel into the panel group is to change the Panel Group
item label and Folder tab label. If there is more than one panel in the panel group,
the Panel Group item labels will be displayed to the application user as a cascading
list from the Menu item label, otherwise just the Menu item label will be dis-

played. The developer will want to enter meaningful Panel Group Folder tab label(s) even if there is just one panel in the panel group as the Folder tab is always displayed at panel run-time. If no Folder tab label is entered, it will default to the Panel Group item label; this may be an acceptable alternative. Refer to Figure 10.3 to see the display of the Panel Group item label and Panel Folder tab label.

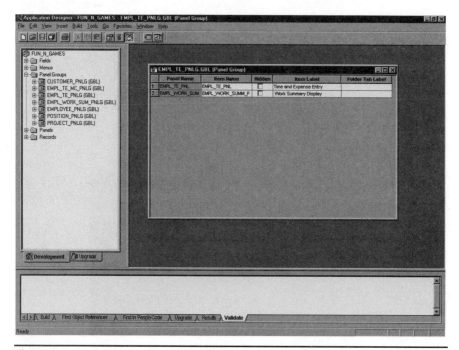

Figure 10.3   *Example of Panel Group item label and Panel Folder tab label*

Another option for the developer during panel group definition is to mark a panel in the group as Hidden. This will remove that panel from the panel group as a valid menu choice and effectively prevent any user from accessing this panel. This option might be useful for a panel that is included in one of the delivered (licensed) PeopleSoft applications if the organization has no intention of utilizing that panel.

Panel Group Properties

Like all other PeopleTools application objects, the panel group has object properties. These may be accessed by clicking on the **Properties** icon while the panel group is open in the Object Workspace or selecting **Object Properties** from the Application Designer menu. Please refer to Figure 10.4 for a look at the extremely important Panel Group Properties dialog box.

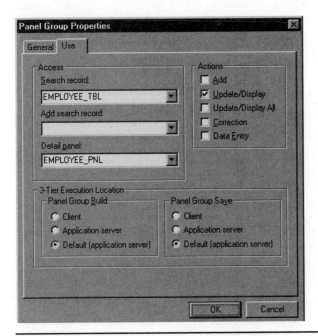

Figure 10.4   *Panel Group Properties dialog box*

Recall that the panel group consists of one or more panels that each contain information related in some way to the same search record (for instance a group of panels related to employee information). Therefore, the first decision to make in Panel Group properties is to name the appropriate search record. The record selected will serve as the only search record for the panel group and will control the display of the Search dialog box *for every panel in the panel group.* This is a frequent source of confusion to new application developers. If the developer wants a different Search dialog box to be displayed for a particular panel, then that panel must be included in a different panel group. The panels in the panel group have the same search record and will share the same row of data selected from the Search dialog box. From the application user's perspective, this row of data will remain current until the user either **Saves** or **Cancels** the panel group or selects the **Next/Previous** row of data (in list).

The selection of the available panel actions is the next decision for the developer to set in panel group properties. There are five possible actions; Add, Update/Display, Update/Display All, Correction, and Data Entry. Not all actions will be appropriate for all panels. However, like the named search record, all panels in the panel group will share the same set of available actions. We use the term "available actions" because not all application users will have access to all available actions defined for the panel group. User access may be restricted by application security (Chapter 16). However the action must be selected to be made available to any user.

In determining the appropriate actions, the developer must consider the search record just selected for the panel group. If panel(s) in the panel group will be used to add a new key value to the search record, then the Add action should be selected. That is to say, if the user will add a new key value/occurrence of that search record, then select the Add action. This is a frequent source of confusion to new PeopleTools application developers. The Add action is *not* necessary for the addition of rows of data or new key values at any level on the panel other than level zero (the search record). New rows of data may be inserted in the scroll bar at levels 1, 2 or 3—but this is *not* considered an Add action.

Update/Display should always be selected as an available action. If the search record is effective dated, the developer should also select the Update/Display All and Correction actions to make these available. These actions should be available for some application users to view and possibly update history rows of data (effective-dated logic). Of course, this is subject to limitations that will be established for operators in application security. The Data Entry action can be made available for the convenience of users who will need to enter many rows of data.

The selection of a Detail panel in Panel Group properties allows the application developer to specify the panel that will be displayed (in display-only mode) to the application user if the user clicks on the Detail button provided within the Search dialog box. The panel selected should be a panel with information that will assist the application user is deciding what row of data to choose from the Search dialog box. In the example in Figure 10.5 taken from our case study application, the Detail button on this Employee Time & Expense Search dialog box will invoke the Employee (detail) panel.

Another set of Panel Group properties are related to three-tier architecture processing. Beginning with PeopleTools version 7 the entirely new three-tier architecture was introduced (as discussed in Chapter 3). A three-tier installation is optional, but offers significant performance benefits compared to the traditional two-tier implementation. In a three-tier implementation, by default some online PeopleTools processes will run on the client workstation and some will run on the new application server. This separation of processing is referred to as partitioning the application. As a general rule, application processes that will require substantial interaction with the database server should be executed on the application server. Within the Panel Group properties the developer may specify where the panel group Build and panel group Save processes will execute. The panel group Build includes all processing and PeopleCode events prior to the display of the panel. The panel group Save includes all processing and PeopleCode events required for the Save of the panel group.

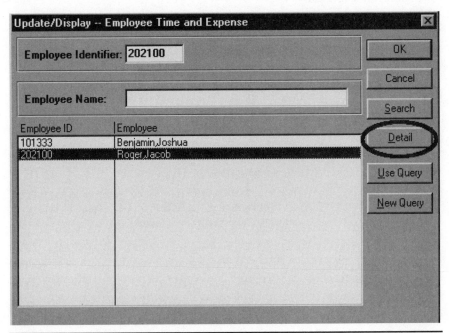

Figure 10.5   *Search dialog box with Detail button*

Buffer Allocation

At the time of initial execution of any panel in a panel group the PeopleSoft application processor retrieves all the rows of data from the application database that will be required for display of *all* panels in the panel group. This allows for subsequent display of any panel in the panel group without retrieving additional data from the database server. From the application user's perspective, the display of the first panel selected in the panel group may seem slow, while the subsequent display of the other panels in the group may seem much quicker (or even immediate). This is because when the initial panel is loaded all information for all panels is loaded.

The process of retrieving data from the database for the panel group is referred to as *panel buffer allocation*. The application processor builds a panel buffer to contain data for every record at every scroll level on every panel in the panel group, following a "depth first" algorithm. The buffer allocation process will include records and fields of data referenced on the panels according to the rules shown in Table 10.1.

Table 10.1   *Buffer allocation process for loading fields and records*

Type of Record	Fields included in the panel buffer
Level Zero	Only the Search key and Alternate Search key fields loaded in buffer, but if any other field from the record is on the panel, then all fields are loaded.
Scroll levels 1,2,3	All fields in the record loaded in buffer, even fields that are not referenced on the panel. All rows of data corresponding to the selected level zero key value.
Related Display	All Related Display fields referenced on the panel loaded in buffer, but additional fields from the same records will be loaded if referenced by PeopleCode.

The panel buffer process has implications for application run-time performance since a large panel buffer can require significant time to build. The developer should consider the requirement to place panels together in a group against the potential for slow execution. For a poorly performing panel, it may be possible to improve performance by placing that panel in another panel group. Certainly the developer is encouraged to experiment with the alternatives. To understand the panel buffer allocation, the developer may wish to start an SQL trace and review the actual SQL Select statements being executed during the Panel Build process. For more information on using the SQL trace please refer to Chapter 17 (Test and Debug the Application). In addition to raising performance consideration, the panel buffer is significant for PeopleCode programs since only record fields in the panel buffer are available during execution. The use of Record fields in PeopleCode programs will be discussed further in Chapter 13.

11

Define Menus

There are two types of menus within PeopleSoft applications, standard menus and popup menus. Standard menus are the basic means for organizing the various application functions that end-users can perform and provide the application navigation. Popup menus are accessed by right clicking from either an application panel or a panel field. Popup menus are typically used to transfer control to another panel and offer application users another form of navigation.

Standard Menus

The standard menus are defined to meet the needs and application security limits of the application user. The PeopleTools application developer must understand the basic menu structure and terminology in order to create a meaningful application user interface. Please refer to Figure 11.1 for a sample menu.

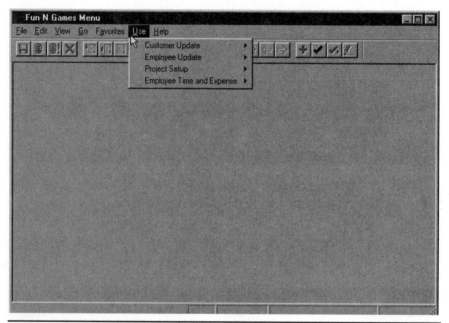

Figure 11.1   *Sample menu*

Selection of a menu group from the **Go** bar item, will reveal the various menu group labels in the drop-down list of menu choices. Upon selection of one menu the application user will see the menu label across the top (blue) bar of the active window. From selection of one of the bar items in this menu, the application user will be presented with the various menu choices, known as menu item labels.

The definition of a menu or modification of an existing menu is the last step required in the development of the user interface. To create a new menu the application developer can simply select **File/New** or the **New** icon in the Application Designer tool and then select the **Menu Object** type. For a new menu the developer must choose a menu type of either Standard or Popup. We will discuss the definition of a standard menu here. To modify a menu the developer may simply open an existing menu. In either case, the new or existing menu will be opened in the Object Workspace, as seen in Figure 11.2.

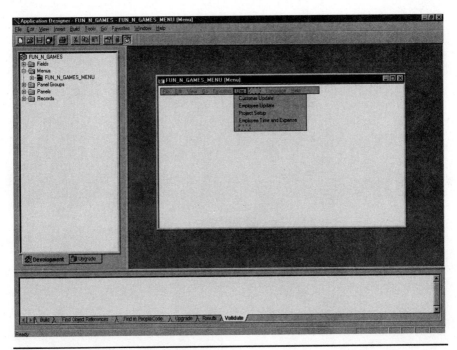

Figure 11.2   *Menu in object workspace*

Every application menu has a number of standard predefined menu bar items, provided by PeopleTools, and one or more custom application menu bar items. The Standard menu bar items include the File, Edit, View, Go, Favorites, and Help menu bar items. In addition to these, the developer may define new custom menu bar items by placing the cursor in a blank menu bar item position (surrounded by dashed lines) and either double clicking or right clicking and then selecting menu **Bar Item Properties**. The developer must name the new menu bar item (internal name for PeopleTools) and provide the menu bar item label to be displayed to the application user. The PeopleSoft convention is to use custom menu bar item labels Use, Process, Setup, Inquire, and Report. Under the custom menu bar item the developer will create the list of menu items. Each menu item will typically correspond to one panel group (as discussed in Chapter 10) and a set of related panels. The simplest way to associate the panel group with the menu item is to drag the desired panel group from the Project Workspace list and drop it into the blank position at the bottom of the list of menu items for that particular menu bar item (again, shown as a blank item enclosed by dashed line). Double clicking on the menu item or right clicking and selecting Menu Item Properties will bring the developer to the Menu Item Properties dialog box seen in Figure 11.3.

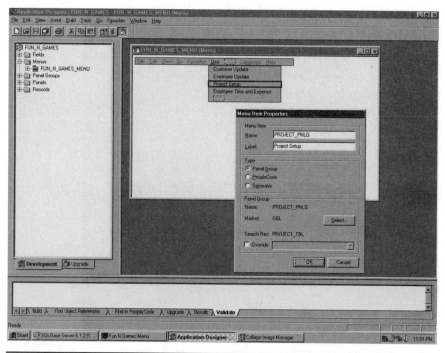

Figure 11.3   *Menu Item Properties dialog box*

Here the developer must name the menu item (internal name) and provide a menu item label that will be displayed to the application user. The developer can create a shortcut key for the application user by placing an ampersand (&) in the menu item label text immediately before the letter that will become the shortcut. That letter will be indicated as the shortcut with an underscore in the menu item label displayed to the application user. For instance, if the menu item label text entered is "&Customer Information" then when the menu is selected by the user that menu item will be displayed as "Customer Information." When executing the application, the user can then select that menu item by simply holding the **Alt** key and hitting that letter (e.g. Alt–C).

The menu item type is panel group by default. If the desired panel group does not exist in the current Project Workspace list, the developer may search for any panel group in the PeopleTools tables by clicking on the **Select** push-button and then choosing the desired panel group from the displayed Open Object dialog box. Finally, in some cases it may be desirable to check Override for the Search Record, and identify a different Search record for the execution of this panel group when invoked by this menu item. For instance, it may be helpful to substitute a Search record that is a view with certain criteria in place of the usual Search record (without criteria).

After defining one or more menu bar items and defining the complete set of menu items for each menu bar item, the application developer must define the overall menu properties. As with other objects, the menu properties is accessed by selecting **File/Object Properties** or choosing the **Properties** icon from the Application Designer. Please see Figure 11.4 for a sample of the menu properties–Use tab.

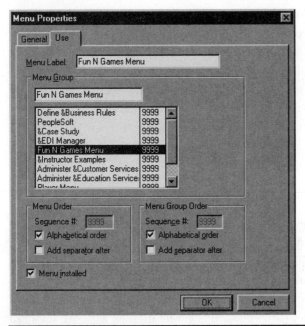

Figure 11.4   *Menu Properties—Use tab*

The application developer must enter the Menu Label text in the box, again with the opportunity to select a shortcut key by placing an ampersand before a letter in the label. This menu label will be the text that appears in the highlighted title bar at the top of the active window. In the Menu Group area, the developer may either select one of the existing menu groups from the list or may simply type in a new menu group into the text box. Recall that the menu group is simply used to group menus together for access from the **Go** menu bar on any PeopleTools application. Typing a new menu group into the text box, this new name becomes an available menu group for another menu. This is an occasional source of confusion to new PeopleTools application developers. It can be particularly awkward at first since the new menu group will not be visible to the application user under the **Go** menu bar until two or more menus are associated with that menu group. If only one menu is associated with a menu group, then the application user will be presented with that menu label under the **Go** menu bar item. The developer may think that the menu group was not entered correctly, but actually it is in "hiding" until another menu is associated with that menu group!

Completing the definition of the standard menu, the application developer may specify the display order of the menu within the menu group and the display order of the menu group within the **Go** menu bar. For the display order of the menu and the menu group the developer has the option of ordering by ascending sequence numbers assigned by the developer, or ordering entries alphabetically, or a using combination of the two options (in sequence number order followed by alphabetical order). The developer may also specify the display of a separator after a menu or after a menu group.

Popup Menus

The definition of new popup menus is very similar to the definition of standard menus. From the **File/New** menu choice or **New** icon in Application Designer the developer selects the **Menu Object** type. Rather than choose the standard menu, the developer indicates the Popup menu type. A new popup menu is opened in the Object Workspace, as seen in Figure 11.5.

Here the developer *cannot* define Menu Bar items, only menu items that will appear in the popup menu (will appear in a single list). As with the standard menu items, double clicking on the menu item will display the Menu Item properties. However for popup menus there is a new menu item type of transfer. If it is selected, the developer will then complete the Transfer Properties dialog box as seen in Figure 11.6.

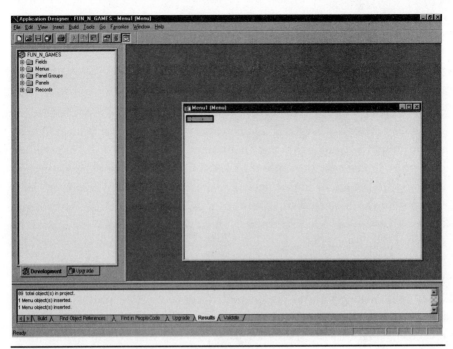

Figure 11.5 *New popup menu in Object Workspace*

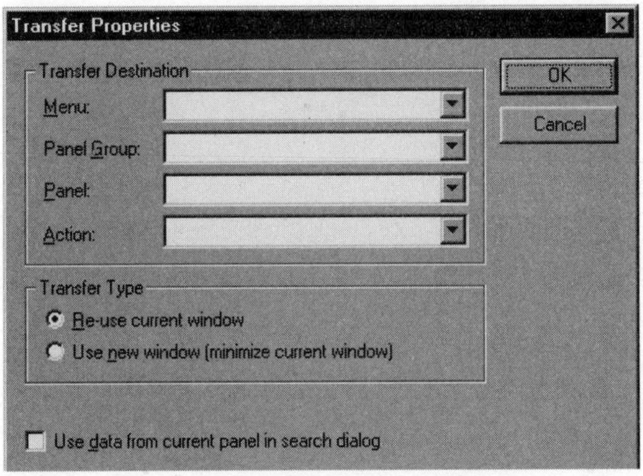

Figure 11.6 *Transfer Properties dialog box*

In the Transfer Properties the developer will identify a "destination" menu, panel group, panel, and action. When the application user selects this menu item type, the named panel and action will be executed. The develop may also specify that the transfer should use data from the current panel in the Search dialog of the destination panel and potentially bypass the Search dialog box entirely, bringing the application directly to the desired panel.

Once the popup menu has been defined and saved in the Application Designer, it must be accessed from somewhere in our application. Unlike standard menus, popup menus are *not* put into a menu group and *not* accessed from the **Go** menu bar. The popup menu is associated with either a panel field or the panel itself (refer to Chapter 9). The menu is associated with a panel field by the developer's naming that popup menu on the Use tab of its Panel Field properties. In that case, the application user will see the popup menu upon right clicking with the cursor in that field. The presence of a popup menu associated with a field can be seen if the application user checks on **Highlight Popup Menu Fields** in the View menu bar. Those fields with popup menus will be surrounded by a solid line. Alternatively, the popup menu is associated with the panel itself by the developer's naming that popup menu on the Use tab of the Panel properties. In that case, the application user will see the popup menu upon right clicking with the cursor located anywhere in the background of the panel (i.e. with the cursor *not* in a field location). The application user therefore must be familiar with the application panels to know that a custom popup menu can be found on the panel.

Part 4

Incorporating Code into Your Application

12

Preview PeopleCode

PeopleCode is PeopleSoft's proprietary programming language that is used to enhance the functioning of the application. PeopleCode includes typical programming statements, assignments, branching, and looping and is used to provide additional logic and controls to the application. PeopleCode is used as the panels are being processed and can therefore limit what a user can do or enhance how the application performs.

As you have learned throughout this book, PeopleTools provides a great deal of built-in functionality. PeopleCode should be used to complement the functionality that can be achieved through PeopleTools. If the function can be handled through PeopleTools, it should be. In fact, if there is ever a "conflict" between PeopleTools and PeopleCode, PeopleTools will always "win." For example, if there was a field default assigned in the record definition (PeopleTools), then PeopleCode record default processing would not function (this will be discussed further in our next chapter). Typically, PeopleCode is used instead of PeopleTools because the desired function of the application is more conditional, i.e., it should occur only under certain circumstances. PeopleTools applies defaults and system edits without regard to any conditions; they are always applied. PeopleCode enables the developer to incorporate more complexity into the application.

PeopleCode is always attached to a record field and a PeopleCode event (with the exception of PeopleCode for menus). A PeopleCode event is the processing event where the code will be executed. In Chapter 13, we will cover the Application Processor and each of the events in detail. The placement of the code within the correct event is critical in terms of the code's "firing" at the correct place in the application. It is possible to have syntactically correct code which does not work because it has been placed in the incorrect PeopleCode event. PeopleCode syntax, commands, and functions will be reviewed in Chapters 14 and 15.

PeopleCode Editor

Before we get into the details of PeopleCode events, we should become comfortable with navigating within the PeopleCode editor. PeopleCode is written in the Application Designer tool. The code is attached to a field and record. There are multiple means of accessing the code, but in the end, the code still remains attached to the field and record. The PeopleCode editor can be accessed from the record, from the Project Workspace, from the panel, or from the output window (refer to the section on Searching PeopleCode).

To access PeopleCode from the record, open the record definition and view the PeopleCode display. PeopleCode display can be accessed from **View/PeopleCode** or by using the icon on the toolbar.

EMPL_TE_TBL (Record)

Field Name	Type	FDe	FEd	FCh	FFo	RIn	RIs	RDe	RSe	SEd	SPr	SPo	Srl
EMPLOYEE_ID	Char					Yes		Yes					
PROJ_ID	Char												
WORK_DT	Date									Yes			
WORK_HRS	Nbr												
CURRENCY_CD	Char												
CUR_EXCH_USD_RT	Nbr			Yes									
WORK_EXPENSES	Nbr			Yes									
WORK_EXPENS_EQUIV	Nbr												

Figure 12.1 *PeopleCode display*

The PeopleCode display (shown in Figure 12.1) will show all the fields with the PeopleCode events across the top. At the intersection of the field and the event, if there is available code, there will be a "Yes." Double click at the intersection of the field and event to view the PeopleCode editor.

To access PeopleCode from the Project Workspace, expand the record so that the field listing can be seen. For fields where code exists, there will be a plus sign next to the field. Expanding on the field will show the PeopleCode events for which code exists; for each event there will be a lightning bolt symbol. Double clicking on the field event will open the PeopleCode editor.

To access PeopleCode from the panel, right click on a panel field or use the menu **View/PeopleCode** and the PeopleCode editor will once again open, as shown in Figure 12.2. Once the PeopleCode editor is opened, note that there are two drop-down lists available. The drop-down list on the left lists all fields in the current record. The drop-down list on the right lists all PeopleCode events. It is not necessary to close out the Editor window to access code on a different field or event. Just changing the values in the drop-down list will change the display in the Editor window. When using the drop-down list for the events, if the event is in boldface, this indicates that there is code available for that field event.

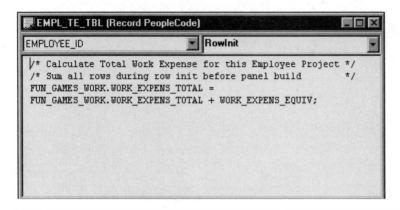

Figure 12.2   *PeopleCode editor*

The PeopleCode editor will allow code to be written for that specific field on the record but will also allow references to other fields and other records. When referencing the specific field on which you are working, use the field name or use the ^. The ^ will be replaced with the field name once the code is validated or saved. For referencing another field that exists on the same record, use the field name. For referencing a field that exists on a separate record, the reference must be made using recordname.fieldname. If it is not, PeopleSoft will show a message indicating that the field is not defined. In the example shown below, the code is written on the WORK_DT field. WORK_DT could be used in the code or the ^ could have been used. Note that ASSIGNMENT_DT exists on a separate record and therefore must be referenced with the record name, EMPL_PROJ_TBL.

```
If WORK_DT < EMPL_PROJ_TBL.ASSIGNMENT_DT then
SetCursorPos(%panel, RECORD.EMPL_PROJ_TBL,
          CurrentRowNumber(1),
RECORD.EMPL_TE_TBL, CurrentRowNumber(2), WORK_DT);
```

Once you open the PeopleCode editor, three new icons are made available (see Figure 12.3).

These icons correspond to functions that can be performed on the code: Find, Replace, and Validate Syntax. The Find icon will allow a search for a specific string to be performed. The Replace icon will also allow a search but will replace the search string with the new specified string. Validate Syntax will validate the syntax of the program. It will indicate such things as an END-IF statement missing or a field not defined. The validation will also take place when the code or record is saved. The Validate icon will allow you to validate prior to saving. Validate will also format the code. Do not spend any time formatting the PeopleCode developed because PeopleSoft only allows one consistent format which it does for you. The formatter will format code by indenting and placing code on new lines, according to the prescribed format. All other edit features are available when working in the PeopleCode editor such as cut, copy, paste, and drag and drop.

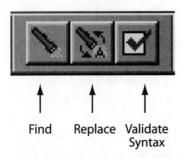

Find Replace Validate
Syntax

Figure 12.3 *PeopleCode icons*

It is important to note that PeopleCode is case *insensitive*. Field names or record names do not have to be capitalized. The only time that case sensitivity is important is when the code includes something in quotations, for example, when the code compares a variable to a constant which is defined inside quotations. In this case, because the value must match exactly what is defined in the quotations, the case must match exactly. PeopleCode treats anything in quotations as a "black box" and will not perform any validations on the value.

Searching PeopleCode

When making changes to PeopleCode, it is often useful to search the code to understand where the code exists and what impact there would be if the code were modified. A search can be performed on PeopleCode from the Edit menu, **Edit/Find in PeopleCode**. A Find in PeopleCode dialog box is illustrated in Figure 12.4.

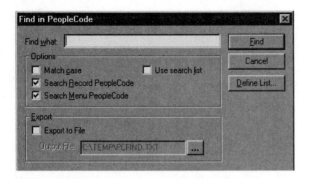

Figure 12.4   *Find in PeopleCode dialog box*

A search can be performed against all records in the application by just typing the search criteria in the Find what entry box. Or, the search can be narrowed to a select list of records. To limit the search, click on the **Define List** button. A Define Search List dialog will be presented. Records and/or menus can then be selected on which the search will be performed. Once records and/or menus are selected, press **OK** and return to the Find in PeopleCode box. Ensure that the Use Search List check box is checked off and the search will be performed on the records and menus specified.

When either a limited or a full search is performed, the output can be displayed to the output window or to a specified output file. To export to a file, click on the Export check box and specify the path and file name the to which output should be written. If output is written to the Output window, the names of the records in which the PeopleCode was found will be displayed. The PeopleCode editor can be directly accessed by double clicking on the entry in the Output window.

13

Understand the Application Processor

As a developer, you realize there is a lot going on "behind the scenes" during the execution of the PeopleSoft application. This processing is being managed by the Application Processor, which controls the flow of the application and creates all SQL Select, Insert, Update, and Delete statements that need to be executed against the relational database management system. Therefore, when a user performs an action, there is a corresponding series of actions that must be performed by the Application Processor.

As introduced in the previous chapter, PeopleCode is attached to a PeopleSoft processing event where the code will be executed. The importance of understanding the Application Processor cannot be overstated. In order for the application to execute correctly, the code must be placed on the appropriate event so that as the processor manages the application flow, the code will be executed at the appropriate time. It may be useful to think of the Application Processor as a large control program with a defined set of entry and exit points. As the Application Processor manages the flow of the application, there are pre-defined processing steps that will occur based upon the actions performed by the user.

As an introduction to the application processor flow, this section will review the flow without the PeopleCode events. In the next section, the events will be introduced and a more complete picture of the Application Processor flow can be presented. (Application Processor flow diagrams are available in PeopleBooks.)

Reset State, Search Processing, and Record Defaults

The Application Processor flow begins with the menu choice Go. Before a user makes any selection, the application is considered to be at the Reset state and the buffer is empty. The Reset state means that no panel has been loaded. Once a user chooses a panel and an action, the application processor determines if this is a new panel group. If it is, it determines the Search record defined for the panel group and builds the Search dialog box.

If a user enters a fully qualified key (i.e., a key which will uniquely identify a row in the Search record) into the dialog box or a unique Alternate Search key, the processor can perform the search processing to retrieve all the rows necessary to populate the panel group. Recall from our discussion of the buffer allocation process that the Application Processor will retrieve all rows of data from the database to fill all panels and scroll levels in the panel group.

If the user does not enter a fully qualified key or a unique Alternate Search key, the Application Processor must build a list of values in the List box. Therefore, prior to the search processing, a separate SQL statement is executed to the RDBMS to select the rows that should populate the List box and then display the values to the user. Once the user chooses the row, the search processing can then begin and the Application Processor can select rows that should be loaded into the buffer.

Once all rows that will be required to display the panel group have been selected, the Application Processor will apply record defaults. At this point, the panel/panel group has not yet been displayed to the user. The record defaults will be applied from PeopleTools (remember, record defaults are defined as part of Record Field properties in the Edit Attributes tab). Record defaults will only be applied if the value in the field is *null*; null is defined as blank for a character field and zero for a numeric field. Defaults will not be applied to fields when data has already been entered into these fields. After the record defaults have been applied, the panel will be displayed to the user. Once the panel has been displayed, the Application Processor waits for the operator to respond. Once the user takes some action, the Application Processor will move down one or more branches of the Application Processor flow. The branches of the flow can be referred to as Field events, Row events, Save events, and Popup menu.

The *Field events* flow is represented by the bottom center branch of the Application Processor flow. This flow will be performed when the user makes a change to a field. If a field changes and there are any system edits that have been defined for the field, the system edits will be executed. System edits include:

▲ Value entered match field type, e.g., numerics have been entered into numeric fields
▲ Required fields are populated
▲ Fields with prompt table edits have valid values
▲ Value entered in correct field format, e.g., Name format
▲ Reasonable date edit.

If the system edit is successful, then the field entry or change will be accepted. If it is unsuccessful, an error or warning message will be displayed to the user and the cursor will be positioned on the field that has failed the edit.

Row events include the actions Row Insert and Row Delete. The Application Processor will either insert or delete rows of data based upon the user request to do so within a panel scroll bar.

Save events are executied if a user changes or adds information on a panel and either presses the diskette, clicks Next/Previous in List, clicks List, or requests a panel outside the panel group. The Application Processor will prompt the user to save the changes made on the panel. Also recall that all panels in the panel group will be saved together. Once the panel group has been saved, the changes will be updated to the database. The user does not have the opportunity to "roll back" the changes after the save has been done.

The *Popup Menu events* occur when a user right clicks in a field and the popup menu becomes active. The standard popup menu includes actions such as Undo, Cut, Copy, Paste, and Delete. Custom popup menus can also be defined which can allow a user to transfer to another panel.

This discussion represents the most basic view of how the Application Processor flow works based on user actions. The Application Processor manages how the application functions. Now that we understand the flow, we will introduce the PeopleCode events and identify where they fall within the Application Processor flow.

PeopleCode events will be fired or executed as the Application Processor is passing through the flow. For each event discussed, we will discuss where it falls within the processing flow, how it can and should be used, and provide an example of how to use the event.

Search, Select, and Default Events

The *SearchInit* event is fired before the Search dialog box is created. This event is used to initialize or preset values for the Search dialog box. The code must exist on the Search record because that is the record the Application Processor reads into the buffer to build the Search dialog. In order for this code to fire correctly, the PeopleCode must be attached to a Search key or Alternate Search key on the Search record. Because the user has taken no action and has not even seen the Search dialog, this event does not accept error or warning messages.

SearchInit might be used to prepopulate values into the Search dialog box. Based on a particular operator signon, the value populated into the Search key or Alternate Search key fields may be customized based on security profile. Therefore, because a user has specific rights, the Search key might be prepopulated so that when the dialog box appears, the value most often used by that user is already selected. Additionally, Alternate Search keys can be hidden in the Search dialog box using the Hide function (this will be discussed in Chapter 15). List box items cannot be hidden with this event.

It is important to note that because the code is attached to the Search record, it will fire every time this Search record is used for a panel group. If this is not the desired effect, then the code should be made conditional based upon the panel group as follows:

```
If %PanelGroup = PANELGROUP.panelgroupname Then
    set values here
End-If;
```

A common function used within the SearchInit code is SetSearchDialogBehavior. This function will allow the developer to force the way the dialog box behaves. The syntax for this function is:

```
SetSearchDialogBehavior(parameter);
```

The parameter can be set to either 0 or 1. The 0 will suppress the display of the dialog box if the box has been prepopulated with a fully qualified search key. The 1 will force the dialog box to display even if there is a fully qualified key. By default, if there is a fully qualified Search key and the SetSearchDialogBehavior function is not used, the Application Processor will display the Search dialog box.

The *SearchSave event* is fired after the dialog box is created. This event is used to validate the values entered by the user in the Search dialog box. Again, for this code to fire appropriately, the code must be attached to a Search key or Alternate Search key on the search record. For this event, the user has taken some action, and therefore, error and warning messages are allowed.

SearchSave might be used to force users to enter some (non-blank) value into a Search dialog field. It is a good event to use if the potential list of values returned would be too large. Recall that PeopleSoft will only return the first 300 rows to the user; SearchSave is an effective way to limit the search within the dialog box.

Again, it is important to note that this code is attached to a Search record which may be used for more than one panel group. If the code should not be executed for all panel groups, there must be some conditional statement limiting when it should be fired (as presented above).

The *RowSelect event* is fired within the search processing flow as the Application Processor is selecting records to be loaded into the panel buffer. RowSelect is fired specifically after each row is selected by the Application Processor. This event is used to filter the rows to be selected into the buffer based on criteria set in the code. This code is not specific to one field and can therefore be attached to any field on the record. It is important to note that if you are interested in performing a selection on a record that is used within the panel group, the code must be placed on that record. For example, within one panel group, there may be multiple scroll levels. Place the RowSelect code on the record where you want to limit the rows selected. For this event, the user has not caused anything to happen; therefore, error and warning messages are not allowed. Error and warning messages can be coded for this field event but will never be seen.

RowSelect might be used to select out rows that meet certain criteria. For example if you only want to select rows that are within a certain date range, you can use RowSelect. When coding for RowSelect, the developer should use the DISCARDROW and STOPFETCHING functions. DISCARDROW will discard the row based on the criteria set but will continue to process the remainder of the rows. STOPFETCHING will stop retrieving rows once the criteria are met. The STOPFETCHING function is typically used when the rows being retrieved are in sort order. Depending on the way the code is developed, this function will usually keep one row of data that is "bad" or does not meet the criteria because that is the last row before the Application Processor realizes that the criteria have not been met. The syntax for these functions is: DISCARDROW(); and STOPFETCHING(); there is no parameter needed.

DISCARDROW and STOPFETCHING functions are new to version 7. Prior to version 7, this functionality was handled through the use of errors and warnings. The error was equivalent to STOPFETCHING and the warning was equivalent to DISCARDROW. In earlier versions of the delivered software, error and warning statements are used. If error or warning messages are coded within RowSelect, they will be suppressed and will not be seen by the user.

One question a developer should ask is why use RowSelect to filter out rows instead of using a view to narrow the scope of the rows brought into the buffer? The answer is that you should favor the use of a view because it is much more efficient. A view will limit the rows of data selected from the database table in the first place. When RowSelect is used, all the rows are selected from the database table and then the selection process begins within your application PeopleCode.

The *FieldDefault event* is fired after all the rows have been selected and after record defaults have been applied. Field defaults will only be applied when a field is "blank." A field is defined as blank depending on its data type:

numerics	zeros
character	spaces
date	null
long character	null

Therefore, if a default is set within record defaults and then PeopleCode is written for the same field, the FieldDefault code will never fire because the record default will be applied first and the field will not be blank. FieldDefault code should be written when the default logic to be applied is conditional; if the default should always be applied, the default should be set in the record. FieldDefault code is specific to one field and therefore must be attached to the specific field on the record. For this event, the user has not seen the panel or taken any action and therefore a warning or error message should not be issued.

FieldDefault might be used to set the value of one field based on another field's value. For example,

```
If profession = "DR" Then
   favoritegame= "GOLF"
End-If;
```

Therefore, before the Application Processor loads the panel, the value of a field will be set based upon another value.

The *FieldFormula event* is fired after default values have been applied to the rows of data. PeopleSoft refers to this event as "retired;" this event is no longer being used as it was originally designed. FieldFormula will fire on every row in the buffer and based upon the Application Processor flow, will fire quite often. Therefore, using FieldFormula code could have a great impact on the performance of the application. That is why this event is no longer used for its original intent. The FieldFormula event is now used to store functions for function library records. Warnings and errors should not be coded into the FieldFormula event.

FieldFormula might be used to define a function that will be shared across the application. Functions do not have to be defined in the FieldFormula event but it has become a common practice to do so, and this is the location where many developers would look to view function definitions.

Once the Application Processor has passed through search and default processing, it is about ready to load the panel. Prior to loading the panel, it determines if the row(s) to be displayed has been displayed before. If not, *RowInit* code is fired. RowInit is also fired when a new row of data is inserted on the panel. The RowInit event is used to initialize values and set the display characteristics of the panel. This event is fired on all fields in the row and all rows in the buffer; therefore, it is not field specific and the code can be placed on any field in the record. Again, this event is not tolerant of error and warnings; the panel has not yet been displayed and the user has not taken any action so it would be inappropriate to display an error or warning.

The RowInit event might be used to set the display of a field on the panel. Based on a value stored in the field, it might be desirable to hide a field or gray out a field so that a user cannot make a change. This is one of the most common uses of the RowInit event.

Because RowInit is fired when a new row is inserted in the panel, it is advisable not to code the same code on both the RowInit event and the RowInsert event (to be discussed later in this chapter). If the same code is placed on both these events, the code will fire twice.

Once RowInit is completed, the panel will be displayed. No other event will be fired until the user takes some action on the panel. Once again, depending upon the action taken by the user, the Application Processor will pass through the different branches of the flow: Field events, Row events, Save events, and Popup menu (all discussed in the following sections).

Field Events

The *FieldEdit event* is used to validate the data entered into the field. It will fire after the standard system edits have been processed, but only when the value of a field has changed. The panel display control will determine whether a field is recognized as having a changed value. A field is recognized as changed as shown in Table 13.1.

Table 13.1   *Field changed as defined by panel control*

Panel control	Recognized as changed when
edit box	value changes *and* user tabs out of field
edit with prompt	new value is selected *and* user tabs out of field
drop-down list	new value is selected from list
radio button	another radio button is clicked
checkbox	the check box is clicked on or off

The FieldEdit event is field specific and therefore the code must be placed on the specific field being validated. The FieldEdit event *cannot* be used to validate data in one field based upon the value of another field in the panel buffer which has a value that can change. That functionality is the use of SaveEdit which will be discussed in the Save Events section. Warnings and errors are commonly used on the FieldEdit event. Because this event is being used to validate the data, the user should be provided with a meaningful message if the data does not meet the validation requirement. If an error or warning is issued, the field will be highlighted and in the case of an error, the cursor will automatically be returned to the field. FieldEdit might be used to validate that a numeric value does not exceed a specific level or that a date is within a certain range of dates.

The *FieldChange event* will fire after the standard system edits and FieldEdits have been passed. Again, it will only fire when the value of a field has changed. Just as for the FieldEdit event, the panel display control will determine whether a field is recognized as having a changed value. The FieldChange event has two primary functions: 1) to assign values and 2) to control panel display. The event is field specific and therefore the code should be placed on the specific field that has changed. Warnings and errors are not tolerated in this event; because the user is not controlling the action taking place in the FieldChange, it would be inappropriate to indicate an error or warning to the user.

FieldChange might be used to affect the display of one field based on the value of another. If a user chooses a value from a drop-down list for one field, the developer may want to display additional information and therefore may ungray other related fields on the panel.

Does the use of FieldChange sound familiar? FieldChange and RowInit perform similar functions. The difference is *when* the code is performed. RowInit performs the panel display changes and/or field calculations when the panel is initialized whereas the FieldChange event performs the code when the value of the field changes. We like to think about FieldChange and RowInit as "partners in code." As a rule of thumb, when there is code on RowInit, similar code is typically repeated on FieldChange.

Many people ask why there is a separate event for validation and then the FieldChange event. PeopleSoft has separated the FieldEdit and FieldChange events so that the validation could first be performed on the field prior to moving on to any other processing. If the value of the field is not valid (as tested in FieldEdit), the Application Processor should not be performing any of the subsequent steps (FieldChange).

Row Events

The *RowInsert event* will fire when the user inserts a new row of data on the panel. It will fire on the entire row and therefore the code does not have to be placed upon a specific field. Warnings and errors are not tolerated in this event. The purpose of this event is to set up new values for a new row such as increasing a value or clearing a DESCRLONG field for an effective dated panel. RowInsert might be used to increment a line counter set on the panel.

The *RowDelete event* will fire when the user deletes a row of data on the panel. Again, it will fire on the entire row and therefore the code does not have to be placed on a specific field. The purpose of using code on this event is to reset or to decrease values you may be calculating on a panel. For example, if there is a counter or a grand total on the panel and a row is deleted which would affect these values, the code on the RowDelete action could reduce these values appropriately.

Save Events

The *SaveEdit event* will fire when the user attempts to save the panel group. The save of the panel may occur by the user taking one of the following actions after making a change on the panel:

▲ clicking **File/Save** or using diskette icon
▲ using the **Next in List/Previous in List** buttons
▲ navigating to a panel outside the panel group (next panel icon, **F6** or **View/Next Panel**).

SaveEdit code will execute on all rows of data and is not field specific; therefore, the code does not need to be placed on a specific field. SaveEdit is used to perform validations across fields that exist on a panel or within a panel group. SaveEdit should be used for cross validation because the user can change multiple fields and therefore the validation should be performed as the user is finished updating the panel group. Because validations are performed and the user can make corrections, warnings and errors can be issued in the SaveEdit code. The messages provided to the user should be informative and may contain any values that were in error. In contrast to errors and warnings used in the FieldEdit event, when errors and warnings are issued in the SaveEdit event, the fields are not highlighted.

The SaveEdit event might be used to validate that a field has a certain value populated based upon the value of another field. If the values do not meet the criteria, you could provide the user with an error or warning message to make the changes.

A function commonly used with the SaveEdit event is `SetCursorPos`. The syntax for this function is:

```
SetCursorPos(panel, field, scroll-level);
```

The `SetCursorPos` function will position the cursor on the row/field where there is a problem with the data. The reason this is important in the SaveEdit code is because this code is firing on all rows in the buffer. The function will point the user to where the problem exists. Otherwise, the user may have to scroll through all the rows to find where the error is located. When using `SetCursorPos` in the SaveEdit code, always place it before the error. Once the processor encounters an error statement, that is the last code to be processed before redisplay of the panel.

The *SavePreChg event* will fire after the panel has been successfully saved, i.e., SaveEdit completed successfully. The SavePreChg event is used to perform any additional processing to the data *prior* to updating the relational database. SavePreChg code is executed on all rows in the buffer and is therefore not field specific. Because the user has no impact on what happens at this point, errors and warnings should not be coded into SavePreChg.

SavePreChg code might be used to assign a high-level key. There are situations on a panel when you do not want the user to assign the high-level key but want to make the assignment based on an incremental value. You do not want to increase the value until the user saves the panel; otherwise, you could assign a value and then the user could cancel the panel and never save it. Therefore, the SavePreChg could process this assignment after the panel has been successfully saved.

Workflow events will fire after SavePreChg and prior to making updates to the database. Workflow is used to kick off other external business processes. Workflow fires on all rows in the buffer and is therefore not field specific. Errors and warnings should not be coded in workflow events. Workflow might be used based on values or flags set in the panel. For example, an electronic mail might be sent out to a group of users using the Workflow event.

The *SavePostChg event* will fire *after* making updates to the database. This event is typically used to make additional updates to the database. These additional changes will update other tables in the database that were not being worked on in the panel. The SQLExec function is typically used to handle this work (this function will be addressed in Chapter 15). The SavePostChg event is not field specific. Errors and warnings should not be used in the SavePostChg event; they will cause runtime errors.

Popup Menu Event

As discussed in the menu chapter, a popup menu can be accessed by either right clicking on a field to which a popup menu is attached or right clicking the panel background. A popup menu provides the user with another form of navigation in the application. The *PrePopup event* will fire prior to the popup being displayed. The PrePopup event allows the developer to control the display of the popup menu. PrePopup code is executed from the specific field to which the menu is attached. Note that because it is field specific, PrePopup code can only control popup menus that are attached to fields; popup menus attached directly to the panel cannot be controlled with this event. Because the user has no impact on what happens at this point, errors and warnings should not be coded in the PrePopup event.

PrePopup code can be used to change the format of a popup menu based upon some condition being met. For example, to disallow access to a menu item based on the value populated in that field, you could place code in the PrePopup event to control this function.

Functions commonly used with the PrePopup event are DisableMenuItem, HideMenuItem, and CheckMenuItem. The syntax for these functions is:

```
DisableMenuItem(BARNAME.menubarname, ITEMNAME.menuitemname);
HideMenuItem(BARNAME.menubarname, ITEMNAME.menuitemname);
CheckMenuItem(BARNAME.menubarname, ITEMNAME.menuitemname);
```

DisableMenuItem will gray out the menu choice on the popup menu; EnableMenuItem will perform the opposite function. HideMenuItem will hide the menu choice altogether; while UnhideMenuItem will perform the opposite function. CheckMenuItem will place a check mark next to the menu item; and UncheckMenuItem will perform the opposite function.

PeopleCode Menu Events

There is one PeopleCode event specific to menus and therefore it can only be accessed from menus. The *ItemSelected event* will fire when a user selects a custom menu item from either a standard or popup menu. The ItemSelected event is used when the menu type is defined as a PeopleCode within the Menu Item properties dialog (refer to Figure 13.1).

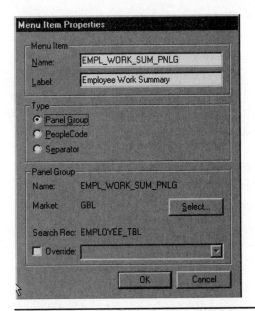

Figure 13.1   *Menu Item Properties window*

The ItemSelected event is typically used from popup menus to allow field values to be passed from one panel group to another. The event manages both the transfer process between the panel groups and the assignment of values to temporary variables and to the field values.

Placement of Code

For each of the events we have reviewed, it has been stated whether or not the code is field specific. When the code is field specific, there is no question about where it should be placed. When the code is not field specific, typically when it is being executed on all rows in the buffer, a decision on the best field for the code to be attached must be made by the developer. There are two schools of thought about where the code should be placed.

One recommends that the code be grouped on one field for a single event. The logic for this recommendation has a lot to do with the way PeopleCode is saved and processed. For each PeopleCode field/event combination, the PeopleCode is saved as a single program. For more efficiency in processing, if there were SaveEdit code on multiple fields, placing all that code on a single field would save and execute it as a single program.

The second school of thought is that if code primarily relates to a field but it is not field specific, it should be placed on that field. Many times developers will expect to find the code on the field most closely related to it. Therefore, placing all code related to a single event on one field may be misleading to developers.

Although we understand the first recommendation in terms of efficiency, in terms of reviewing another developer's PeopleCode, it is much easier to refer to the field where that code is expected. Therefore, we recommend that the code be placed on the field most closely associated with the code that has been written. If the developer does note a degradation in the application's performance, experimentation is in order to determine if moving the code to a single field/event will allow for improvements.

Errors and Warnings

As we reviewed each of the PeopleCode events in the previous section, we indicated when it would be appropriate to use errors and warnings. For the most part, the explanation given was that if a user has not performed an action to warrant an error or warning message then it should not be used in the event. As a developer, you may still be tempted to place an error or warning into an event that we have suggested does not make sense. Not only does the code not make sense placed in these events, but it will also "break" the panel and cause your user to have to cancel out of the panel and return to the Reset state. PeopleSoft considers events that should not have errors and warnings coded as not "tolerant" of errors and warnings.

In the PeopleCode editor there is nothing stopping you from coding with an error or warning. In fact, you can put the code in and execute the panel. The panel may appear to operate successfully at first, but if the error or warning condition executes, your user will receive an error message, as shown in Figure 13.2, stating that the panel must be closed due to an error.

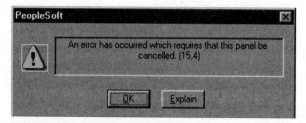

Figure 13.2   *Panel Error message*

This message may not occur until after the user has made quite a number of changes to the panel and all of those updates will be lost.

PeopleCode Event Summary

Table 13.2 depicts the PeopleCode events, whether they are field specific and whether they are tolerant of errors and warnings.

Table 13.2   *PeopleCode event summary*

Event	Definition	Field Specific?	Error/warning Tolerant?
FieldChange	Assigns values and sets panel display	Yes	No
FieldDefault	Applies default values	Yes	No
FieldEdit	Validates data entered into a field	Yes	Yes
FieldFormula	Stores functions	No	No
ItemSelected	Manages transfer between panels	No—Menu PeopleCode	No
PrePopUp	Controls display of popup menu	Yes	No
RowDelete	Resets calculated values	No	No—system delivered
RowInsert	Sets up values for a new row	No	No
RowInit	Initializes values and sets panel display	No	No
RowSelect	Filters rows to be selected into buffer	No	Yes (backward compatibility only)
SaveEdit	Performs validations across fields	No	Yes
SavePostChg	Performs additional updates to the database	No	No
SavePreChg	Performs additional processing prior to updating the database	No	No
SearchInit	Initialize values for a search dialog box	Search, Alt. Search keys	No
SearchSave	Validates values entered into search dialog box	Search, Alt. Search keys	Yes
Workflow	Starts other external business processes	No	No

PeopleCode and Buffer Allocation

As we discussed in Chapter 10, when a panel group is loaded, all the information needed to build all panels in that panel group is loaded into the buffer. This is critically important for PeopleCode. PeopleCode will only execute successfully if the information needed for the code is available in the buffer. Therefore, if the developer writes code on a record field that requires information from another record field not represented in the panel buffer, the Application Processor will be unable to execute the code.

If a field is unavailable when the code is trying to execute, the Application Processor will issue an error message that the field could not be found. The message will be seen by the user as the code is being executed. For example, if the code is on the RowInit event and not all the information is available to execute the code, the user will see a panel processor message (refer to Figure 13.3) as the panel is trying to get loaded. If the code is on the Fieldedit event, the message will appear when the user tabs out of the field (and the field is recognized as changed).

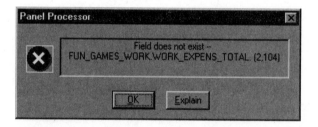

Figure 13.3   *Panel Processor error message*

How does a developer know if data is available in the buffer for code to execute? Remember from Chapter 12, at level 0, only the Search Key fields will be loaded to the buffer unless there are additional fields from the Search record on the panel; in that case, the entire row will be loaded to the buffer. At levels 1, 2 and 3, the entire row of data is loaded to the buffer and therefore will be available for code. PeopleCode written on related display fields will not execute. Interestingly enough, related display fields referred to in the PeopleCode of another field will execute and any other field that exists on the related display record can also be referenced in the PeopleCode. For derived/work record fields, the code will execute only on the fields available on the panel; a derived field only loads that specific field into the buffer.

To avoid having problems with data unavailable to execute the code, carefully consider whether the information is available in the buffer. If the information is not available in the buffer because it is not relevant for the user to see on the panel, the information should be placed on the panel and should have a Panel Field property Use Attribute of Invisible. This way, the data will be loaded into the buffer but will not be visible or accessible to the user.

Another consideration for PeopleCode and buffer allocation is the PeopleCode that exists on the search record. As we have learned, the Search record populates level 0 on a panel. This means that any PeopleCode that is attached to any of the record fields at level 0 will be executed on any panel that uses that record as the search record. It might be the case that a developer does not want the code to execute every place this record is used as a search record. To avoid this issue, write code with conditions based upon the panel or panel group where the code should execute. For example, if SEARCHREC is the search record on PANELA, PANELB, and PANELC but you only want the code to fire on PANELA, structure your code as:

```
If %PANEL=PANELA then
   statement 1;
   statement 2;
End-if;
```

14

Syntax and Message Catalog

In Chapter 12, we introduced the PeopleCode editor and the steps for working within the editor. Chapter 13 followed with an introduction to the Application Processor and actual processing sequence of the code. The purpose of this chapter is to prepare you to write syntactically correct PeopleCode.

Before beginning to write code, ask yourself a few questions. *Where* should the code be placed (in terms of fields and records)? *When* should the code fire (in terms of events)? *What* should the code be doing? The Where and the When should now be clear to you based upon the Application Processor flow and the PeopleCode events we introduced. This chapter will focus on the *What*. By introducing the proper syntax, the logical statements that can be used, and the message catalog, you will be prepared to begin to develop code. The next chapter will take one step further and introduce built-in functions that can be incorporated into PeopleCode.

PeopleCode Syntax

In terms of general syntax, there are a few things to consider; these include syntax for PeopleCode statements, referencing fields and records, and using comments. When writing PeopleCode, you must end all statements with a semicolon. Making reference to fields and records within your code will depend on where your code is placed. When writing code on a specific field on a record, you can refer to that field by using the field name or by using the ^ notation (which will then be converted to the field name when the code is validated or saved) as shown in Figure 14.1.

When writing code on a record, you can refer to any field on that record just by using the field name in the code. If you refer to a field that exists on another record, the record name must also be used in the code (see Figure 14.2).

For example, if the code is being written on recordA and referring to a field on recordB, the syntax for referring to that field would be `recordB.fieldname`. If this syntax is not used, when validating (or saving) the code, PeopleSoft will not recognize the field.

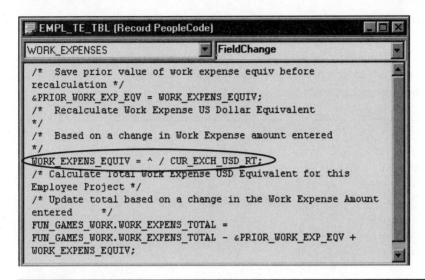

Figure 14.1   *Field reference in PeopleCode*

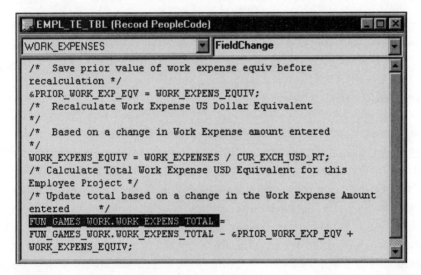

Figure 14.2   *Record reference in PeopleCode*

Operators

PeopleSoft supports all the common operators for use within PeopleCode. The most common operators are presented in Table 14.1. Refer to PeopleBooks for additional operators available.

Table 14.1 *PeopleCode operators*

Operator	Definition
=	equal to
<>	not equal to
<	less than
>	greater than
<=	less than or equal to
<=	greater than or equal to
NOT	can precede any of the operators to negate the meaning
AND	Boolean expression AND
OR	Boolean expression OR

Code Documentation

As with any other programming language, documentation of the code is strongly encouraged. Comments should be added to code to explain how the code is being used and why the code exists. We strongly recommend that any code added to an application have comments added with a unique string of characters that can be easily identified when performing a search in PeopleCode. Consistently using this unique string of characters, will allow the developer to perform a search to locate any customizations made to the application.

Comments can be added to code using two different notations. Using the REM syntax requires that statements be ended with a semicolon, just as in any other PeopleCode statement. Until the semicolon is encountered, everything following the REM statement will be considered a comment. Using the /* notation does not require a semicolon at the end of the statement. But, again, PeopleCode will recognize everything that follows the /* as comments until it encounters the end of the comment block which is noted by */. Below are examples using both forms of notation:

```
REM It is good practice to document your code;
/* It is good practice to document your code */
```

Errors and Warnings

PeopleSoft allows error and warning messages to be issued to alert the user to a potential problem with the data that was entered into the application. There is a distinct difference between an error and a warning. An error will not allow the user to progress; it will force the user to correct the error condition or cancel the panel. In contrast, a warning will issue a message to the user but will allow the user to continue (by clicking **OK**). The proper syntax for errors and warnings is:

```
IF condition then
   error ("Error statement to user");
end-if;
IF condition then
   warning ("Warning statement to user");
end-if;
```

Error messages should be used when you do not want to allow the application user to proceed without correcting the mistake. Warnings should be used to alert the user to a potential mistake or data out of range even though you will allow the user to continue with the panel.

Logical Statements

Logical statements you may be familiar with from other programming languages can also be used within PeopleCode. Some of the most common statements are IF, WHILE, and EVALUATE.

The *IF statement* is used for conditional logic. The syntax for this statement is:

```
IF condition then
   statement 1;
   statement 2;
else
   statement 3;
end-if;
```

The IF and End-If are required for this statement; else is optional. All statements must be followed by a semicolon. In the previous example, if the condition is true then statements 1 and 2 will be executed, otherwise, statement 3 will be executed. It is acceptable syntax to have nested IF statements within PeopleCode. Figure 14.3 shows an IF statement in PeopleCode.

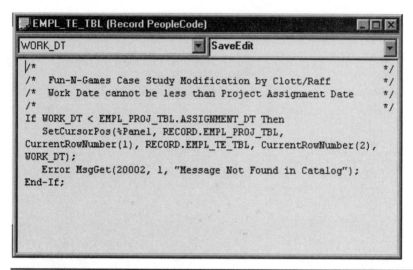

Figure 14.3   *IF statement in PeopleCode*

The *WHILE statement* will execute logic while a logical statement holds true. The syntax for this statement is:

```
WHILE logical statement
    statement 1;
    statement 2;
End-While;
```

The WHILE and End-While are required for this statement. Again, all statements must be followed by a semicolon. WHILE the logical statement remains true, the loop will continue. Once the logical statement is found to be false, it will exit from the loop. Within the WHILE loop, a BREAK statement can be used. This will force the end of the processing of the loop. The BREAK statement might be added within the loop using an IF statement to determine if the BREAK should occur; i.e., based on some condition, BREAK out of the loop. Refer to Figure 14.4 for an example of a While statement in PeopleCode.

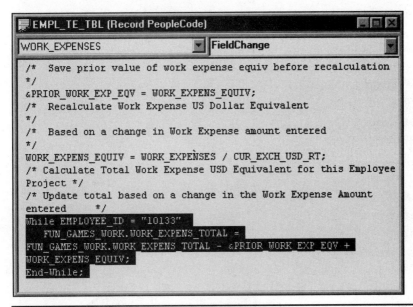

```
/* Save prior value of work expense equiv before recalculation
*/
&PRIOR_WORK_EXP_EQV = WORK_EXPENS_EQUIV;
/* Recalculate Work Expense US Dollar Equivalent
*/
/* Based on a change in Work Expense amount entered
*/
WORK_EXPENS_EQUIV = WORK_EXPENSES / CUR_EXCH_USD_RT;
/* Calculate Total Work Expense USD Equivalent for this Employee
Project */
/* Update total based on a change in the Work Expense Amount
entered     */
While EMPLOYEE_ID = "10133"
   FUN_GAMES_WORK.WORK_EXPENS_TOTAL =
FUN_GAMES_WORK.WORK_EXPENS_TOTAL - &PRIOR_WORK_EXP_EQV +
WORK_EXPENS_EQUIV;
End-While;
```

Figure 14.4   *WHILE statement in PeopleCode*

The EVALUATE statement will assess the conditions and perform logic based upon the conditions being true. The EVALUATE statement is used when there are multiple values to be assessed. The syntax for this statement is:

```
EVALUATE field
  WHEN value
    statement 1;
  WHEN value
    statement 2;
    statement 3;
End-Evaluate;
```

The EVALUATE, WHEN, and End-Evaluate are required for this statement. Again, all statements must be followed by a semicolon. The BREAK statement is commonly used in an EVALUATE statement. In evaluating a number of terms without a BREAK statement, the statements will continue to be performed even after one of the values has already been found to be true. A BREAK statement will immediately exit the Evaluate logic. WHEN-OTHER is also commonly used within the EVALUATE statement. It allows a statement to be performed when none of the conditions has been met and the code requires something to be done for all other situations.

Here is an example of an EVALUATE statement:

```
EVALUATE number
  WHEN = 7
    statement 1;
    BREAK;
  WHEN ≤ 12
    statement 2;
  WHEN-OTHER
    statement 3;
    statement 4;
End-Evaluate;
```

In this example, we are evaluating the field number. If the field is equal to 7, the program will execute statement 1 and will immediately exit out of the evaluate statement. If the field is less than or equal to 12, the program will execute statement 2 but will continue to evaluate the field, even though it has already found the valid value. In this example, it was important to have a BREAK statement after statement 1 was executed; otherwise, a number equal to 7 would have met the conditions =7 and ≤12. This may not have been the logic the developer wanted. This is the reason that the BREAK statement is very commonly used with EVALUATE. WHEN-OTHER is used when the logic test should be conducted for a few situations and then, for all others, the program should perform another statement. There is no reason the EVALUATE statement had to be used in this situation; the same logic could have been accomplished using the IF statement. Figure 14.5 shows an EVALUATE statement in PeopleCode.

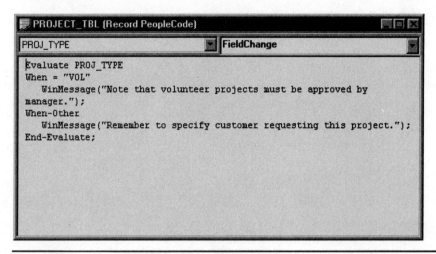

Figure 14.5 *EVALUATE statement in PeopleCode*

Message Catalog

Thus far, we have given examples of providing the user with messages by "hard coding" messages into the error and warning statements. As most developers realize, this type of hard coding often leads to more maintenance down the road. PeopleSoft provides a utility, like a library for messages, called the Message Catalog. This is a centralized location for messages so that they can be reused but maintained at a single point.

The Message Catalog is organized into message sets, groupings of messages that are similar or will be used in similar parts of the application. PeopleSoft delivers each of its applications with message sets that will be used within that module. These message sets have been reserved for their use. Message sets that can be used for customization are message sets 20,000–29,000. Not to worry, there will be enough for all of your customizations; within each message set, there is a maximum of 32,767 messages.

Setting up messages in the Message Catalog is done through the use of Utilities. To access the Message Catalog, **Go/PeopleTools/Utilities**. From the Utilities menu, select **Use/Message Catalog/Update Display** (or **Add**). The Search dialog box will be presented (Figure 14.6).

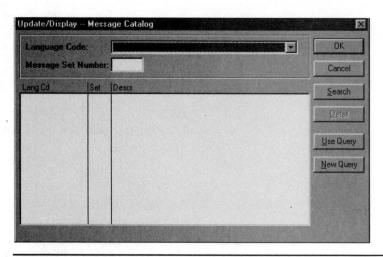

Figure 14.6   *Search dialog box for Message Catalog*

Note that the Message Catalog is organized by language. One of the strong benefits of using the Message Catalog is that for a global implementation, messages can be saved in different languages. Depending on the operator's language preference, the messages will be displayed to the user in that language. If the messages were hard coded into the application, this would be difficult to maintain.

Each message set has a message set number which uniquely identifies that set. Within the set, each message also has a unique message number. Multiple messages can be inserted into a message set, as shown in Figure 14.7

When a new message set is set up, the language and message set number are defined in the Add dialog box prior to coming into the panel. Once these key values are defined for the message set, the panel allows a description and short description to be entered for the message set. The description entered here should represent the description for the overall message set and should describe the types of messages that will be contained within this set.

The scroll area on the panel allows for insertion of multiple messages within the set. For each message, a message number, severity, message text, and explanation can be entered. The message number uniquely identifies the message in the set.

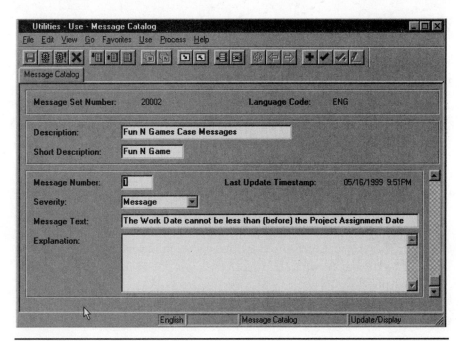

Figure 14.7   *Message Set panel*

The severity can be set to Cancel, Error, Warning, or Message. It should be used *only* when using the MessageBox function in PeopleCode. If MsgGet or MsgGetText are used, the severity should always be set to Message and the severity will be controlled from within the code. In contrast, for the MessageBox function, the severity is set and controlled within the Message Catalog, not within PeopleCode. (MsgGet, MsgGetText, and MessageBox functions are discussed in detail in the next section.) The severity options and results are presented in Table 14.2.

Table 14.2   *Message box severity*

Severity	Results
message	A message will display to the user; processing will continue
warning	A message will display to the user; same treatment as a warning
error	A message will display to the user; same treatment as an error
cancel	A message will display to the user; the panel will be canceled

The message text is what the user will see in the message box when the message is issued. A bind variable can also be included in the message text so that the value of the field can be included for the user to see. To use a bind variable, an input field is included in the PeopleCode (discussed in Message Function section). An example of using a bind variable is:

```
The value you entered of %1 does not meet the field criteria.
```

The result to the user will be:

```
The value you entered of 85 does not meet the field criteria
```

where the value of 85 was what the user entered into the field.

Finally, the explanation is the more detailed explanation of the message text and will be displayed when the user clicks on the **Explain** button in the Message dialog box.

After messages have been entered into the Message Catalog and have been saved, they can be referenced in the Message functions used in PeopleCode.

Message Functions

Once the messages have been established in the Message Catalog, they are referenced in the code using the message set and message numbers. There are three Message functions that can be used within PeopleCode. Note that these should only be used in PeopleCode events that can support warnings or errors; if these functions are used elsewhere, they will cause panel errors and will force the user to cancel work. The three functions are MsgGet, MsgGetText, and Messagebox.

MsgGet and MsgGetText are very similar in function. They allow the developer to use the error or warning keyword within PeopleCode and can reference a message stored within the Message Catalog. The distinct difference between MsgGet and MsgGetText is that the MsgGetText will not display the message set number and message number in the dialog box displayed to the user (notice the difference in Figures 14.8 and 14.9). From the developer's perspective, it is useful for the user to be able to reference the message set number and the message number when asking questions and therefore it is recommended that MsgGet be used.

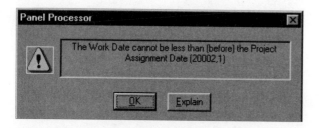

Figure 14.8   *Dialog box for MsgGet*

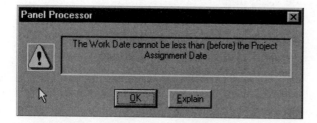

Figure 14.9   *Dialog box for MsgGetText*

The syntax for MsgGet and MsgGetText is the same:

```
Error MsgGet (messageset #, message #, "default message",
       input variable);
Warning MsgGetText (messageset #, message #, "default
        message", input variable);
```

The *message set* is the group to which the message is member. The *message number* is the number to be used for the message. The default message should be used just in case something is wrong with the Message Catalog or the entry cannot be found. That way, some message will be displayed to the user. The *input variable* is a field value that can be used as a bind variable and "passed in" to the message so that the value can be displayed in the message itself. An input variable must be included in the MsgGet or MsgGetText syntax and also must appear in the message catalog in the message text (as discussed earlier).

MsgGet and MsgGetText will display a standard message box. The message box will have OK and CANCEL buttons and will display an exclamation mark as the icon. Using either of these message functions offers no choices in terms of modifying the format of the message box.

The advantage of using the MessageBox function is the capability of formatting the message box icon, the message box title bar, and the buttons. The syntax for MessageBox is:

```
MessageBox (style #, "titlebar", messageset #, message #,
           "default message", input variable);
```

Note that there is no error or warning used in this statement. For the MessageBox function, the severity is controlled not by the PeopleCode statement but from the Message Catalog severity. Also notice that two new parameters need to be specified, style # and titlebar. The style # is the control for the buttons and the message box icon. The titlebar is the text that will appear in the titlebar of the messagebox. These options will *only* hold when the severity within the Message Catalog is set to message; all other times, the message box will inherit the characteristics that are default to the severity level.

The style number which controls the icon and the buttons displayed is a numeric parameter. This number represents the sum of values assigned to individual icons and buttons. Table 14.3 shows a list of values and their associated control.

Table 14.3 *Control values for buttons and icons*

Style Number	Control for Buttons and Icons
0	OK button
1	OK and CANCEL buttons
2	Abort, Retry, and Ignore buttons
3	Yes, No, and Cancel buttons
4	Yes and No buttons
5	Retry and Cancel buttons
0	First button is default
256	Second button is default
512	Third button is default
0	No icon
16	Stop-sign icon
32	Question-mark icon
48	Exclamation-point icon
64	Information icon (lowercase letter "I" in a circle)

Because the message box allows different buttons to be included, it therefore allows the user to make choices in which a return value is provided back to the Application Processor. This allows the developer to develop conditional logic or branched logic based upon the returned value. This type of capability is not possible with either MsgGet or MsgGetText. Table 14.4 presents the values that would be returned based upon the user selection.

Table 14.4 *Using return values with Message Box*

User Selection	Return Value
Warning Issued	−1
No Button	0
OK	1
Cancel	2
Abort	3
Retry	4
Ignore	5
Yes	6
No	7

15

Functions, Commands, and Variables

Understanding the Application Processor flow and the proper syntax for PeopleCode are critical to developing PeopleCode. But beyond the basics are many PeopleSoft-delivered functions that will allow the developer to create more complex code.

PeopleSoft provides an almost limitless number of built-in commands and functions. It would not be possible to cover each command or function within this discussion. We have identified the commands and functions commonly used throughout applications. For additional commands and functions, the developer should refer to the PeopleSoft online help tool, PeopleBooks. This tool covers every command and function that exists for use in the PeopleTools environment.

The commands and functions have been grouped into categories for ease of discussion. The categories that will be discussed include: panel display, panel control, scroll buffer functions, logical functions, date and time functions, effective-date functions, search dialog functions, menu functions, and the SQLExec function.

Panel Display Functions

Panel display functions manage how objects get displayed on the panel. They are most commonly used in the RowInit and Fieldchange PeopleCode events because these events control the initial setup of the panel and any changes that need to be made based on a user action.

Hide and *Unhide* functions control the field display by actually forcing the field to be hidden or unhidden on the panel. If a field is hidden, it is unseen by the user. These functions are typically used when the developer does not want the user to see a field or set of fields based on some condition. The syntax for these functions is straightforward.

```
Hide (fieldname);
Unhide (fieldname);
```

Gray and *Ungray* functions cause a panel display to be changed to gray or ungray. The display of a grayed field is similar to display only on a panel (discussed in Chapter 9). These functions are typically used to control whether a user can enter data into a field based upon a value set in another field. The panel in Figure 15.1 shows the Project Priority Rating field in the gray mode.

The syntax for these functions is quite simple.

```
Gray (fieldname);
Ungray (fieldname);
```

By default, panel display is set to Ungray and Unhidden. Therefore, no code needs to be developed if these defaults are acceptable.

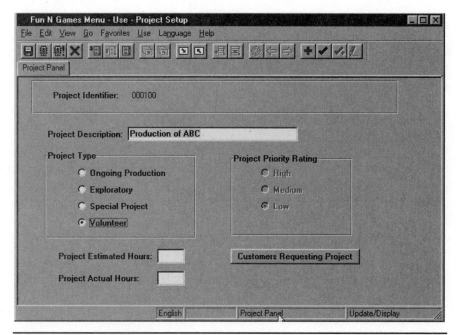

Figure 15.1   *Grayed field*

Panel Control Functions

Panel control functions control how the data in the buffer can be referenced and actions that can be taken on those rows. The following represent a selected number of functions that fall into this category.

ActiveRowCount provides a count of active rows of data for a record within a scroll level on a panel. The ActiveRowCount function is most often used to set the upper end of a loop function.

```
For &I= 1 to ActiveRowCount()
   statement 1;
   statement 2;
End-For;
```

The syntax for the function is:

```
ActiveRowCount(recordname)
```

CurrentRowNumber returns the row within the current buffer scroll level. This function may also be used to determine the CurrentRowNumber of a parent or grandparent scroll level (it cannot be used to reference a child-level scroll). The syntax for the function is:

```
CurrentRowNumber (scrolllevel)
```

If the scrolllevel parameter is not provided, the current scroll will be assumed.

The *PriorValue* function returns the last value of the field. This function is typically used within FieldEdit or FieldChange events to compare the current value of the field with the prior value of the field. PriorValue will be the most recent prior value; this has nothing to do with the last time the panel was saved. The syntax for the function is:

```
PriorValue(fieldname)
```

An example of how PriorValue could be used is:

```
Grand_Total = Grand_Total - PriorValue(fieldA) + fieldA
```

In this example, the grand total field is being recalculated to subtract out the prior value of fieldA and add in the new value of fieldA. This type of code might be placed on the Fieldchange event for fieldA so that when the value of the field changes, the grand total is recalculated.

SetDefault sets the field to a null value, based upon the field type. When the Application Processor passes through the default processing, the field will now be set to its default value. The syntax for the function is:

```
SetDefault(fieldname);
```

SetDefaultAll performs the similar function but will set the default for the field for all rows in the buffer. The syntax for this function is the same:

```
SetDefaultAll(fieldname);
```

%Menu, %Panel, and *%Panelgroup* allow the developer to reference the current menu, panel, or panel group. These functions are commonly used to check the

current menu, panel, or panel group to determine if logic should be performed. The syntax used for these functions is:

```
If %Menu = menuname
```

SetCursorPos positions the cursor in the record.field after an error or warning has been issued. This function is typically used in the SaveEdit event when there are multiple rows in the buffer. With this command, the cursor is positioned to the first row where the error or warning was found. It is important to position this function prior to the error statement in the code because otherwise it will not get executed. (PeopleCode does not execute any lines of code after the error statement.) The syntax for the function is:

```
SetCursorPos(panel, field, scroll-level);
```

DiscardRow and *StopFetching* are used within the RowSelect event to filter out rows that do not meet the criteria to be loaded into the panel buffer. DiscardRow will discard a row based on the criteria but continue to process other rows. StopFetching will stop retrieving rows after the criteria are met and is typically used when the rows are known to be in sort order. The syntax for these functions is:

```
DiscardRow();
StopFetching();
```

Scroll Buffer Functions

Scroll buffer functions are used to control the data loaded into the scroll buffer areas. Common scroll buffer functions are ScrollSelect and SortScroll.

ScrollSelect selects data into the scroll area and uses an imbedded SQL statement to set conditions on which rows should be selected. The syntax for this function is:

```
ScrollSelect (level #, recordname, "SQL statement", bind
              variables)
```

For example, to select from the product table all products where the price was less than 5, the syntax would appear as:

```
ScrollSelect (1, PRODUCT_TBL, "where price <5");
```

SortScroll sorts the data loaded into the scroll area. Many times this function is used on a panel attached to a field that is set up with radio buttons. The radio buttons provide the user with sort choices; each time the radio button is changed (fieldchange), the Sortscroll function is executed. The syntax for this function is:

```
SortScroll (level #, recordname,sortfield, "A/D");
```

The last parameter indicates whether the sort will be ascending or descending; either "A" or "D" should be specified. The sort parameter must be included in quotations and is case sensitive.

Logical Functions

Logical functions allow field values to be tested to determine whether they are populated or blank. The most commonly used logical functions are ALL and NONE.

ALL tests a field to determine if it is populated. ALL will return true if the field is populated and will return FALSE if it is not populated. NONE also tests a field to determine if it is populated. NONE will return true if the field is not populated and will return FALSE if it is populated. The syntax used for these functions is:

```
ALL(fieldname)
NONE(fieldname)
```

To test the condition for multiple fields, multiple fields can be included in the parentheses; the fields should be separated by commas. If you are testing multiple fields it is important to understand that there are implied "ands" so when using ALL, all fields must be populated in order to get a return value of true. For NONE, all fields must not be populated in order to get a return value of true.

There are other functions which are variations of ALL and NONE:

▲ ALLORNONE will return true if all fields have a value or if all fields are null.
▲ ONLYONE will return true only if one of the fields has a value; if more than one field has a value, then this function will return false.

▲ ONLYONEORNONE will return true if only one of the fields has a value or if none of the fields has a value; otherwise, it will return false.

Date and Time Functions

Date and time functions allow calculations and functions to be performed on fields with date and time formats.

The *%date* function returns the system date. %date is typically used as a default for date entry fields when it is common that the date to be entered will be the system date. Effective-date fields usually have %date set as the default value.

AddToDate allows you to take a date and add (or subtract) years, months, and days to determine a future (or historical) date. The syntax for this function is:

```
AddToDate(date, num_years, num_months, num_days)
```

Days365 calculates the number of days between two valid dates based upon a 365-day year. The syntax for this function is:

```
Days365(date1, date2)
```

There is also another function that performs the same calculation based upon a 360-day year. The syntax for this function is the same, just substituting 360 for 365.

Effective-Date Functions

Effective-date functions allow calculations and determination of rows based upon effective date and effective sequence number.

The *CurrentEffDt* function will return the current effective date of the current scroll area. This function might be used to compare another date with the current effective date of the scroll level. The syntax of the function is:

```
CurrEffDt(scrolllevel);
```

PriorEffDt will return the field value of the row with the prior effective date. This function is usually used to compare the value of the specified field with the value of the field on the prior effective dated row. This function is obviously only relevant for effective dated records. The syntax of the function is:

```
PriorEffDt(fieldname);
```

Search Dialog Functions

The Search Dialog functions control how the Search dialog appears. The most common function (previously discussed) is the *SetSearchDialogBehavior*. This function will allow the developer to force the way the dialog box behaves. The syntax for this function is:

```
SetSearchDialogBehavior(parameter);
```

The parameter can be set to either 0 or 1. The 0 will suppress the display of the dialog box if the box has been prepopulated with a fully qualified search key. The 1 will force the dialog box to display even if there is a fully qualified key. By default, if there were a fully qualified search key and the SetSearchDialogBehavior function were not used, the Application Processor would display the Search dialog. Therefore, this function is typically used to suppress the dialog.

Menu Functions

As we reviewed during the discussion of the PrePopUp event, some functions can be used to control menu appearance. The functions commonly used for menu control are DisableMenuItem, HideMenuItem, and CheckMenuItem. The syntax for these functions is:

```
DisableMenuItem(BARNAME.menubarname, ITEMNAME.menuitemname);
HideMenuItem(BARNAME.menubarname, ITEMNAME.menuitemname);
CheckMenuItem(BARNAME.menubarname, ITEMNAME.menuitemname);
```

The DisableMenuItem will gray out the menu choice on the popup menu; EnableMenuItem will perform the opposite function. HideMenuItem will hide the menu choice altogether; while UnhideMenuItem will perform the opposite function. CheckMenuItem will place a check mark next to the menu item and UncheckMenuItem will perform the opposite function.

SQLExec Function

The SQLExec function allows an SQL statement to be executed directly to the relational database without using the Application Processor. This function is very powerful but should be used with caution. If data is selected using the SQLExec function, the return can only be one row of data. If data is updated directly to the database using SQLExec, the function can only be used in the SavePreChange, WorkFlow, and SavePostChange events. The syntax for this function is:

```
SQLExec ("SQL statement", bind variables, output variables)
```

One output variable must be provided for each column selected in the SQL statement. Note that no validation will be performed on the SQL statement; therefore, if the statement is incorrect or inefficient, it will still be executed to the database.

Derived/Work Records

We introduce the topic of a derived/work record in the PeopleCode section because this record type is typically used for PeopleCode development. A derived/work record stores temporary fields whose values can be shared across multiple PeopleCode programs and/or across panel groups.

Derived/work records are not defined to the underlying RDBMS. This record type is not built nor does it contain key fields. In fact, the fields on this record are typically sequenced in alphabetical order. The PeopleSoft naming convention for a derived/work record is DERIVED_recordname.

The two most common uses of derived/work records are: 1) to store temporary variables that can be presented on panels for calculations or display and do not need to be maintained in the database, and 2) for transferring between panels so that a value or values can be passed from one panel group to another.

Variables

As with any development language, variables can be used within PeopleCode. Both local and global variables can be defined for a PeopleCode program. Local variables keep their value only for the life of a PeopleCode program. In contrast, global variables keep their value for the life of the session in which the application user is working. Because a global variable maintains its value through the life of a session, the value can be passed between panel groups. Global variables are difficult to maintain and keep track of; if the intent is to have a variable that can be shared across PeopleCode programs and across panel groups, we encourage you to use the derived/work record fields.

Variables should be declared prior to the PeopleCode program and specify a data type. If no data type is specified, then PeopleSoft will choose the data type based on how it is being used. The data type ANY can be used if the developer is unsure what type of data will be stored within the variable. Syntax for declaring a variable is:

```
Local/Global datatype &variablename
```

For example:

```
Local Number &amount
Global String &lastname
Global Any &valueA
```

Although global variables are defined for the life of a session, they must be declared in each PeopleCode program in which they are to be used.

Multiple Scroll Levels

When you work with code on panels with more than one scroll area, it is important to understand where the code must be placed in order to execute properly and it is also important to reference the scroll areas appropriately. Basically, the developer must tell PeopleSoft where the data is being stored in the buffer so that the code can be executed. Remember that PeopleSoft loads data into the buffer based on a top-down approach, level 0, level 1, level 2, level 3 and then back to level 1 to get the next high-level key.

The easiest way to handle code on a panel with multiple levels is to place the code at the level at which you want it to execute. If you are performing a validation at level 2, place your code on the level 2 record. Sometimes, though, things are not that easy; based on what you are trying to accomplish, the code must be placed at a different level. In that case, the rule is to access the child-level record through the parent-level record. What that also means is that when you are writing code, you need to provide PeopleSoft with a path to find the child record from the parent record.

So, for functions that require a record name as a parameter, both the parent record name and the child record name must be provided. The syntax for a function in this case would be:

```
function (parentrecordname, childrecordname);
```

An example would be ActiveRowCount, which requires the record as the parameter. If the code is written at the parent-level record, then the scroll path must be specified. For example,

```
ActiveRowCount (parentrecord, childrecord);
```

The same approach holds true if the function requires a record name and a row number as the parameter. In that case, the record name and row number of the parent must be specified before the record name and row number of the child.

Part 5

Completing the Application

16

Administer Security

Once the PeopleTools application is developed, security must be defined to allow access to the application. Although it might seem unusual, even someone who has developed or modified the application must be provided with security access to execute and test the functionality. Consequently, before the application can be fully tested, the developer must be given security rights.

Types of Security

There are various levels of information system security, inside and outside PeopleSoft. Aside from network security and database security, which are managed outside the PeopleSoft environment (and are outside the scope of this book), PeopleSoft applications have various levels of security. Access can be managed at the field, row, query, object, and application levels. The focus of this chapter will be a discussion of application-level security. We will introduce the other security types but will not review them in depth.

Field-level security is managed through the use of PeopleCode and panel display. If a field should not be available to an application user, the developer can use PeopleCode to hide it based on the operator's signon to the system. Field security can be very tedious to develop and maintain; there should be strong justification for securing at a field level.

Row-level security is commonly used in the PeopleSoft delivered applications. In Human Resource applications, row-level security is used to limit the information a user employee can view and modify. Within Financial applications, row-level security is used to limit what information a user can view and modify about a particular business unit or department. Row-level security is managed by setting up security views which limit the data loaded into the panels by using the security view as the search record.

Query security is used to limit what types of queries a user can develop and run within the Query tool as well as to limit the tables to which the user has access. Limiting a user's access to a table within the query tool will not affect whether that same user has access to that information in the online application. These are separately managed security tools.

Object security limits access of developers to specific database objects in Application Designer. There is a separate Object Security tool which requires that object groups be created before users or user groups are granted access to the object groups.

Application security provides security access to the application including the menus and panels the user can access. It also grants rights to the application user for when he/she can sign onto the system or how long he/she can stay logged on but not be actively working. To provide a thorough coverage of application security, we must first introduce the Security Administrator tool. This will be followed by a discussion of access types and security properties.

Security Administrator Tool and Access Types

The Security Administrator is the tool which allows the definition of application security profiles. To access the tool, use **Go/PeopleTools/Security Administrator**. Once the tool is open, a profile needs to be opened or created. A profile can be opened (**File/Open**) to review it or to make modifications. If **File/New** is selected, a new profile will be created. A profile can be an operator or a class of operators. These are two different types of PeopleSoft security.

An operator definition should be thought of as an individual user logon. For each application user, there should be an operator ID established. An operator either has its own unique attributes or may inherit attributes from a class.

A class of operators can be thought of as a security group. A class cannot be used to sign onto PeopleSoft. A class is typically created when there are multiple users who should have the same security profile. Instead of setting up each operator ID with the same attributes, the class can be setup and then the operators can be assigned to the class and inherit the attributes of the class. This allows for easier maintenance because if the group's access needs change, the change can be made to the class and each the operator will inherit the change.

A new feature of version 7 is that an operator can be assigned to more than one class. One class must be identified as the primary class for that operator. Differences in terms of how attributes will be inherited from primary or other classes are dependent upon the type of attribute. The way that an operator inherits attributes from multiple classes will be discussed later in this chapter.

Security Attributes

The security attributes that can be defined for an operator or a class are very similar. For an operator, the following attributes can be defined: General, Menu Items, Signon Times, Process Groups, and Classes. Obviously, the attribute that is not defined for a class is the Class attribute (a class cannot be assigned to another class).

General attributes, shown in Figure 16.1, are set up for an operator to define the operator description, the disconnect interval and time-out minutes (only set for an operator if the operator is not linked to a class), the operator password, language preference, access profile (for access to the underlying relational database management system), and the employee ID (if operator will be restricted from access to his/her own employee information).

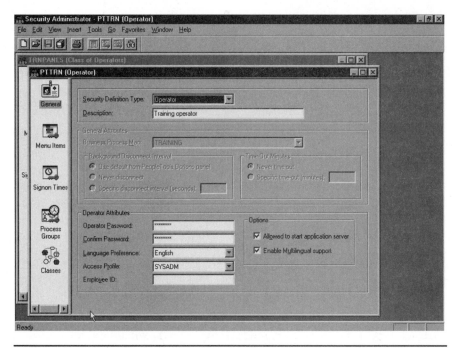

Figure 16.1   *General Attributes panel*

The background disconnect will disconnect the user session from the database if the user has not used the application in the interval specified; once the user begins to work in the application again, the connection will be reconnected. In contrast, the time-out minutes will actually log out the user from the PeopleSoft application when there has been no activity in the session. The logout process is uneventful; in fact, no warning will even be issued to the user prior to logout. The time-out minutes should be used with caution because a user could be logged out in the midst of making a large number of changes.

The menu items (Figure 16.2) provide a view of the menus to which the operator has some level of access. The operator may have access to all panel groups and actions within that menu or to only a single panel and action within that menu. To understand the menu security provided to the operator, double click on one of the menu items. Another window will open up to display the Authorized Menu Items for that particular menu, as shown in Figure 16.3.

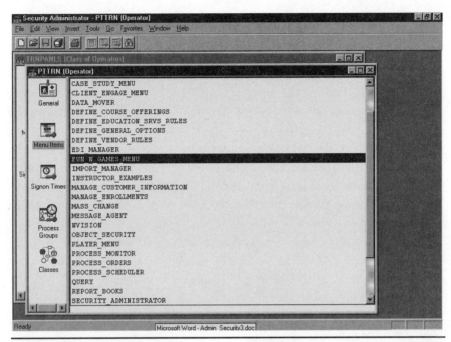

Figure 16.2 *Menu Items panel*

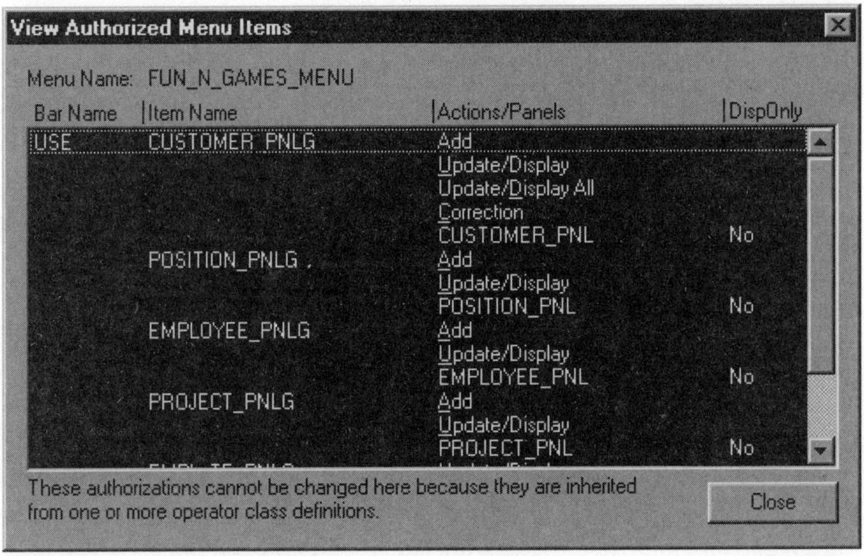

Figure 16.3 *Authorized Menu Items panel*

Any panel or action item highlighted in blue indicates that the operator has access. If an item is highlighted blue, clicking on that line will remove access. To provide access to any action on a panel, the action must be highlighted along with the panel name. It is important to note that if an operator is linked to a class, it will inherit the menu access set up for that class. In this case, changes to an operator's menu access cannot be managed at the operator level but must be done at the class level.

If a new menu is created and access needs to be provided to an operator, the menu must first be inserted into the list of menu items (**Insert/Menu Name**). The list of menus displayed from Insert/Menu will be a list of all menus to which the user currently has no access. Once the menu has been inserted, access to the panels and actions within the menu can be granted.

The signon times restrict when an operator can access the application. By default, a new operator will have access to the application 24 hours a day, 7 days a week. To modify the signon access, double click on the day and modify the access times (see Figure 16.4).

Figure 16.4   *Signon Times panel*

To add additional signon times, from the insert menu, **Insert/Signon Time** and make the appropriate modifications to the access times. Although it is not displayed, the value for the seconds for any time will be 59. Therefore, to provide an operator with access until 11:00am, the time should be entered as 10:59 because the system interprets this as 10:59:59.

Process groups allow the operator to be assigned one or more processes that the operator has rights to run. Double clicking on a process group allows the properties to be set. An operator assigned to a class will be unable to double click on the process group listing. To grant access to a new process group, add it to the list from the insert menu (**Insert/Process Group**).

The class view allows the operator to be linked to one or more class. As mentioned earlier, if the operator is linked to more than one class, the primary class must be identified. It is important to understand how an operator inherits security access if the operator is a member of more than one class. Table 16.1 depicts how this is handled.

Table 16.1 *Operator security access*

Security Attribute	Controlled by
Disconnect Interval	primary class
Time-out Minutes	primary class
Menu Items	all classes
Signon Times	all classes
Process Groups	all classes

Therefore, if an operator is assigned to more than one class, the disconnect interval and time-out minutes will be inherited from the primary class. For menu times, signon times, and process groups, the operator will inherit the attributes from *all* classes to which it is assigned; we may consider the operator as getting the "best of all" classes in this case.

For example if an operator is only assigned to a single class, that operator will inherit all the security attributes from that class. If another operator is assigned to multiple classes, the disconnect interval and time-out minutes will be inherited from the primary class but all other security attributes will be a combination of the attributes from the multiple classes.

Changes to Security Profiles

Security changes made to an operator or a class will not take effect until the user signs out of the application and signs back in. The security change will take place when the user signs back in because the new profile can now be retrieved into cache (on the client machine) from the database.

Test and Debug the Application

17

One of the final and most critical steps in the development process is thoroughly testing the application. The application must be tested to ensure that it functions as expected and that there are no unforeseen issues. There are various types of testing such as unit testing, application testing, and integration testing. Unit testing is performed to test a self-contained program. Unit tests are discrete and independent of any other development for the application. For application testing, the entire system or application is tested to ensure that once all the pieces are brought together the system performs as expected. Finally, integration testing is used to test the application along with other applications with which it interfaces. The focus of this chapter is application testing, but the same concepts apply to whatever type of testing is performed.

There are no specific PeopleSoft-provided tools used for application testing, but there are PeopleSoft tools that can be used to assist with the debugging process. In the sections that follow, we will suggest steps to test the PeopleSoft application and then introduce some of the debugging tools.

Test Cases and Test Plans

Just as with any other application development project, a thorough test plan should be developed to test all potential scenarios. Much of the testing can be performed in the user front end (by executing the application) to ensure that the menus and panels are performing as expected. Testing that the underlying relational tables are populated with data from the PeopleSoft application should also be conducted.

The test cases should be developed based on the specifications for the application. They should test for both positive and negative scenarios, i.e., the test should ensure that the application performs "positive" or required functions and prevents "negative" or undesired functions. Test cases may be constructed for increasing levels of difficulty and complexity. A common scenario would test for a complete "typical" business event or sequence of events.

Because a large majority of what we have covered in this book has focused on front-end application development, the focus here will be on online testing. It should be understood that online testing only is one piece of the testing that needs to be performed on an application. Other areas of testing include database testing, performance and stress testing, testing of batch processes, and testing of interfaces (movement of data between applications).

Online Testing

When online testing is performed, consideration must be given to the specifications for the application. During the design process the business requirements were translated into design specifications which were then addressed in the development process. The test plan that is developed should refer to the design specifications. To the extent that there were changes to the design during the development process and these changes were not reflected in the design specifications, these changes must also be incorporated into the test plan.

One of the first steps in testing the online application is to test the navigation. At this step, the goal is to ensure that the menus are organized into the desired menu groups, that the panels are organized into the desired panel groups, and that the appropriate actions are available for each of the panel groups. Questions the developer should ask at this point include:

▲ Are the menus appearing where and as expected?
▲ Are the panel groups appearing where and as expected?
▲ Does it make sense that all the panels should appear in the same panel group?
▲ Are the appropriate actions available for the panels?

Once the navigation of the application appears to be acceptable, the next step is to test the search processing or the use of the Search dialog box. At this point, we want to ensure that the appropriate Search dialog box is presented and that the Search keys and Alternate Search keys "make sense" for the panel which is about to be launched. Some of the questions that should be asked include:

▲ Is the correct Search dialog box created for the panel group?
▲ Are the expected Search and Alternate Search keys available?
▲ Is the code created for the Search dialog executing properly?
▲ Are the appropriate rows of data returned?

When we enter the panel, the panel testing needs to be comprehensive. This is where the user does most of the work and where most of the data validation is performed. It is critical that the panels function as expected. Again, questions that should be asked and cases that should be tested include:

▲ Are validations on the panel available as expected (prompt table, yes/no, translate)?
▲ Are all related display fields appearing; with the correct values?
▲ Is the effective-dated functionality of the panel operating correctly?
▲ Are required field edits in place?
▲ Are record defaults in place?
▲ Can multiple children rows be inserted into a parent record and saved successfully?
▲ Can the panel be successfully saved after data has been entered?
▲ Is PeopleCode executing based on the conditions coded?

Each of these areas of the online test should be clearly documented in a test plan so that a thorough test can be conducted. Often, there is a separate testing or quality team that performs the testing. This is helpful because team members can approach the test from an unbiased perspective; they have not performed the development tasks and might try something "unexpected" just as an application user would.

Database Testing

To ensure that the PeopleSoft application is correctly inserting and updating data stored in the RDBMS, queries should be written and executed directly at the database. Once data has been entered or updated in the application, use an SQL tool to query against the relational tables. Of particular interest should be whether all data rows and columns are being properly stored in the tables. Basic queries can be performed to ensure rows were inserted as expected. Also of interest is to ensure that rows of data in parent child tables are reflected correctly.

Performance Testing and Stress Testing

When testing the application for "real-life" application performance, the quantity of data that will be expected within the application must be tested. Often, the most important performance consideration will be database size and other physical characteristics. Performance testing will ensure that the database is tuned properly and that the table sizes have been appropriately defined. This task should be performed jointly by the developer and the database administrator. To perform this test properly, estimations will have to be made about the volume of data that is expected to be handled by the application. This estimate can be based upon existing systems or on known transaction volumes that a company processes within a given timeframe. Although it is outside the scope of this book, there are third-party tools that can be used for performance and stress testing.

Debugging

During the testing process, issues or problems are typically uncovered. Although PeopleSoft does not have testing tools, there are a few tools available that can assist the developer with the debugging function. The Application Reviewer tool (refer to next section) will allow the developer actually to execute the application and understand what is happening in PeopleCode as the user performs the various tasks within the application. SQL Trace (refer to section on SQL Trace later in this chapter) will allow the developer to understand what SQL is getting performed as the user executes the application. SQL Trace writes the SQL to a file which can then be reviewed by the developer. Each of these tools is discussed in more detail in the sections below.

Application Reviewer

The Application Reviewer tool will allow the developer to review the PeopleCode as it is executing online. The benefit of this tool is it helps the developer to understand the step-by-step execution of the code and to view the values of local and global variables as the program is executing. Application Reviewer replaces the utility known as PeopleCode Trace.

To use the Application Reviewer tool, the first step is to execute the panel (or panel group) that will be under scrutiny. Once the panel group is open, the Application Reviewer tool is accessed by **Go/PeopleTools/Application Reviewer**. At this point, there is a "blank" screen. The most useful next step is to use the Break at Start function, which can be accessed from **Break/Break at Start**. This command will cause the Application Reviewer to become active when the PeopleCode in the application begins to execute. To use this feature, once Break at Start has been selected, switch back to the panel being tested and begin to navigate the panel. As soon as any PeopleCode is encountered, Application Reviewer will "take over" and you will be brought back to the tool. A new window will be opened; the window titlebar will have the name of the field and event on which code is currently executing (refer to Figure 17.1). To test the code, pass through the code step by step by using **F8** or **Run/Step**. The step process will execute the code line by line and the developer can review what is occurring.

Break points can also be specifically set in the code to force Application Reviewer to break during the execution of the code. To set break points, select **File/Open**. A list of records and fields will be listed. Choose the record and field and then choose the program or PeopleCode event (note that an event must exist on that record.field in order for any programs to be listed). Highlight the appropriate program and select **Open**. This will open the PeopleCode program in Application Reviewer. Break points can be inserted either using the menu **Break/Break at Cursor** or by using the **F9** key. Break points are not visible in the code window. To view the break points, **Break/List** will open a window, Figure 17.2, which will list all breaks that have been established. Break points can be cleared using the clear button.

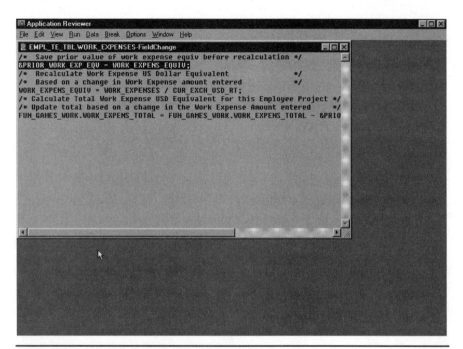

Figure 17.1   *PeopleCode program window*

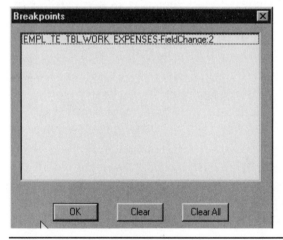

Figure 17.2   *Listing of all breaks*

In addition to executing the code line by line, Application Reviewer will also allow the developer to view the values of local and global variables. To view the local and global variables, open up the local and global variable windows by selecting **View/Local** or **View/Globals**. The values of the variables displayed in the windows (as shown in Figure 17.3) will be automatically updated as the values change during program execution. To review multiple windows concurrently, cascade or tile from the Windows menu.

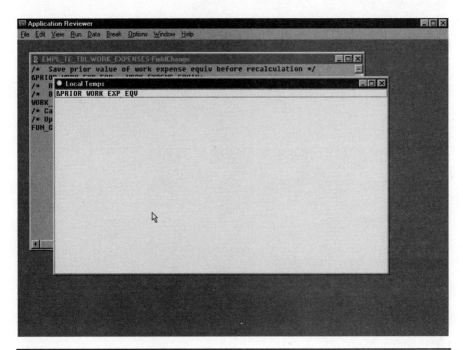

Figure 17.3   *Local variables window*

The values of PeopleSoft fields can also be reviewed within Application Reviewer. To determine the current value of a field, select **Data/ PeopleSoft Variable**. This will open a display variable window (Figure 17.4). The variable name must be typed into the Edit box (there is no drop-down list available). The variable must be typed in the format recordname.fieldname. Once the field name is entered, press the Display button and the value of the field will be displayed.

The results of the review can also be written to a log file. To specify what details are written to the log file, set the log options, **Options/Log** as seen in Figure 17.5.

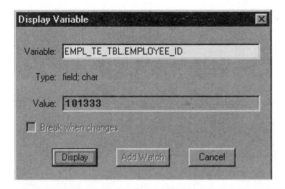

Figure 17.4   *Variable window*

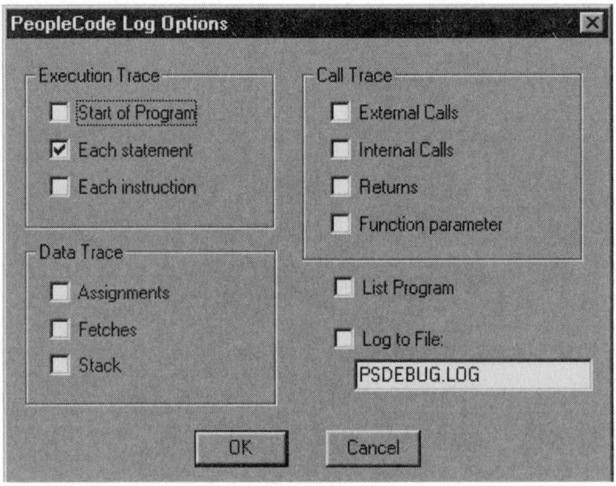

Figure 17.5   *Log window*

SQL Trace

The SQL Trace tool allows the SQL statement executed by the Application Processor to be traced and recorded. The trace will be recorded in a specified trace file. The SQL trace can be "turned on" from either Configuration Manager for the workstation or from **Utilities/SQL Trace** for the server. There is a significant difference if the trace is turned on for the workstation versus for the server; the server will perform the trace for all users, whereas for the workstation, the trace will only be conducted for that particular workstation. The Utilities menu will not provide as many trace options. When setting up the trace through either of these paths, note that the trace will degrade the performance of the application. Therefore, after the trace has been performed ensure that you turn the trace off.

When accessing the SQL Trace from Configuration Manager, there will be a number of options in terms of what can be traced. The SQL Trace options are shown in Figure 17.6. Accessing the SQL Trace from the Utilities menu will have some but not all of the same options available.

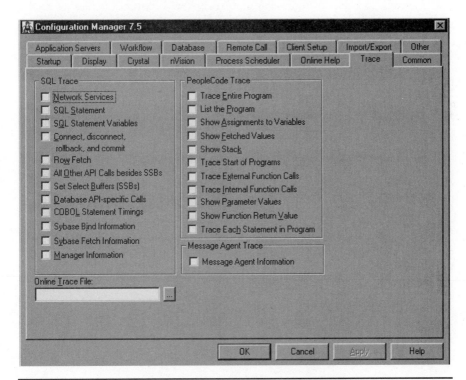

Figure 17.6   *SQL Trace options (from Configuration Manager)*

The SQL Statement and SQL Statement Variables options will capture the full SQL statement and the variable value(s) will also be recorded. Other options relate to the database and buffer selects. For more detailed information on each of these options, refer to PeopleBooks. Once the SQL Trace options have been selected, the Trace file should be specified. The information requested will be written to the Trace file.

The application should then be executed. As the application is executing, the SQL details are being written to the Trace file. (This is why having the trace on during application execution will degrade performance.) Once the developer has completed tracing the portion of the application, the trace should be turned off. The Trace file can then be reviewed to understand what SQL statements were being executed to the relational database management system. This tool is particularly useful in resolving data retrieval issues. It is also useful to look at the relative timing of statements to identify any long-running SQL, which may indicate potential performance problems that may need to be addressed with database tuning (such as additional indexes) or with potential changes to the application design.

18

Globalization

PeopleSoft applications can be implemented to support users with different national language and currency requirements. PeopleSoft application packages can be licensed and installed in nine different international languages, including: Canadian French, Dutch, English (U.S.), French, German, International English, Japanese, Portuguese, and Spanish. Translated versions of the applications display all application text, including menu text, panel text, message text, and even some of the application data in one of the translated languages.

239

This process of implementing and potentially customizing the applications to support different languages and currencies is termed the "globalization" process. In this section we discuss the concepts of globalization and introduce how operators can select a language preference. In subsequent sections we discuss the process of globalization as it relates to the different types of application objects. Note, the Application Designer tool and other development tools are (presently) only available in English.

For each PeopleSoft application database a single "base" language is selected at the time of installation. This should be the language that will be most commonly required by application users. Additional, "non-base" languages can also be supported within the same database. If additional non-base languages are installed, then each application user can select a personal language preference. The PeopleSoft application objects and data will be displayed in the non-base language of preference if that particular language is available, otherwise the application will be displayed in the base language. This model supports numerous concurrent users with different language preferences, all working in a single PeopleSoft database with translated versions of (essentially) the same functioning application.

Aside from the visible difference in language, another difference between an application used in the base language compared to the same application used in a non-base language *may be* the run-time performance. This is because during execution of the application for a non-base language, database views are used to join the base tables to Related Language tables to bring in the non-base language data values (see discussion of Related Language records later in this chapter). This makes the PeopleSoft database larger and the performance of the application slower. The change in the size of the database and the impact on the performance of the application will be a function of the number of non-base languages supported and other factors and is difficult for us to predict. It would be prudent to allow time in your globalization work effort for performance analysis and (perhaps) database tuning.

Selecting Language Preference

There are two types of language preferences that may be set for a given PeopleSoft application session. The first is the language preference for PeopleTools "system" resources, including the PeopleSoft signon screen and the PeopleSoft system menus such as the File, Edit, and View menus. The second type is the language preference for application-specific resources, such as application menus and application panels. The first type of language preference is initially set in the Configuration Manager tool on the Common Settings tab, as seen in Figure 18.1.

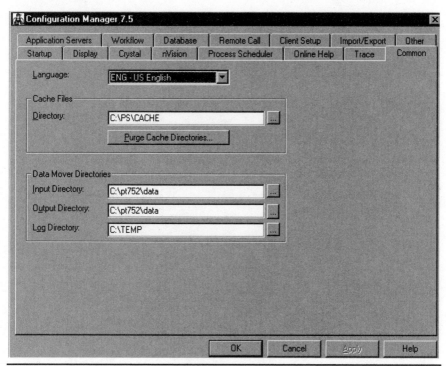

Figure 18.1 *Configuration Manager—Common tab*

Here, the language for the PeopleSoft system resources is established through the selection and execution of a language-specific DLL at startup. This language preference, like all other Configuration Manager settings, is set for the given workstation session regardless of the application user. The second type of language preference, for application-specific resources, is established for the individual operator in Security Administrator. Please see Figure 18.2 for an example of an operator profile.

The individual's language preference is set among other Operator attributes on the General display of the Operator profile. Beginning in PeopleSoft version 7.5 there is also the option to permit the operator to "Enable Multilingual Support." This feature allows the operator dynamically to switch between different languages for application resources while in the application. The switch is made using the new **Language** menu bar now found on language-sensitive panels. Figure 18.3 shows the Language menu bar active on a panel taken from our case study application.

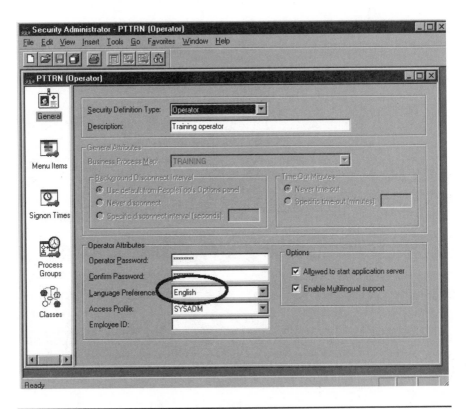

Figure 18.2   *Operator attributes in Security Administrator*

The language preference for application resources can also be reset while the operator remains logged on to the PeopleSoft database. This is extremely useful for application developers working on a globalization effort. Go to the **PeopleTools/Utilities/Use/International Preferences** panel to reset your language preference, as seen in Figure 18.4.

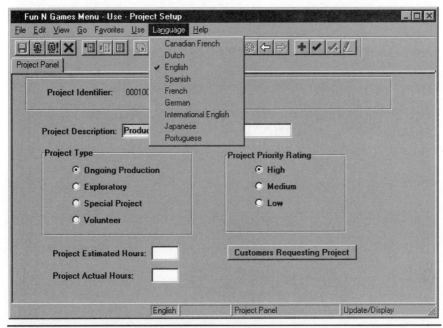

Figure 18.3   *Language menu bar on a sample application panel*

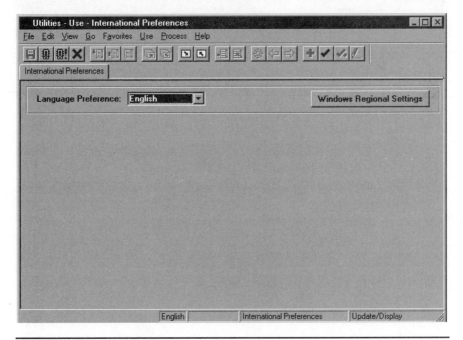

Figure 18.4   *PeopleTools utilities—International Preferences panel*

Here the operator can reset the Language preference. This change will take effect for the next panel group started by the operator. From the International Preferences panel the operator can also start the Windows Regional Settings dialog box to set the display of numbers, currency, date, and time display (see more discussion of currency later in this chapter).

Translating Applications

The complete PeopleTools application displayed to an end-user is composed of numerous application objects, including menus, panel groups, panels, records, and fields. Basically, each of these application objects has a text label for display to the application user during panel execution. Figure 18.5 shows a panel taken from our sample application, with the labels "translated" into a non-base language (Spanish).

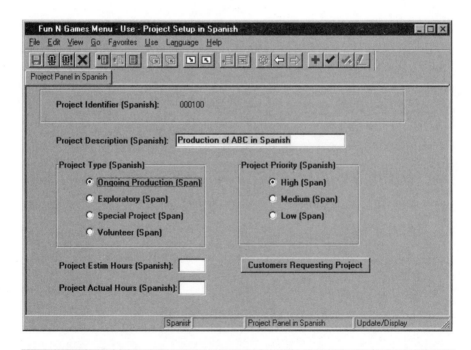

Figure 18.5 *A non-base language panel*

These text labels are defined by the application developer and by default are defined and stored in the PeopleTools database and displayed to the application user in the selected base language. However, the text labels associated with each application object can be translated and stored by the developer in the PeopleTools tables in one or more non-base languages. These application object text labels can be defined in non-base languages by the developer working either with Application Designer or with Translate Utilities. To define them in Application Designer, the developer must set his/her own language preference to the specific non-base language desired. Then each application object type can be modified and saved to define and store the non-base language text labels. Alternatively, Translate Utilities provides a convenient way to update a number of application object labels in one session. Use of both Application Designer and Translate Utilities will be discussed in the following section for each important application object type (for globalization).

Translating Fields

As discussed above, each of the application objects including menus, panel groups, panels, and fields has a text label for display. For the field, the text labels for display are the field long name and the field short name. These names will be used by default on panels as the field labels.

To translate the field labels, the developer can simply change language preference to the non-base language desired (**PeopleTools/Utilities/International Preferences**) and then open the field in the Object Workspace of Application Designer. The developer can then change the field long name and short name to the appropriate translated labels and save the field definition as seen in Figure 18.6.

Alternatively, the developer may **Go** to the **PeopleTools/Translate** menu and **Use/Translate Fields** panel to change a large number of field labels in a single translation session. Each of the Translate utility panels works in a similar fashion. The application developer selects a target language and performs a search to list a set of application objects for label translation. Fields may be searched for based on panel field usage and on whether or not a Target language translation already exists. Please refer to Figure 18.7 for an example of the Translate Fields search option dialog box.

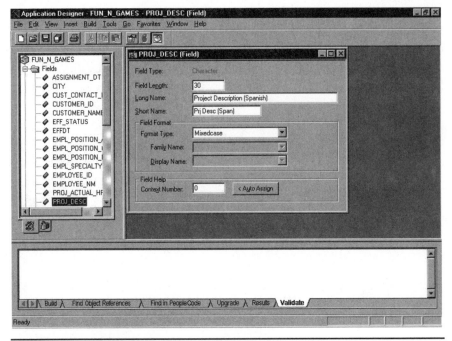

Figure 18.6   *Field definition with names in another language*

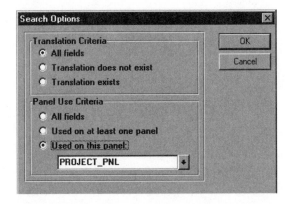

Figure 18.7   *Translate Fields search options*

It is probably useful to limit the search in this manner to avoid listing all fields
in the PeopleTools database. The resulting panel is a display of fields that meet
the search criteria, showing the base language field labels. The developer
(translator) will enter the Target Language field labels on the Translate fields
panel as seen in Figure 18.8.

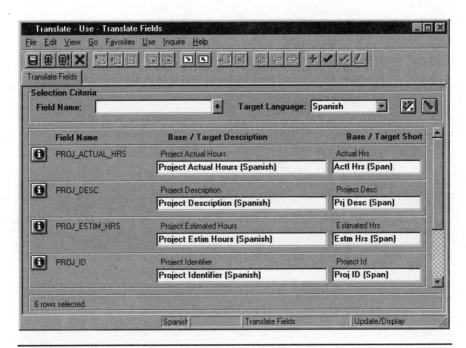

Figure 18.8   *Translate Fields panel*

Either way the field names are translated, the base language version of the field labels will *not* be changed, but the non-base language field labels will be saved in the PeopleTools tables. A panel that includes this field with a default field label will now display the non-base language field label when the panel is executed by an operator with language preference set for that non-base language. However, the application developer will probably want to create a non-base language specific panel (discussed later).

Translate the Translate (XLAT) Field Values

The XLAT long and short name values for fields with XLAT values defined will often be displayed on panels, typically in drop-down list boxes or as radio buttons. Therefore the XLAT long and short name values may also be translated into non-base languages. This can be accomplished using Application Designer. As before, set the language preference to the desired non-base language and open the field in the Object Workspace. Select the Translate Values tab in the field properties to display the current (base language) XLAT values. Click the **Change** button, overtype the long name and short name associated with the XLAT values, and **Save** to store the desired non-base language XLAT value descriptions.

Alternatively and probably simpler, the **PeopleTools/Translate/Translate Xlats** panel may be used to define and save the non-base language XLAT value long and short descriptions. Please see Figure 18.9.

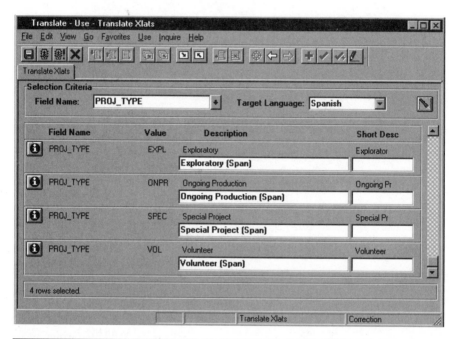

Figure 18.9   *Translate Xlats panel*

On this panel the developer will select the field with XLAT values and select the target language for the translation. The valid XLAT values will be displayed. The developer can enter long and short names (descriptions) in the target language and save the panel.

Creating Translated Panels

For the panel object, a new translated panel will be created for each non-base language. However, after changing/translating the field names (labels) and XLAT values, much of the work in creating a translated panel is already complete. The developer resets the language preference to the desired non-base language and opens the panel in the Object Workspace. The translated non-base language field labels and XLAT values are immediately displayed on the panel. Please see

Figure 18.10 for a panel from our case study, opened up in Application Designer with non-base language field labels and XLAT values (Spanish).

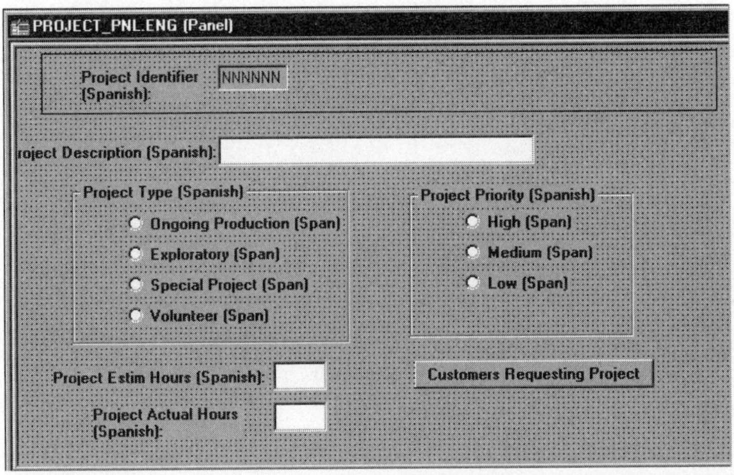

Figure 18.10   *Panel opened in Application Designer with Non-Base Language preference set*

Any static text or field labels input as text, rather than as the RFT long or short names, must now be translated by the developer. This shows the maintenance benefits of using the RFT long or short names as the panel field labels. Since non-base language text may be of different size/length, the panel alignment may need adjustment. Use **Save As** to save the panel with the same panel name but with the desired non-base language selected as shown in Figure 18.11.

Upon execution of this panel by an application user, the language-specific panel will be displayed to the operator with a language preference set to that specific non-base language. As a tip to developers, if you expect that your application will require "globalization" it is wise to allow extra space on the panel for non-base language labels. This will simplify the alignment of labels on the translated panels.

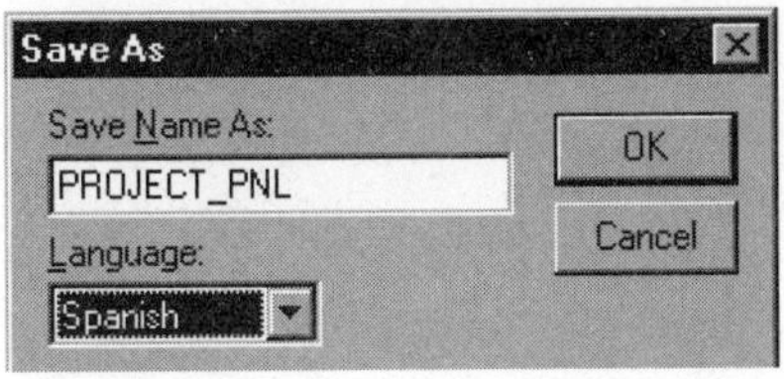

Figure 18.11   *Non-Base Language panel—Save As box*

Translating Panel Groups

For panel groups, the text labels displayed to application users are the panel group item labels and panel group folder tab labels. Each of these types of labels can be changed either in Application Designer itself or by using one of the Translate utilities. As before, to make the translation in the Application Designer tool, the developer can set language preference to one of the desired non-base languages and then modify the panel group label text. When the developer saves the panel group the desired non-base language labels will be saved in the PeopleTools tables.

Using the **PeopleTools/Translate** utilities allows for translation of panel groups into different non-base languages in one session without the developer resetting language preference. The **Translate Panel Group** utility panel, shown in Figure 18.12, can be used to update both the Panel Group item label and folder tab label text.

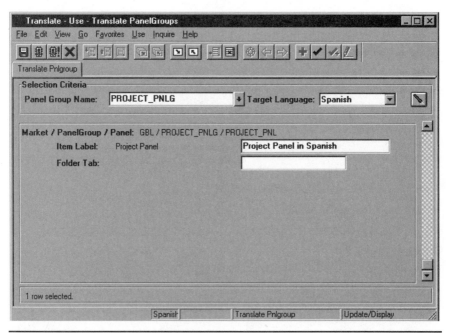

Figure 18.12   *Translate Panel Group panel*

As with the other Translate utility panels, the developer can specify a particular panel group, set a target language, and search for translated values. After entering new translated label text, the developer will save the utility panel to save the associated non-base language labels. During application usage, the new non-base language panel group labels will be displayed to an operator with a language preference set to that non-base language.

Translating Menus

For menus, the text labels displayed to application users are Menu Group Name, Menu Label, Menu Bar Label, and Menu Item Label. Each of these types of labels can be changed either in Application Designer itself or by using one of the Translate utilities. As before, to make the translation in the Application Designer tool the developer must set language preference to one of the desired non-base languages and then modify the menu label text. When the developer saves the menu, the desired non-base language labels will be saved in the PeopleTools tables.

Using the **PeopleTools/Translate** utilities allows for translation of menus into non-base languages. There are two utility panels used for translation of menu objects. The **Translate Menu** utility panel is used to update the Menu Group and Menu Label text. The **Translate Menu Items** utility panel, shown in Figure 18.13, is used to update the Menu Bar Labels and Item Labels.

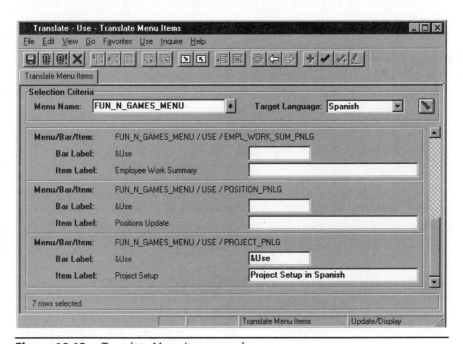

Figure 18.13   *Translate Menu Items panel*

As with the other Translate utility panels, the developer can specify a particular menu, set a target language, and search for translated values. After entering new translated label text, the developer can save the utility panel to save the associated non-base language labels. During application usage, the new non-base language menu labels will be displayed to an operator with a language preference set to that non-base language.

Related Language Records

To translate an application into a different language, not only must the display of the text (labels) on application panels be translated, but it may also be necessary to translate some of the application data. This might apply especially to character data values that represent the names or words used in the application. Use of the Related Language Record allows the selective translation of application data fields. A Related Language Record can be defined for any application database table that contains one or more character fields that need to be translated. Each Related Language Record has the key of the corresponding base language record, plus the LANGUAGE_CD field as another key field. Please refer to Figure 18.14 for the PROJECT_LANG Related Language Record taken from our case study application.

Aside from the key fields, the Related Language Record contains only those character fields that are desired for translation—*not* all of the fields of the base record. The Related Language Record may be thought of as a "shadow" of the Base Language Record for those translated character fields. The Related Language Record is of type SQL Table, and the corresponding database table must be created through the Build command. The Base Language Record then has the Related Language Record named on the Use tab of the Record properties, as shown in Figure 18.15 for the PROJECT_TBL record in our case study.

These record fields are now ready for translation into a non-base language. When an operator with a non-base language preference uses a panel with one of these record fields, the initial value will be taken from the base language. However, if the operator changes (translates) the field value it will be stored in the related language record. Subsequent use of that panel by an operator with the same non-base language preference will display the translated field value from the Related Language Record.

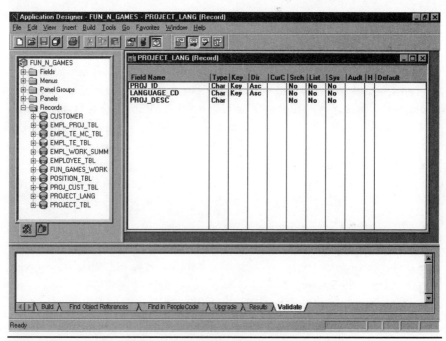

Figure 18.14 *Record fields display of Related Language Record*

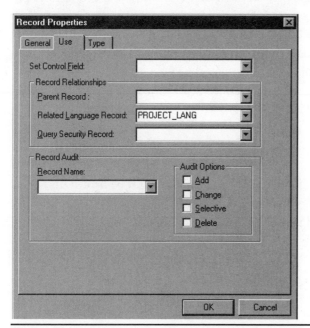

Figure 18.15 *Base Language Record Properties—Use tab*

Multi-currency Support

In addition to support for different national languages, PeopleTools also provides support for development of applications that will maintain monetary amounts in multiple national currencies. The capability to display currency amounts in different currency notations is provided within PeopleTools. Certain common application objects (panels, records, fields) for setup and maintenance of currency codes and currency exchange rates are also provided. The discussion here will focus on currency codes and notation. The logic required for multi-currency application processing such as currency conversion or revaluation is related to the specific application requirements (e.g. General Ledger).

Display Currency Format

The Display Currency format includes the display of a particular currency symbol (e.g. $) and the decimal precision of the amount (e.g. 2 digits). The display of a currency amount in a specific national currency format is maintained through the use of a Currency Control field. The Currency Control field indicates the (ISO) currency code of the corresponding currency amount. For example, the value of "CAN" in the currency control field indicates that the corresponding currency amount is Canadian dollars.

Setting up the Display Currency format using the Currency Control field is relatively simple. The Currency Control field must be placed on the same record as the corresponding Currency Amount field. The Currency Control field must have a prompt table edit defined in Record Field properties against the CURRENCY_CD_TBL for valid currency codes. Please see Figure 18.16 for an example taken from our case study.

The Currency Amount field is the number field that contains the actual monetary amount. In the Record Field properties for the Currency Amount field, the Currency Control field on the same record must be named. In Figure 18.17, the CURRENCY_CD field will be the Currency Control field for the WORK_EXPENSE field in our case study.

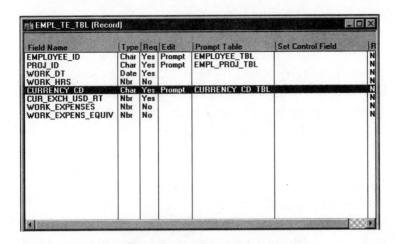

Figure 18.16   *Record Field properties—Edits tab*

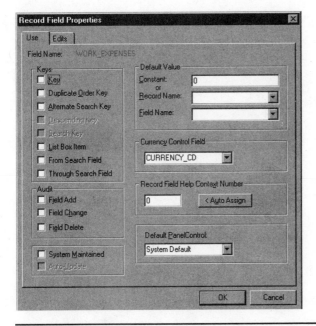

Figure 18.17   *Record Field properties—Use tab—Currency Control field*

Naturally, in most applications the developer will want to display the Currency Control field on the panel alongside the corresponding Currency Amount field.

Once the Currency Control field is defined, the display of the Currency format depends on the selection of the Multi-Currency option on the **PeopleTools/Utilities/PeopleTools Options** panel shown in Figure 18.18.

If the Multi-Currency option is *not* selected, the currency format (symbol) will be based on the Windows Regional Setting and will display the same regardless of the value of the Currency Code field. If the Multi-Currency option is *not* selected, then any panel fields marked as Multi-Currency fields on Panel Field properties will *not be displayed at all*. Please see Figure 18.19 for the Panel Field Properties dialog box.

Of course, when the Multi-Currency PeopleTools option is selected, all panel fields marked as Multi-Currency are displayed in the desired Currency format.

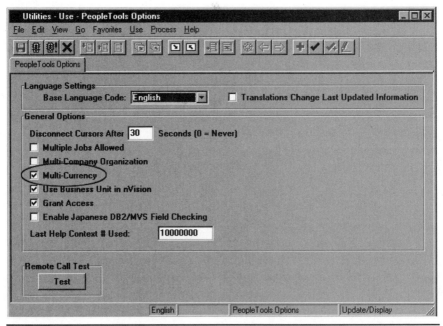

Figure 18.18   *PeopleTools Options panel—Multi-Currency*

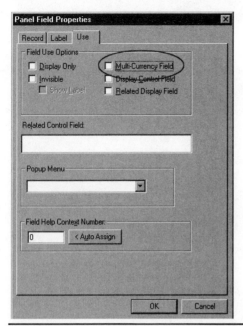

Figure 18.19 *Panel Field properties—Multi-Currency field*

Multi-Currency Functions

As we remarked previously, the logic required for multi-currency application processing is related to the specific application requirements—and can become rather complex. Considerations may include decimal precision, rounding, and other business requirements for currency conversion. Common PeopleTools application objects (panels, records, fields) provided to the developer to support the maintenance of currency amounts include the Currency Code, Rate Type, and Exchange Rate tables. Several PeopleCode functions are also available, notably the **ConvertCurrency** function used to convert an amount in one currency to an equivalent amount in another currency. If your globalization work effort includes multi-currency functions, we suggest further reading in PeopleBooks on this complex subject.

Part 6

Case Study

19

Planning the Application

Part 6 will reinforce all the skills you have learned throughout the book. The objective is to provide hands-on activities to develop a sample application. Those who read through this chapter will learn about the business requirements for the new application. In the chapters that follow, the application will be developed.

Before getting started, there are a few items you will want to ensure are available or set up. First, be sure that you have access to Application Designer in PeopleSoft version 7.0 or greater. Recall that this is where all the application development work is performed. You will be unable to perform the development steps without this access. Next, ensure that you have access to a database environment where this development work can be performed. You want to be certain that it is acceptable to develop this sample application and that it will not affect any other work being performed in the same environment. You should contact your database administrator to assist with this step. Alternatively, this work can be performed using PeopleSoft's Single User Install which can be installed as a stand alone version of the software.

Finally, you will want to set your Project Options. Recall from Chapter 3 that you can access the project options within Application Designer from the menu, **Tools/Options** and then refer to the Project tab. Figure 19.1 provides the suggested settings to be used during development.

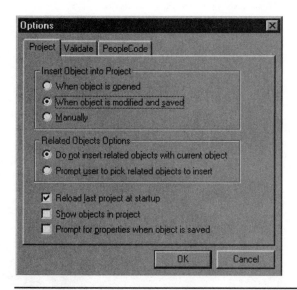

Figure 19.1   *Project Options settings*

Now that we have set our options and have the appropriate access, we can introduce the sample application we will be developing.

Client Organization

The sample application will be developed for our client organization, a rapidly growing toy company, Fun-N-Games. They sell a standard list of toys and games but they also create "custom" toys based on requests from their customers. Because the company develops unique custom toys that cannot be found in most large retail stores, they have created a niche market and have become well respected in the industry. Although the toys are sold based on different pricing strategies, the time and expenses of employees are always captured. It is especially important to capture the time and expenses for toys that are considered "custom" products because many times, the cost of the product is based on the actual costs of production.

Statement of Business Problem

You have been hired to work for Fun-N-Games to assist them in developing a business application. The company has an urgent need to capture employee time and expenses on various projects. Currently, each employee is asked to track this information individually and there is very little consistency or correctness in the results. Because the company needs to understand this information in order to prepare invoices and track revenues, this has become a high-priority requirement.

The focus of this business application is the time and expense capture functionality. The client has assured us that the invoicing, personnel tracking and financial functions are being managed outside the scope of this effort. Further, we have been asked not to worry about any interfaces between the time and expense application and these other functions; this will be managed by another internal technology team.

Business Requirements and Processes

Currently, Fun-N-Games maintains its records of customers, projects, staff time, and expense with simple spreadsheets. They really need an improved system to support the growing volume of business and better plan for the future of the company.

Interviews with many of the business managers identified the major business processes for the company: maintain customer information, maintain employee information, manage project information, manage employee time and expense, and summarize employee T&E. After some discussion, the following description of the processes and associated business information was understood.

Maintain Customer Information process is how general customer information can either be added (new customer) or updated. The information needed about a customer is the customer name, the contact person at the company, and customer address. Also, because the contact information typically changes, Fun-N-Games wants to ensure that they can maintain this historical information in case there is ever a question of who they dealt with.

Maintain Employee Information process is how the general employee information can be added or updated (recall that this is separate from the employee tracking system). The information needed about an employee is employee ID, name, specialty, and position within the organization.

Manage Project Information process is really the focal point of this new business application. A project is defined as any work effort performed at Fun-N-Games. The process to manage this information is particularly important because the company wants to track information by different projects and by the project types defined. During this process, projects are defined (added) or updated. The different types of projects include: ongoing production, volunteer, exploratory, and special project. Ongoing production includes the normal production of toys from the standard stock. Volunteer projects are efforts that have been established to design, produce and deliver toys as a service to the community. Exploratory work is work done to experiment with new ideas in the hope of developing new products. Special projects are efforts commissioned by one or more customers to develop a specially designed toy. Our client is interested in capturing a good deal of information about the projects, such as project ID, project description, effort type, priority rating, status, total estimated hours of effort, actual hours of effort, and customer (if effort is specifically requested by one or more customers).

Manage Employee Time and Expense process is how the employee time and expense information can be added or updated. The information needed about an employee's time and expense include employee ID, project ID, work date, work hours, and work expense.

Summarize Employee T&E process will allow the employee's time and expense to be summarized across all projects. This is in contrast to the Manage Employee Time and Expense process which only allows the employee's time and expenses to be tracked project by project. The information needed is an employee's ID, name, project ID, project description, and total work hours.

Data Model

Based on the business information requirements, a basic entity relationship model was developed. As we develop the design with Fun-N-Games, we may identify changes to the model. Discussion of the data requirements revealed four data entities: employee, project, customer, and employee time and expense. As the data model was further defined, it was noted that there were some many-many relationships. To "resolve" these many-many relationships, two additional entities were added: employee-project and project-customer. The working assumption is that each of the data entities identifies a data table in our application. Figure 19.2 presents the data model.

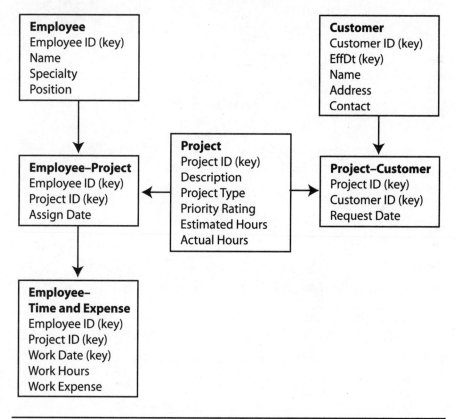

Figure 19.2   *Entity relationship model*

Designing the User Interface

Once the business processes and information requirements are understood, we can begin to sketch out the user interface for Fun-N-Games. It is important that we gain agreement from the users of the application on the design before we move forward with any of the development. Figures 19.3 through 19.8, present mock-ups of the panels that have been agreed upon based on initial discussions. It is more than likely that there will be changes to the design as we "uncover" new or changing business requirements.

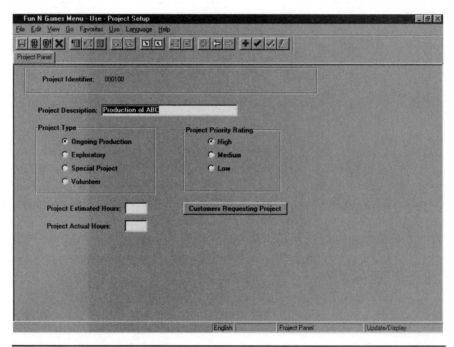

Figure 19.3   *Project Setup panel*

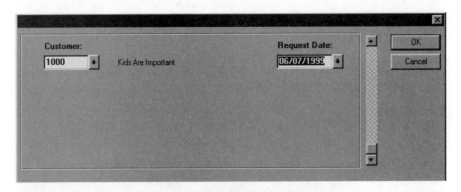

Figure 19.4 *Project-Customer Request (secondary) panel*

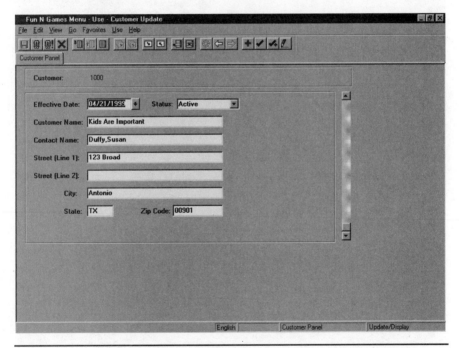

Figure 19.5 *Customer Update panel*

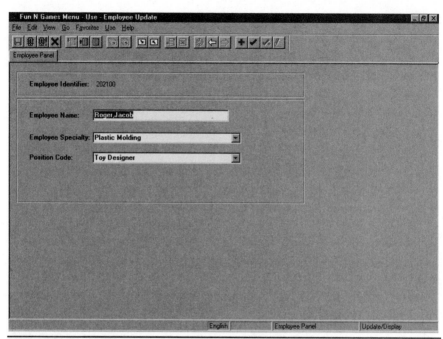

Figure 19.6   *Employee Update panel*

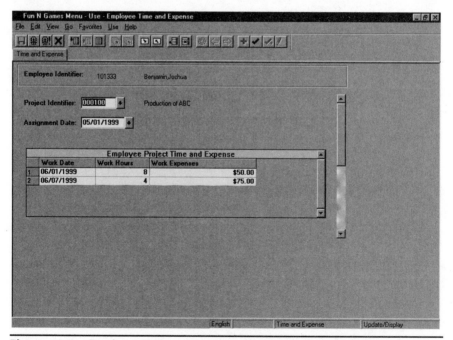

Figure 19.7   *Employee Time and Expense panel*

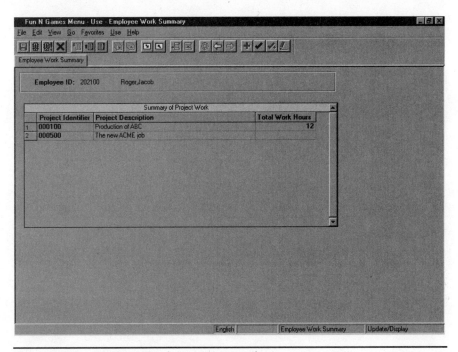

Figure 19.8 *Employee Work Summary panel*

Moving Forward with the Application

Now that we have an understanding of the application requirements, the next few chapters provide an opportunity to "get our hands dirty" working with PeopleSoft and actually perform the development steps. Chapters 20, 21, and 22 provide the development steps needed to create the Project record, panel, and menu, and enable security. In these three chapters, there will be detailed step-by-step instructions on how to perform this development. By following these steps, you should be able successfully to execute the Project part of the application.

Chapters 23 through 27 discuss the steps necessary to develop the Customer, Project-Customer, Employee, Employee T&E, and the Work Summary records, panels and menus. Because the reader has already practiced his/her skills with the Project application, the objective is to perform this development work more independently.

Chapters 28 and 29 provide additional challenge and allow readers to incorporate PeopleCode into their application and to "globalize" the application by introducing an additional language and enabling the use of multi-currency. Because these are new topics with which readers have not yet had any practice, these chapters provide more detailed walk-throughs of the steps necessary to perform this development.

To serve as a guide to help with the development steps, Table 19.1 presents the business processes that were discussed earlier in this chapter along with their associated panels.

Table 19.1   *Business processes and associated panels*

Business Process	Panel Group	Panel Actions
Manage Project Information	Project Setup	Add Project
		Update Project
		Customer Requests Project
Maintain Customer Information	Customer Update	Add Customer
		Update (Update All, Correct) Customer
Maintain Employee Information	Employee Update	Add Employee
		Update Employee
Manage Employee Time & Expense	Employee T&E	Update Employee T&E
Summarize Employee T&E	Employee T&E	Update Employee Work Summary

Figure 19.9 indicates the chapter in which each entity is discussed and developed.

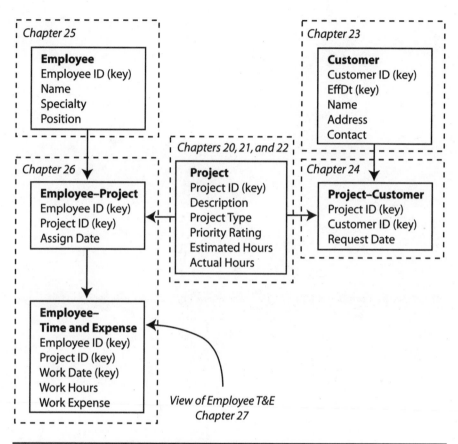

Figure 19.9 *Data model with chapter references*

20

Understanding the Data: Project Panel

Once the planning and design stages of our application have been completed, we can begin the initial stages of development. Our first big step is to translate our data model into the fields, records, and database objects necessary for the PeopleSoft application. This chapter will walk through these steps for the project data. Chapters 21 and 22 will continue to focus on the development of the Project panel.

Defining Fields

In reviewing the data elements identified during the planning stage, we need to think about what type of information we will be capturing about these elements so that we can appropriately define the field types. We are going to make the assumption that none of these fields exists. In a "real-life" application, prior to defining new fields, the first step would be to evaluate existing fields to determine if there are existing fields that would be appropriate.

The *Proj_ID* will be a unique identifier of the project. The ID value will not have significance except that it will uniquely identify that piece of work. It might be useful to have a sequenced number assigned to this value. But, because no mathematical functions will be performed on this field, we can make this field a character type and assign it a Numbers Only format. A field length of 6 should provide us with the availability of enough values for this field. The *description* will be a textual explanation of the work effort. In this field, we would expect the application user to type some meaningful description. This can therefore be a character field with a field length of 30. The *project type* will be used to capture the type of work defined for our business: ongoing production, volunteer, exploratory and special project. Because these types are relatively consistent, we can use translate values to store these values in the XLATTABLE, PeopleTools table. Therefore, we know that we must use a character field with a length less than or equal to 4. This field will be defined with a field length of 4. The *priority rating* indicates the level of preference for this work. Again, because there is a short list of stable values, we can store these values in the translate table. This field will be defined with a length of 1. The *estimated hrs* and *actual hrs* fields will be used to capture the work time spent in total for all employees working on this work effort. The estimated hours will be established at the start of the work and the actual hours will be updated as the employees enter their work time into the application. Because both these fields will capture a number of hours, the fields are defined as number with a field length of 4. Table 20.1 summarizes the fields to be created and their attributes. When beginning a PeopleSoft application or modification, you may find it useful to put together a worksheet such as this to assist with the development process.

Table 20.1   *Development Worksheet for Fields*

Field Name	Type	Format	Length	Translate	Values
PROJ_ID	Char	Number	6		
PROJ_DESC	Char	Mixed	30		
PROJ_TYPE	Char		4	EXPL	Exploratory
				ONPR	Ongoing Production
				SPEC	Special Project
				VOL	Volunteer
PROJ_PRIORITY_RT	Char		1	H	High
				M	Medium
				L	Low
PROJ_ESTIM_HRS	Number		4		
PROJ_ACTUAL_HRS	Number		4		

Walk-Through of Creating Fields

Now that we understand the fields needed and the field attributes, let's go ahead and begin to create these new fields.

1. **File/New** or use the **New** icon from the toolbar.

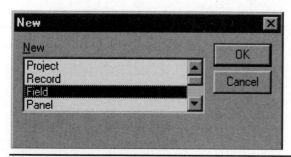

Figure 20.1   *File/New dialog box*

2. Select **Field** from the New dialog box (Figure 20.1).
3. From the New Field drop-down list, select the field type. For PROJ_ID, choose character (Figure 20.2).

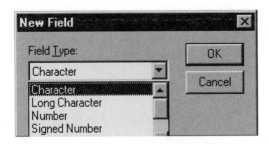

Figure 20.2   *New Field dialog box*

4. Define the field by completing the field length, short name, long name, and format type (Figure 20.3).

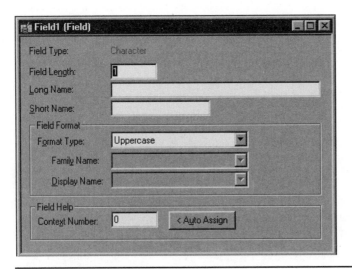

Figure 20.3   *Field definition*

5. The field definition for PROJ_ID will be defined as shown in Figure 20.4.
6. The final step in defining the PROJ_ID field is to set the field properties. The object properties can be accessed either from **File/Object Properties** or from the **Properties** icon on the toolbar. The only properties tab for the PROJ_ID field is the General tab. Complete this tab to provide documentation about the field (Figure 20.5).

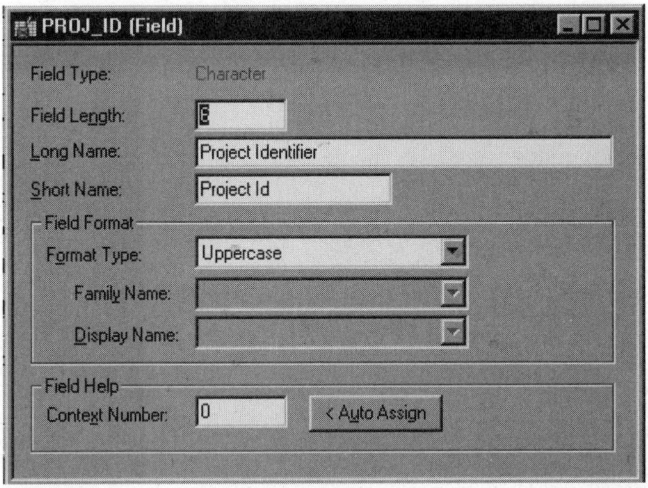

Figure 20.4 *PROJ_ID field defined*

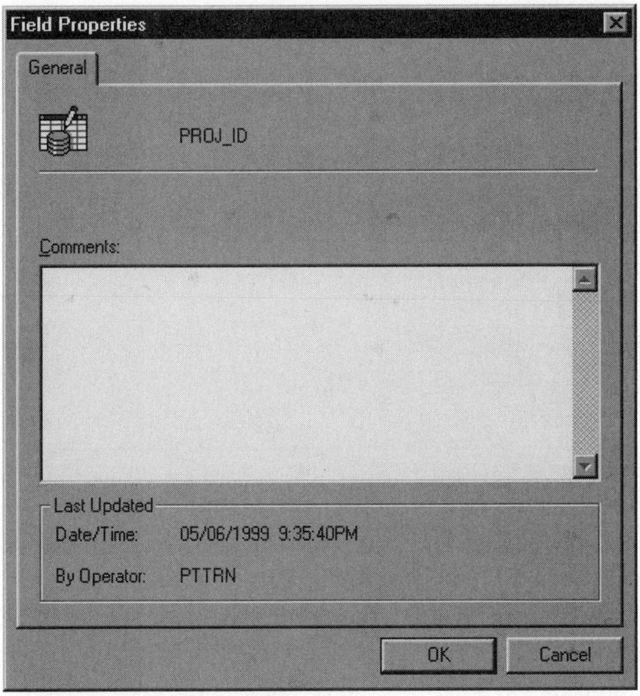

Figure 20.5 *Field properties*

The walk-through of creating the Description field will follow the same steps as the PROJ_ID field. But let's take a look at creating a field with translate values such as the Project Type field.

1. **File/New** or use the **New** icon from the toolbar.

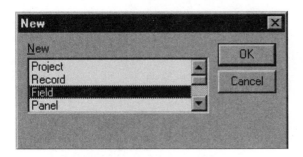

Figure 20.6   *File/New dialog box*

2. Select **Field** from the New dialog box (Figure 20.6).
3. From the New Field drop-down list, select the field type. For project type, choose character (Figure 20.7).

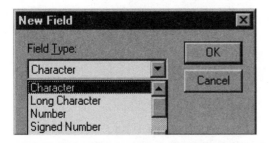

Figure 20.7   *New Field dialog box*

4. Define the field by completing the field length, short name, long name, and format type (Figure 20.8). Remember in this case because our field will have translate values defined, we must define the field length to be less than or equal to 4.
5. The field definition for PROJ_TYPE will be defined as shown in Figure 20.9.

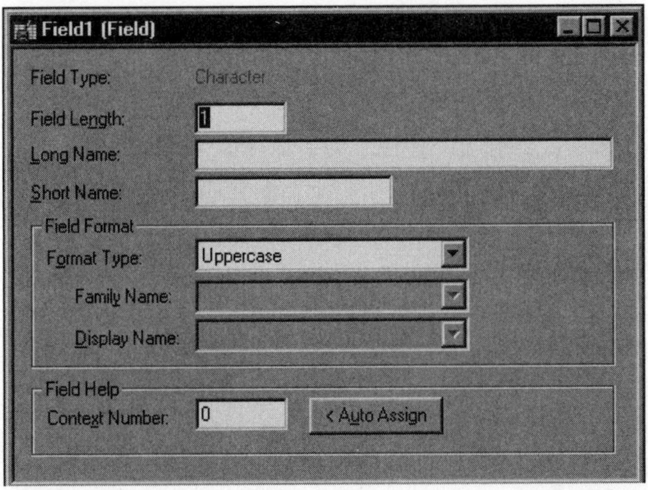

Figure 20.8 *Field definition*

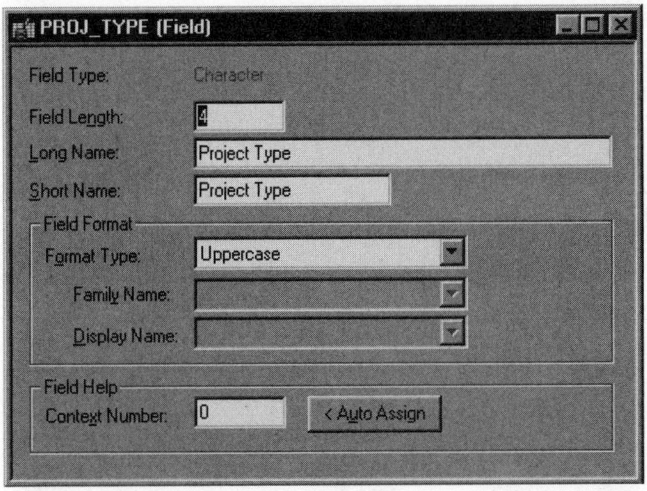

Figure 20.9 *PROJ_TYPE field defined*

6. The final step in defining the project type field is to set the field properties. The object properties can be accessed either from **File/Object Properties** or from the **Properties** icon on the toolbar. Notice that now, in addition to the General tab, there is also a Translate Values tab (Figure 20.10).

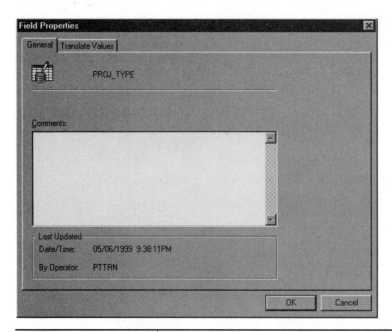

Figure 20.10   *Field properties*

7. Switch to the Translate Values tab to add the translate values (Figure 20.11).

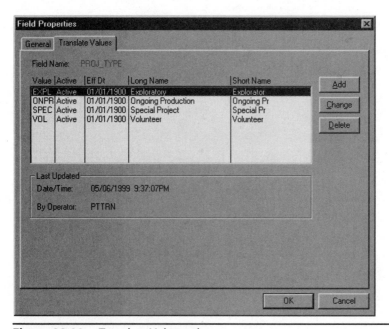

Figure 20.11   *Translate Values tab*

8. To add values, click the **Add** button. You will be presented with an Add Translate Table Value window (Figure 20.12). Complete the value (or the code) and the long and short name for this value. Notice that the translate values are effective dated. Recall that the recommendation for effective dates for Translate values is 1/1/1900. Once the value has been added, click **OK** and the value will now appear in the list of values.

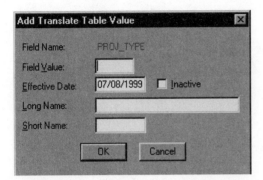

Figure 20.12   *Add Translate Values windows*

Complete the definition of the remainder of the fields for the Project entity on your own, including the Project Description, Priority Rating, Estimated Hrs, and Actual Hrs.

Defining Records

With the data elements or fields developed, we can begin to develop the record definition. Remember, the record definition will be used by the relational database management system to create the relational table where the application data will be stored. It is important when defining the record to think about how the relational table will be used and therefore what the necessary keys and indexes required for the record definition are.

The Project entity will capture information about projects for the Fun-N-Games Company. To uniquely identify a project, we will use the PROJ_ID. Therefore, PROJ_ID will be the key to the record. We will also use the PROJ_ID as part of the Search dialog box, as a Search key. The description will also be used as part of the Search dialog box as an Alternate Search key to allow users to search on the description of the project if they do not know the

PROJ_ID. Project Type and Priority Rating both have translate values so when we define the record, we want to ensure the edit attributes are set correctly. Table 20.2 summarizes the characteristics that should be defined when creating the record definition. Again, this is a useful worksheet for those first performing development in PeopleTools.

Table 20.2   *Development Worksheet for Records*

Field Name	Key	Defaults	Required?	Edits
PROJ_ID	Key, Search key		Yes	
PROJ_DESC	Alt. Search key		Yes	
PROJ_TYPE		ONPR	Yes	Translate
PROJ_PRIORITY_RT		H	Yes	Translate
PROJ_ESTIM_HRS				
PROJ_ACTUAL_HRS				

Walk-Through of Creating the Record

Now that we understand the characteristics we need to set on the record definition, let's go ahead and begin to create the Project record.

1. **File/New** or use the **New** icon from the toolbar.
2. Select **Record** from the New dialog box (Figure 20.13).

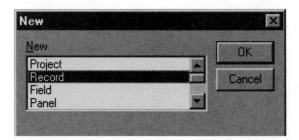

Figure 20.13   *New dialog box*

3. You will be presented with an "empty" record definition (Figure 20.14).

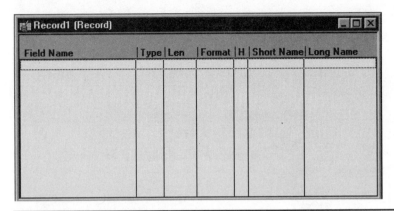

Figure 20.14   *Record definition*

4. The next step is to place the fields required for the record into the record definition. This can be accomplished either by "drag and drop" from the Project Workspace, fields folder, or from the menu, **Insert/Field....** Because the "drag and drop" feature provides ease in development, it is good to use this method. Select the first field, PROJ_ID, from the project workspace and drag it over to the record definition, as shown in Figure 20.15.

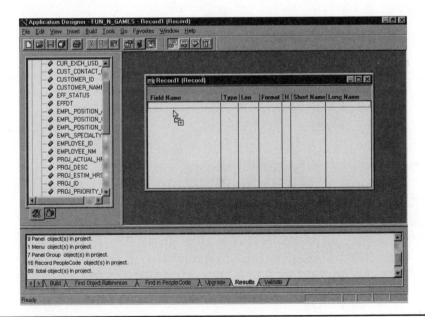

Figure 20.15   *Inserting fields into record definition*

Once you release the mouse, the field will be placed in the record definition (Figure 20.16).

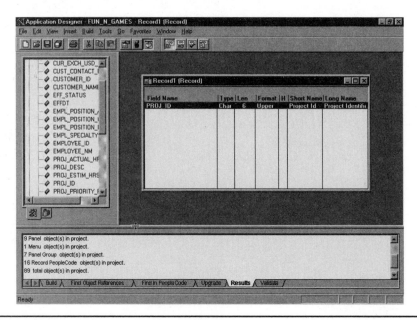

Figure 20.16   *Field placed in record definition*

5. Place the remainder of the fields into the record in the same manner. Once all the fields are in the record, it is a good idea to save the record definition. Either use the menu **File/Save** or click on the **Save** icon in the toolbar. Because this is the first time the record has been saved, you will be prompted to save the record and assign a name (Figure 20.17). Save the record as PROJECT_TBL.

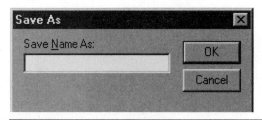

Figure 20.17   *Save dialog box*

6. Now that the fields exist within the record definition, the Record Field properties must be defined. Remember, there are Use attributes and Edit attributes that can be defined for each field.

7. Starting with PROJ_ID, double click on the field in the record (or right click, **Record Field Properties**) to open the Record Field properties. Either way, you will be presented with the Record Field Properties box (Figure 20.18).

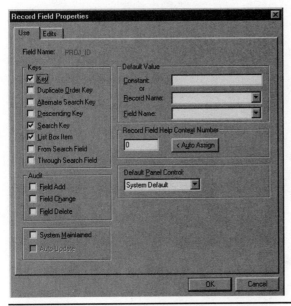

Figure 20.18   *Record Field properties—Use tab*

8. For PROJ_ID, it was determined this field would be a key, a search key and should also show as a list box item. Each of these attributes is set on the Use tab (Figure 20.18).

9. Attributes should also be set on the Edits tab (Figure 20.19). The PROJ_ID is a key field; all key fields should be marked as required. Other than that, there are no other edits performed on the field.

10. Click **OK** and move onto each of the fields in the record.

11. After you have completed the Use and Edit attributes for each of the fields, compare the Use and Edits display with those presented in Figures 20.20 and 20.21.

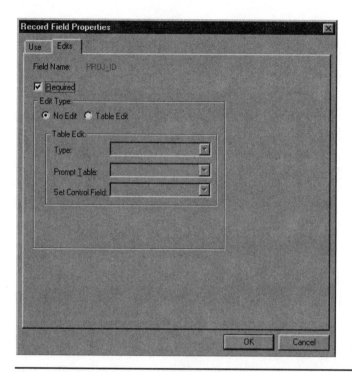

Figure 20.19   *Record Field Properties—Edits tab*

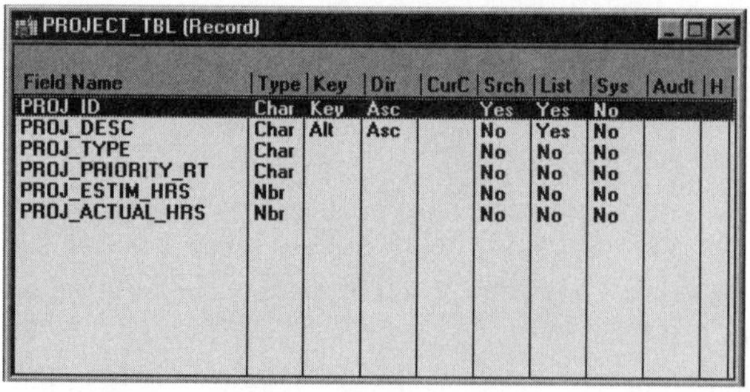

Figure 20.20   *Record Use display*

12. The final step in defining the record is setting the record properties. We just set the Record Field properties, which are specific to each field on the record. Now we want to set the overall record properties. The Object properties can be accessed either from **File/Object Properties** or from the **Properties** icon on the toolbar. Record properties have the General, Use, and Type tabs (Figure 20.22).

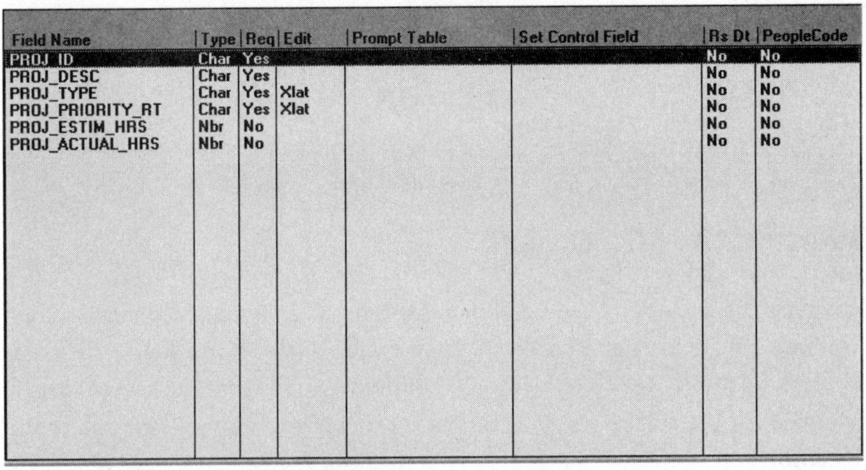

Field Name	Type	Req	Edit	Prompt Table	Set Control Field	Rs Dt	PeopleCode
PROJ_ID	Char	Yes				No	No
PROJ_DESC	Char	Yes				No	No
PROJ_TYPE	Char	Yes	Xlat			No	No
PROJ_PRIORITY_RT	Char	Yes	Xlat			No	No
PROJ_ESTIM_HRS	Nbr	No				No	No
PROJ_ACTUAL_HRS	Nbr	No				No	No

Figure 20.21   *Record Edits display*

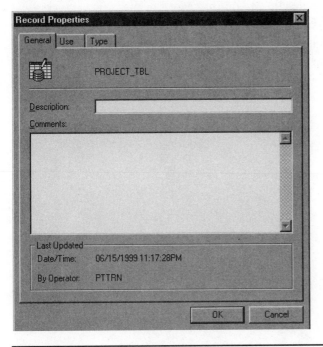

Figure 20.22   *Record properties*

In this case, we want to set General properties to provide any documentation and we want to ensure that the record type is set to SQL table on
the Type tab.

13. Save the record definition.

Building the SQL Object

Now that the project record is defined, we can build the record definition. Up
until now, the fields and records are known to PeopleSoft (to the PeopleTools
tables) but the underlying relational database management system is not
"aware" that the record exists. The build process will define the table to the
RDBMS.

1. Open the record to be built either by **File/Open**, the **Open** icon on the
toolbar or by double clicking on the record in the project workspace.
Let's open PROJECT_TBL.

2. Once the record is open in the object workspace, select **Build/Current
Object** or use the **Build** icon on the toolbar. Either of these will open
the Build dialog box (Figure 20.23).

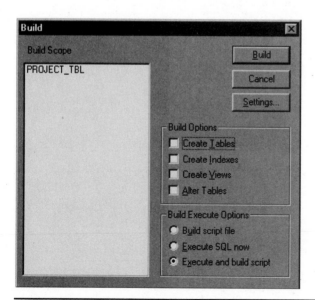

Figure 20.23   *Build dialog box*

3. Because the Project record is a new record, we can choose Create Table and Execute and Build Script for the Build options and the Build Execute options, respectively (Figure 20.24).

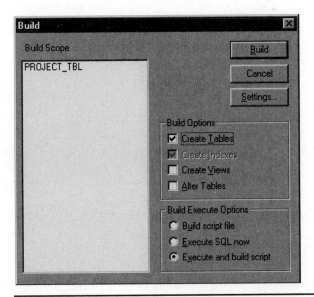

Figure 20.24   *Build options and Build Execute options*

4. It is always a good idea to check the Settings. Click on the **Settings** button. Ensure that the appropriate settings are defined in each of the tabs. Click **OK**.

5. Click the **Build** button to build the record, PROJECT_TBL.

6. Review the output window to ensure that there were no warnings or errors during the build process.

7. Verify that the table was defined to the RDBMS by using an SQL tool and performing the following SQL statement:

```
Select * from PS_PROJECT_TBL
```

At this point, because no data has been entered, the table will exist but there will be no rows of data in the table.

The data definition is now complete. With data elements and records defined, the next step is to move onto developing the user interface.

Sample Solution

Refer to Figure 20.25 for the printout of the PROJECT record.

```
Field Name          Type  Length Format  Long Name                Short Name       Key  Req TblEdt AU Dt PC Aud Prompt Table  Default Value
Related Language Record Name: PROJECT_LANG
Last Updated Date/Time: 07/15/1999  9:01:13PM
Last Updated by Operator: PTTRN


PROJ_ID             Char   6    Upper   Project Identifier       Project Id       KALS Yes
PROJ_DESC           Char  30    Mixed   Project Description      Project Desc     AAL  Yes
PROJ_TYPE           Char   4    Upper   Project Type             Project Type          Yes Xlat                                'ONPR'
     Values: EXPL Active 01/01/00     Exploratory              Explorator            05/06/1999 9:37:07PM  PTTRN
             ONPR Active 01/01/00     Ongoing Production       Ongoing Pr            05/06/1999 9:37:23PM  PTTRN
             SPEC Active 01/01/00     Special Project          Special Pr            05/06/1999 9:37:40PM  PTTRN
             VOL  Active 01/01/00     Volunteer                Volunteer             05/06/1999 9:38:00PM  PTTRN
PROJ_PRIORITY_RT    Char   1    Upper   Project Priority Rating  Priority Rating       Yes Xlat                                'H'
     Values: H   Active 01/01/00      High                     High                  05/06/1999 9:39:41PM  PTTRN
             L   Active 01/01/00      Low                      Low                   05/06/1999 9:39:57PM  PTTRN
             M   Active 01/01/00      Medium                   Medium                05/06/1999 9:39:49PM  PTTRN
PROJ_ESTIM_HRS      Nbr    4            Project Estimated Hours  Estimated Hrs
PROJ_ACTUAL_HRS     Nbr    4            Project Actual Hours     Actual Hrs
```

Figure 20.25 *Printout of the PROJECT_TBL record*

291

21

The User Interface: Project Panel

Our next step in the development stage is the user interface. Remember, we have already defined the data elements and the records. Now, we are ready to develop the application windows for our users to enter and view data. The user interface will be based on the design document prepared at the start of our project for Fun-N-Games. In Chapter 19, we presented the mock-ups of the screens.

The user interface has a few aspects that need to be considered. First, the actual screens on which the user will enter data or from which they will view data must be easy to understand and navigate. Once the panels are developed, the navigation of the application is important to the user. Navigation of the application is accomplished through the use of panel groups and menus. Recall that panel groups organize one or more related panels and menus organize the panel groups. Let's start with defining the Project panel and then we will move into the navigational aspects.

Defining Panels

Continuing with the Project example, we need to present the user with a means of capturing and viewing project information. The project information will be stored in the PROJECT_TBL record. The panel developed to maintain this information will be reading and writing from/to this record.

Walk-Through of Creating the Panel

Based on the design, we have a good idea of how the panel should appear. Let's begin to develop the Project panel.

1. **File/New** or use the **New** icon from the toolbar.
2. Select **Panel** from the New dialog box (Figure 21.1).

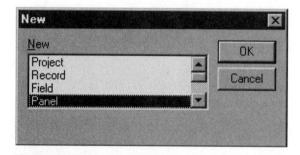

Figure 21.1   *New dialog box*

3. You will be presented with an "empty" panel (Figure 21.2).

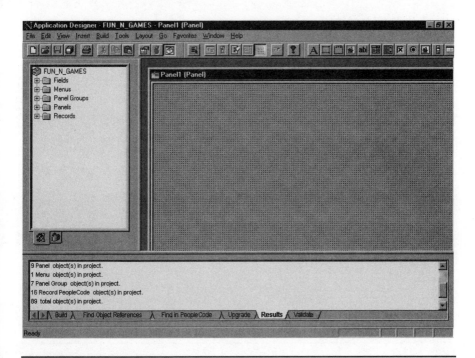

Figure 21.2 *New panel*

You can size the project workspace and output window to provide space to view the panel in its entirety.

4. The next step is to place the record fields onto the panel. This can be accomplished either by "drag and drop" from the project definition, records folder, using the icons from the toolbar, or from the menu, **Insert**. Again, because the "drag and drop" feature provides ease in development, its use is encouraged.

5. Select the first field, PROJ_ID, from the PROJECT_TBL in the project workspace and drag it onto the panel.

   Once you release the mouse, the field will be placed on the panel as seen in Figure 21.3. Place the remainder of the fields onto the panel in the same manner. Once all the fields are placed on the panel, it is a good idea to save the panel definition. Either use the menu **File/Save** or click the **Save** icon in the toolbar. Because this is the first time the panel has been saved, you will be prompted to assign a name in the Save dialog box (Figure 21.4).

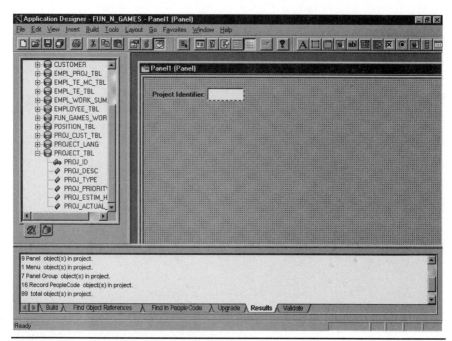

Figure 21.3   *Object placed on panel*

Figure 21.4   *Save dialog box*

6. Now that you have saved your panel, you might notice that some of the panel objects are not the same as the ones presented in the mock-ups. Recall that by default, fields that have Translate values will be placed on the panel with drop-down lists if the fields are dragged and dropped from the record definition. From our mock-up (refer to Figure 19.3), we know that we want the project type and priority rating fields to appear as radio buttons. To change these panel objects to radio buttons, we must delete the existing objects from the panel and re-add the objects. In this case, instead of dragging and dropping the record fields from the project workspace, we will

insert the objects from the menu, **Insert/Radio Button** or by using the icon on the toolbar. Note that when a radio button is added, the label is marked "dummy name." This label indicates that a record and field have not yet been specified for this panel object; the panel object must be associated with some record and field so that the information can be properly recorded. In one of the next steps, we will review the Panel Field properties and address how this can be corrected.

7. Note that the Project panel has a push button to a secondary panel which displays the customers who have requested this work. The push button will be added to the panel in Chapter 24.

8. Once the fields are placed on the panel, the Panel Field properties must be defined. They can be accessed either by double clicking on the field itself or by right clicking and accessing the Panel Field properties from the popup menu (Figure 21.5).

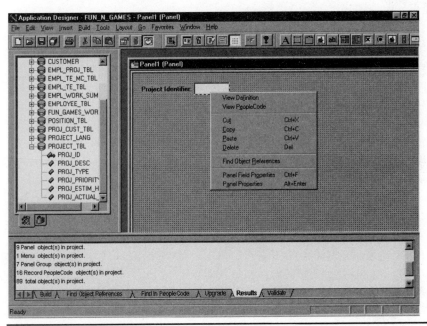

Figure 21.5   *Panel Popup menu*

Either way, you will be presented with the Panel Field Properties dialog box (Figure 21.6).

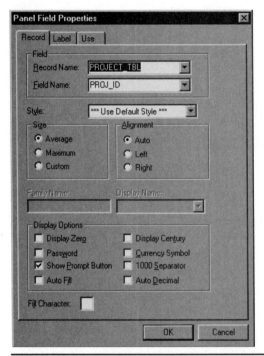

Figure 21.6   *Panel Field Properties dialog box*

Starting with the Project ID, double click on the field in the record (or right click, Panel Field Properties) to open the Panel Field properties.

9. All the fields on the project panel are from the Project record. Therefore, on the *Record tab*, the Record Name should be defined as PROJECT_TBL for all fields. The field name should correspond to the field within that record. On the *Label tab*, we should try and use either the RFT Long or RFT Short as the label type. We will see the most variation on attributes on the *Use tab* because this is where we set how the field will be used on the panel.

10. We know from the mock-up that Project ID should be display only. We set this attribute on the Use tab. No other changes need to be made to this field once it is placed on the panel.

11. We still have work to do on the radio buttons for both the Project Type and Priority Rating fields. Once we have inserted the radio button onto the panel, we need to set the Panel Field properties. When we open the Panel Field Properties window, we note that the record and field name

are not complete (that is why it displays on the panel as dummy name) as shown in Figure 21.7.

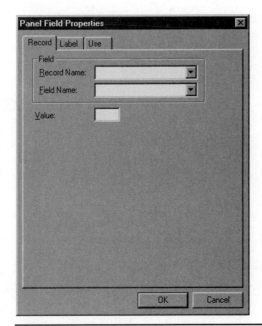

Figure 21.7 *Panel Field Properties—Record tab*

The record name should be defined as PROJECT_TBL and the field name should be defined as PROJ_TYPE. Also on the Record tab, we must define the value. The value is the radio button value and must correspond to one of the values stored in the translate table. If the value does not correspond to a value that exists in the translate table, a warning message will be issued (Figure 21.8).

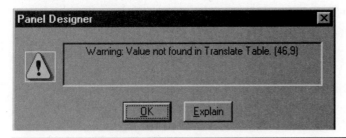

Figure 21.8 *Translate Value warning message*

Once complete, the Record tab for Project Type should appear with the characteristics shown in Figure 21.9.

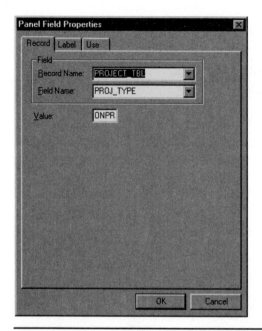

Figure 21.9   *Panel Field Properties— Record tab*

Once one of the radio buttons is set up on the panel, the short cut is to copy and paste the radio buttons for as many values as will be displayed. By cutting and pasting, all the attributes of the radio button will be copied over. After each paste, be sure to change the value on the Record tab.

12. Complete the Panel Field properties for all the panel objects on the Project panel. Remember, if this panel had Display Control/Related Display fields (which it does not), the display control would be placed before the related display in the panel order. The Display Control field would be pulled from the main record within the scroll area, in this case, the Project record and the Related Display field would be from another record.

13. The final step in defining the panel is setting the panel properties. In the previous steps, we set the Panel Field properties specific to each field on the panel. Now we want to set the overall panel properties. The Object Properties can either be accessed from **File/Object Properties**, from the

Properties icon on the toolbar or by right clicking on the panel itself. Panel properties have General and Use tabs (Figure 21.10).

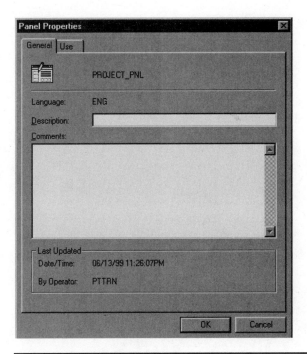

Figure 21.10   *Panel Properties*

In this case, we want to set General properties to provide any documentation and we want to ensure that the panel type is set to standard panel on the Use tab.

14. Save the panel definition.

Defining Panel Groups

Now we are ready to move onto the navigation of the application. For defining panel groups, we recall that panels can be placed in the same panel group *if and only if* they share two of the same attributes, Search record and Actions. When we think about our application, the only other panel related to project information would be the panel used to assign employees to a project. But in that case, the Search record is the Employee record. Therefore it does not make sense for this panel to be in the same panel group. We conclude that the Project panel will be the only panel in a new panel group.

Walk-Through of Creating Panel Groups

Let's begin to develop the Project panel group.

1. **File/New** or use **New** icon from the toolbar.
2. Select **Panel Group** from the New dialog box.
3. You will be presented with an "empty" panel group (Figure 21.11).

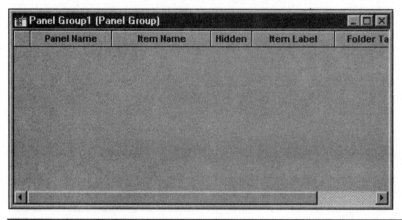

Figure 21.11   *Empty panel group*

4. The next step is to insert the panel(s) into the panel group. This can be accomplished either by "drag and drop" from the project definition, panel folder, by using the icon from the toolbar, or from the menu, **Insert/Panel into Group**. Again, because the "drag and drop" feature provides ease in development, its use is encouraged.
5. Once the panel is placed in the panel group (shown in Figure 21.12),

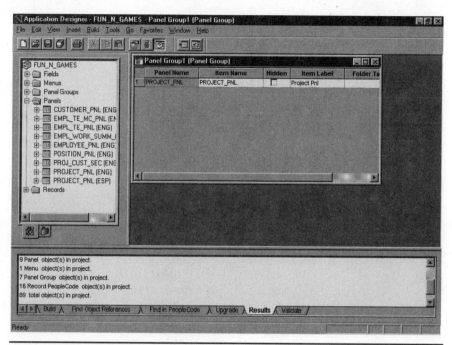

Figure 21.12 *Panel in panel group*

there are a few changes we can make. The item label should be changed to make it readable and understandable for our users. The folder tab label can also be entered although if it is left blank, it will default to the item label. The panel name and item name should *not* be changed; these control which panel will be accessed by the system. The only time this information should be changed is if the panel to be accessed within the panel group is being changed; this is not the recommended approach—it is best to delete the unwanted panel and then reinsert the necessary panel.

6. The Panel Group properties must be defined before the panel group can be saved. They can be accessed from **File/Object Properties**, from the **Properties** icon on the toolbar, or by right clicking on the panel group. The properties box will be displayed (Figure 21.13).

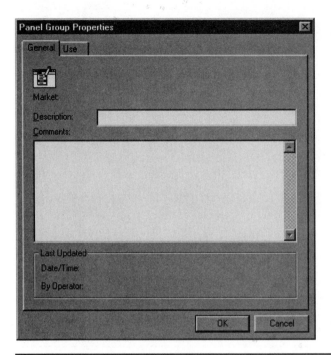

Figure 21.13 *Panel Group properties*

7. Again, the General tab should be used for documentation. The Use tab is where the Search record, Actions, and detail panel are set. For the Project panel group, the Search record is PROJECT_TBL because this is where the list of valid projects are stored for the application. The Actions are Add and Update/Display because we want the user to be able to add a new high-level key, or Project, and also to make any changes to existing projects. The record is not effective dated so the other actions do not apply. The detail panel will be defined as the Project panel, although in this case, it will not make much of a difference because this panel would have displayed by default. The Panel Group properties Use tab should appear as shown in Figure 21.14.

8. Save the panel group.

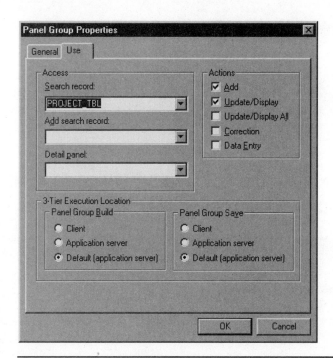

Figure 21.14 *Panel Group properties—Use tab*

Defining Menus

Once the panel group has been developed, we can organize the panel groups into menus. Again, menus organize the application navigation for the user. Organizing our application, we need to think about the logical groupings of panel groups into menus. The approach to accomplishing this is to put together groups which have related information or belong to the same business process.

Walk-Through of Creating Menus

Let's begin to develop the menu for the Project panel.

1. **File/New** or use the **New** icon from the toolbar.
2. Select **Menu** from the New dialog box. Select the **Standard** menu type from the New Menu dialog box (Figure 21.15).

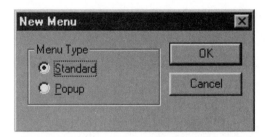

Figure 21.15   *New Menu dialog box*

3. You will be presented with an "empty" menu (Figure 21.16).

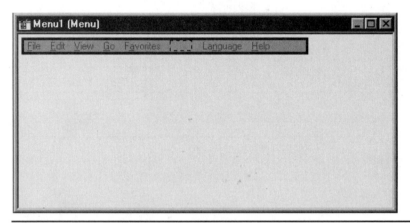

Figure 21.16   *Empty menu*

4. The next step is to define the bar item label(s). This can be accomplished either by double clicking on the dotted rectangle or by right clicking on the dotted rectangle and choosing **Bar Item Properties** from the popup menu.

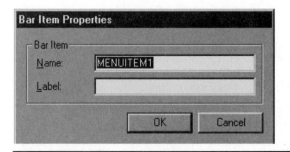

Figure 21.17   *Bar Item properties*

5. The bar item has both a name and a label that must be defined (Figure 21.17). Recall that the name is what PeopleSoft uses to execute the menu and the label is what the user will see during navigation. Typically, the name and the label are given the same name but the name is all capitals and the label is in mixed case with a hot key (assigned by using an ampersand before the hot key letter). For our example, we are going to create the bar item called Use. Figure 21.18 shows the properties for this bar item.

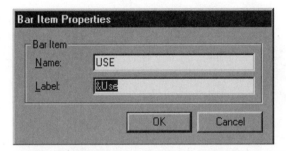

Figure 21.18   *Bar Item properties for USE*

Once the bar item information is defined, we click **OK** and the bar item will appear on the menu (Figure 21.19).

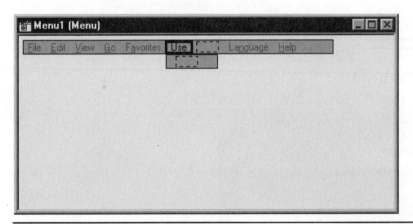

Figure 21.19   *Use bar item in menu*

6. Once the bar item exists, we can place the panel groups into the menu. To assign panel groups to the menu, we can use the "drag and drop" capability or right click on the rectangle underneath the Use bar item and choose the Menu Item Properties. It is recommended that the drag and drop approach be used because it is much easier and avoids mistakes. When dragging from the project workspace into the menu, be sure to drag the panel group underneath the bar item until the empty rectangle is highlighted in blue; once the highlight appears, release the mouse and the panel group will be inserted.

7. Once the panel group is placed in the menu (refer to Figure 21.20), there are a few changes we can make. Double click on the panel group in the menu and the Menu Item Properties window will display, as can be seen in Figure 21.21.

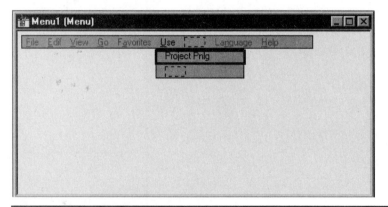

Figure 21.20   *Panel group in menu*

Figure 21.21   *Menu Item properties*

The panel group name should *not* be changed; the name controls which panel group will be accessed by the system. The only time this information should be changed is if you are changing panel group to be accessed from the menu. The menu item label should be changed to make it readable and understandable for our users. Click **OK.**

8. The menu properties are the final step in defining the menu and can be accessed from **File/Object Properties**, from the **Properties** icon on the toolbar, or by right clicking on menu. The Properties box will be displayed. Figure 21.22 displays the Menu Properties window.

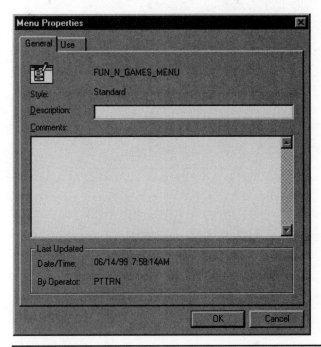

Figure 21.22   *Menu properties—General tab*

9. Again, the General tab should be used for documentation. The Use tab is where the menu label and the menu group are set. The developer also has the option to sequence the menus and menu groups from this dialog box. Let's assign the label "Fun-N-Games Menu." Recall that the menu group will group multiple menus together; if there is only one menu assigned to the menu group, the user will never see the menu group label, they will only see the menu label. For our application, we are going to assign the menu and the menu group with the same label (Figure 21.23).

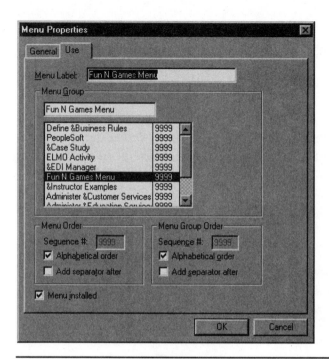

Figure 21.23   *Menu properties—Use tab*

10. Save the menu.

The development of the Project panel is now complete. Now that we have developed the panel, panel group, and menu, the next step is to administer security and test the Project application.

Sample Solution

Refer to Figure 21.24 for the printout of the PROJECT panel.

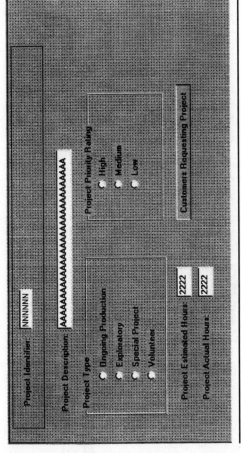

Figure 21.24 *Printout of the PROJECT_PNL panel (Page 1)*

311

Printed: 07/15/99 8:56:44PM   Database: FUNGAMES   PS Panel: PROJECT_PNL   Version: 1556

Num	Field Type	Label Text	Label Type	Record Name	Field Name	Siz	Alg	On	Off	DSP	INV	CTL	REL	RelNum	CUR	DER	OccLvl
Last Changed:	06/13/99 11:26:07PM																
1	Frame	Frame	None														
2	Edit Box	Project Identifier	RFT Long	PROJECT_TBL	PROJ_ID					Yes							
3	Edit Box	Project Description	RFT Long	PROJECT_TBL	PROJ_DESC												
4	Group Box	Project Type	RFT Long	PROJECT_TBL	PROJ_TYPE												
5	Radio Button	Ongoing Production	XLAT Long	PROJECT_TBL	PROJ_TYPE			ONPR									
6	Radio Button	Exploratory	XLAT Long	PROJECT_TBL	PROJ_TYPE			EXPL									
7	Radio Button	Special Project	XLAT Long	PROJECT_TBL	PROJ_TYPE			SPEC									
8	Radio Button	Volunteer	XLAT Long	PROJECT_TBL	PROJ_TYPE			VOL									
9	Group Box	Project Priority Rating	RFT Long	PROJECT_TBL	PROJ_PRIORITY_RT												
10	Radio Button	High	XLAT Long	PROJECT_TBL	PROJ_PRIORITY_RT			H									
11	Radio Button	Medium	XLAT Long	PROJECT_TBL	PROJ_PRIORITY_RT			M									
12	Radio Button	Low	XLAT Long	PROJECT_TBL	PROJ_PRIORITY_RT			L									
13	Edit Box	Project Estimated Hours	RFT Long	PROJECT_TBL	PROJ_ESTIM_HRS												
14	Push Button	Customers Requesting Project	Text	PROJECT_TBL	PROJ_ID	Cus											
15	Edit Box	Project Actual Hours	RFT Long	PROJECT_TBL	PROJ_ACTUAL_HRS												

Figure 21.24 Printout of the PROJECT_PNL panel (Page 2)

22

Security and Testing: Project Panel

In this final chapter on the Project panel, we will complete the development and see our finished application. As with the two previous case chapters, we will provide a detailed walk-through of the development activities.

Application Security

Recall from our discussion of PeopleSoft application security that an operator is given access to an application on the basis of selected menus, panels, and actions. As the developer, you will want to have complete access to all the menus, associated panels and actions in order to test and demonstrate the application you have created. Hence, the definition of application security will be relatively simple, as illustrated in the following steps:

1. Select **Go/PeopleTools/Security Administrator** to open the Security Administrator tool, as shown in Figure 22.1.

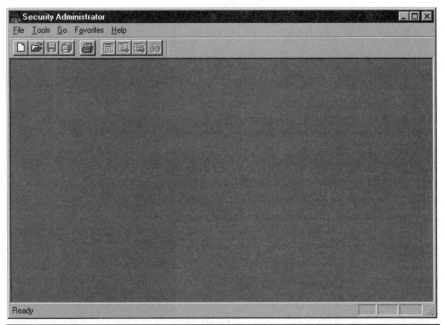

Figure 22.1   *Security Administrator tool*

2. Select **File/Open** and depress the "squiggly down arrow" to display a list of security profile classes and operators. Select either the operator you are using for PeopleTools access, or the class that your operator is assigned to. In our case we are using the operator PTTRN assigned to the class TRNPANLS. Notice in Figure 22.2 that we will select the class TRNPANLS. Recall that if an operator is assigned to a class, then all menu access is inherited from the class profile and *cannot* be modified in the operator profile.

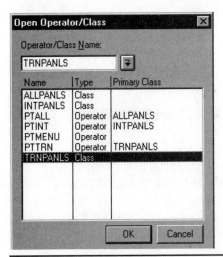

Figure 22.2   *Security Administrator—Open class TRNPANLS*

3. From the General display in Security Administrator shown in Figure 22.3, select **View/Menu Items** or click the **Menu Items** icon on the left side of the display.

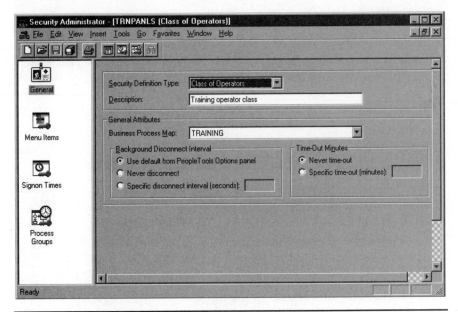

Figure 22.3   *Security Administrator tool—General display*

4. From the Menu Items display in Security Administrator shown in Figure 22.4, examine the list of all menus to which the selected operator or class already has some access. Any menu from this list can be selected by double clicking on the menu name.

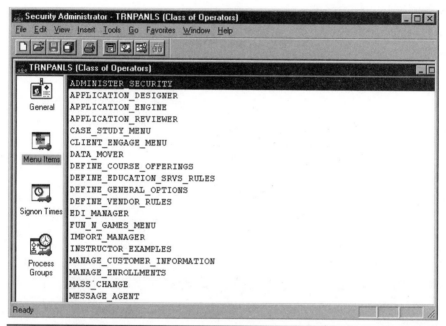

Figure 22.4   *Security Administrator tool—Menu Items display*

5. To provide access to a newly defined menu, select the **Insert/Menu Name** command for a display of all menus to which the operator or class has no access. Highlight the new menu and click **OK**. Select the menu named FUN_N_GAMES_MENU as shown in Figure 22.5.

6. You will now be presented with the **Select Menu Items** dialog box as shown in Figure 22.6. The simplest method to provide access to all panels and all actions on the menu is to click the **Select All** pushbutton in the lower left corner of the dialog box. Notice that all panels and actions turn blue, indicating that they have been selected for access. In our case, the only item that will be listed is the PROJECT_PNLG. Once other panel groups are assigned to the FUN_N_GAMES_MENU, they will then be available.

Figure 22.5 *Security Administrator—Insert Menu Name*

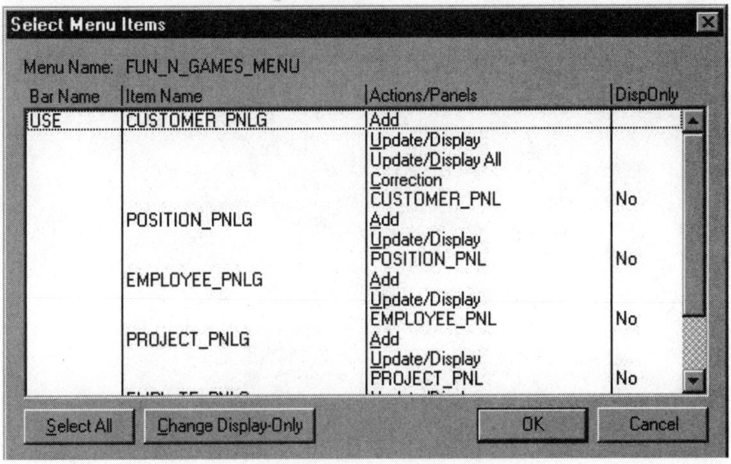

Figure 22.6 *Security Administrator tool—Select Menu Items*

7. Select **File/Save** or use the **Save** icon to save the Operator or Class security profile.
8. Select **File/Exit** or simply close the Security Administrator tool.
9. Exit from all open PeopleTools windows and then sign on to PeopleTools with the Operator profile that has been modified, or an operator assigned to the class that has been modified. You should now have access to the FUN_N_GAMES_MENU and the Project panel.

Application Testing

We will perform two stages of testing of our case application: we will test the function of the online application and then we will test the contents of the application data tables. As discussed in Chapter 17, testing may begin with the development of a formal written test plan, including the development of test cases/data and application test scripts with expected outcomes. In the walk-through that follows, we will illustrate the concepts using a fairly informal process to test the Project Setup application.

1. Check the menu navigation. Ensure that the application menu can be found within the desired menu group, and that the desired menu bars and menu items are present. Please see Figure 22.7 for our sample application **Use** menu bar and menu items.

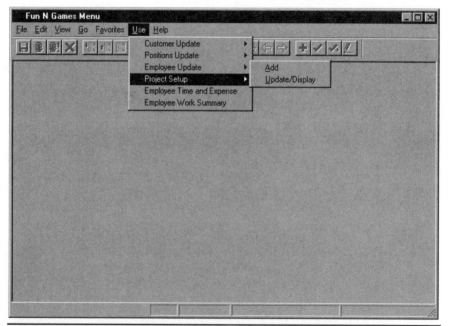

Figure 22.7   *Sample application menu bar and menu items*

2. Since this application has not been executed previously, there are no rows of data in the application data table. Select the application panel **Project Setup** and choose the **Add** action. Enter a new key value for Project Identifier in the Add dialog box as shown in Figure 22.8 and press **Enter**.

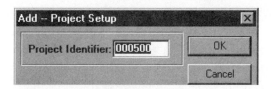

Figure 22.8 *Project Setup—Add dialog box*

3. Ensure that the correct panel is displayed. The Project panel should be blank except for the newly assigned Project Identifier key value. This key value should be display only. Please see Figure 22.9 for our sample Project Setup panel.

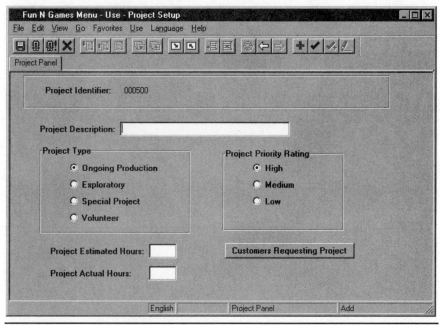

Figure 22.9 *Sample Project Setup panel*

4. Test the function of each field on the panel. Check that fields intended to be required are in fact required, that field formats are appropriate, that field defaults are appearing correctly, and that edit or prompt tables are working properly. Aside from testing editable fields, check that related display fields on the panel are appearing correctly. Finally, make sure that the panel data can be saved without error.

5. Select the application panel to be tested, again the Project Setup, and test the function of the Search dialog box by selecting the **Update/Display** action. Ensure that the appropriate Search keys and Alternate Search keys are found in the Search dialog box in the desired order. Perform unqualified searches with no data entered as in Figure 22.10. Try full-key and partial-key searches. Check the contents of the List box area after each of the searches.

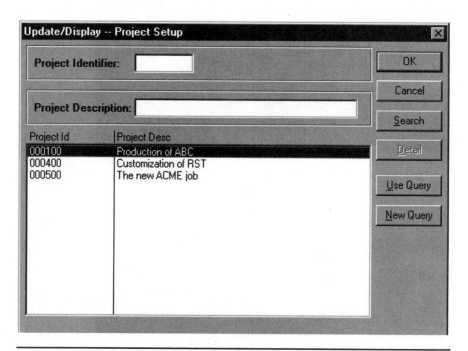

Figure 22.10 *Project Setup Search dialog box*

6. Select a row of data from the Search dialog box and click **OK** to bring up the panel for that high-level key value. You may wish to retest the function of the panel fields (step 4). Make one or more field changes to a row of data and ensure that the panel data saves.

7. If the application is effective dated (Project Setup is *not*), ensure that the Update/Display All and Correction actions are working as well.

8. If the application has associated PeopleCode (Project Setup does *not*), ensure that the PeopleCode is producing the desired results in terms of edits, messages, panel changes, and any calculations.

9. Test the contents of the application data tables by developing and executing SQL statements using an appropriate interactive SQL tool to query the underlying database. Ensure that the rows of data that have been added and/or changed are stored in the database. Shown below is a sample query of the PROJECT_TBL with sample output.

```
Select PROJ_ID, PROJ_DESC, PROJ_TYPE, PROJ_PRIORITY_RT from
PS_PROJECT_TBL;
```

PROJ_ID	PROJ_DESC	PROJ_TYPE	PROJ_PRIORITY_RT
000100	Production of ABC	ONPR	H
000400	Customization Job	SPEC	H
000500	The new ACME job	EXPL	H

23

Developing the Customer Panel

As described in the initial design of our Fun-N-Games application, one of the basic business processes is to maintain information about our customers. The Customer panel will be the part of our application used to add, display, or change customer information. The basic customer information includes a unique Customer Identifier (key), Name, Contact Name, and Address details. In order to maintain a history of changes to customer data this panel is effective dated. Notice the Effective Date and Effective Status fields on the panel and the scroll bar to support multiple rows of data for the same Customer Identifier. Please refer to Figure 23.1 for a sample of the completed Customer panel.

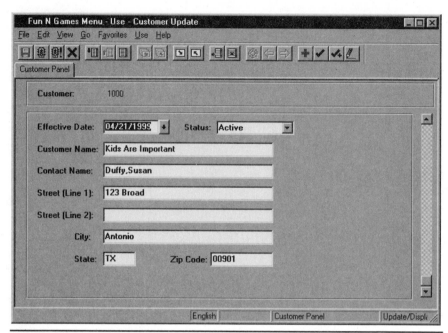

Figure 23.1   *Sample Customer panel—notice the effective date, effective status and scroll bar*

Understand the Data: Customer Panel

Having seen the Customer panel, we have a good idea of the data requirements for the Customer data. Please refer to Table 23.1 for details of the new fields required for the application.

Table 23.1   *Development worksheet—New fields required for customer panel*

Field Name	Type	Format	Length	Translate Values (if any)
Customer ID	Char	Upper	6	
Customer Name	Char	Mixed	30	
Cust Contact Nm	Char	Name	30	
Street Line 1	Char	Mixed	30	
Street Line 2	Char	Mixed	30	
City	Char	Mixed	30	
State	Char	Upper	5	
Zip	Char	Zip/Post	10	

These fields will all be included in the Customer record. Recall that we must use the PeopleSoft provided EFFDT and EFF_STATUS fields to make the record effective dated. Please refer to Table 23.2 for further details of the Customer Record field properties.

Table 23.2 *Development worksheet for customer record*

Field Name	Key	Defaults	Required?	Edits
Customer ID	Key, Search		Yes	
EFFDT	Key, Desc.	%date	Yes	
EFF_STATUS	A		Yes	Xlat
Customer Name	Alt Search		Yes	
Cust Contact Nm				
Street Line 1				
Street Line 2				
City				
State				
Zip				

To complete the data section of our activity, let's not forget to Build the Customer record to create the corresponding relational database table.

Develop the User Interface: Customer Panel

We have seen the Customer panel from the user's view. Now let's take a look from the application developer's view. Please see Figure 23.2 for a sample of the CUSTOMER_PNL open in the Application Designer tool.

For simplicity, we dragged all fields from the expanded Customer record in the Project Workspace and dropped them onto the panel. We accepted the RFT long or short name for the panel field labels. Aside from the frames, the only other panel control that we had to insert was the scroll bar—with an occurs level of 1 and an occurs count of 1. We made sure to place the scroll bar after the Customer Identifier but before the Effective Date in panel layout order. Please see Figure 23.3 for the Order Panel display.

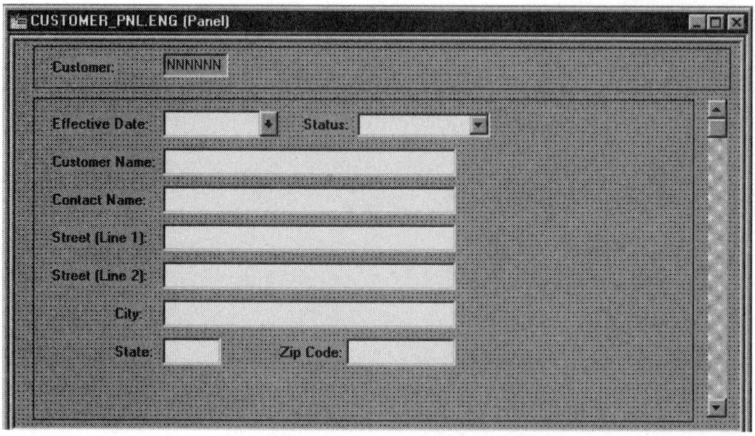

Figure 23.2 *Sample CUSTOMER_PNL open in the Application Designer tool*

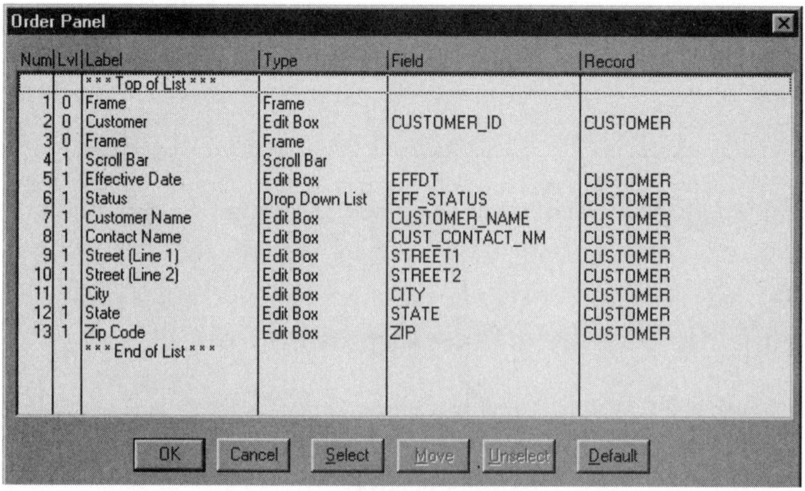

Num	Lvl	Label	Type	Field	Record
		*** Top of List ***			
1	0	Frame	Frame		
2	0	Customer	Edit Box	CUSTOMER_ID	CUSTOMER
3	0	Frame	Frame		
4	1	Scroll Bar	Scroll Bar		
5	1	Effective Date	Edit Box	EFFDT	CUSTOMER
6	1	Status	Drop Down List	EFF_STATUS	CUSTOMER
7	1	Customer Name	Edit Box	CUSTOMER_NAME	CUSTOMER
8	1	Contact Name	Edit Box	CUST_CONTACT_NM	CUSTOMER
9	1	Street (Line 1)	Edit Box	STREET1	CUSTOMER
10	1	Street (Line 2)	Edit Box	STREET2	CUSTOMER
11	1	City	Edit Box	CITY	CUSTOMER
12	1	State	Edit Box	STATE	CUSTOMER
13	1	Zip Code	Edit Box	ZIP	CUSTOMER
		*** End of List ***			

Figure 23.3 *Order Panel display for CUSTOMER_PNL*

Now, we must place CUSTOMER_PNL within a panel group and then associate the panel group with a menu item. We will create a new panel group called CUSTOMER_PNLGP. Please refer to Figure 23.4 for the panel group properties. Note the search record that we have selected, and the actions assigned for an effective dated record.

We will now open FUN_N_GAMES_MENU and place this panel group under the Use bar item. Open the Menu Item Properties dialog box to change the menu item label (e.g. to read "Customer udate").

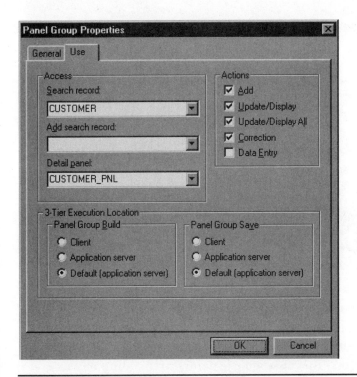

Figure 23.4 *Sample CUSTOMER_PNLGP properties dialog box*

Complete the Application: Customer Panel

Finally, we must give ourselves access to the new Customer panel in order to use and test the application. We start with **Go/PeopleTools/Security Administrator** to begin the process. Now open either the operator you are using, or preferably, the class that is the primary class for your operator. View the Menu Items list and select FUN_N_GAMES_MENU. Notice in Figure 23.5 that initially the newly created menu item is *not* highlighted in the Select Menu Items dialog box.

Just click the **Select All** pushbutton to give your class or operator access to the new menu item. After saving the security profile, exit the Security Administrator and Application Designer tools and log off from all PeopleTools application panels. The next time you sign on to PeopleTools you should have access to the new Customer Panel menu item. Now we can begin to test our new panel.

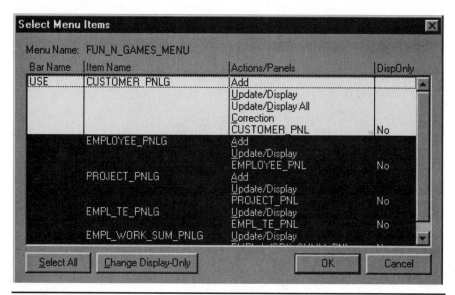

Figure 23.5   *Select Menu Items dialog box*

As before, we will not present a formal test plan or process here. Rather, we suggest that you test the Customer panel by first adding one or more Customers, each with a unique Customer Identifier. Then test each field on the panel to ensure the correct data type, etc. Since the Customer panel is effective dated, test the differences between Update/Display, Update/Display All, and Correction actions. You may want to use an interactive SQL tool to query the PS_CUSTOMER table after your online tests to check the contents of the database.

Sample Solution

Here we present our sample solution for the CUSTOMER application. You may want to print the record and the panel that you developed and compare it to our version of the case application. As a reminder, select **File/Print** with either the record or panel open in the Object Workspace to get a printed report. Please refer to Figure 23.6 for the printout of our CUSTOMER record and Figure 23.7 for the printout of our CUSTOMER_PNL.

Printed: 07/16/99 8:02:47AM

Database: FUNGAME2   PS Record: CUSTOMER   Version: 6458

Field Name   Type Length Format Long Name   Short Name   Key Req TblEdt AU Dt PC Aud Prompt Table Default Value
Last Updated Date/Time: 07/05/1999 1:03:22PM
Last Updated by Operator: PTTRN

Field Name	Type	Length	Format	Long Name	Short Name	Key	Req	TblEdt	AU Dt PC Aud	Prompt Table	Default Value
CUSTOMER_ID	Char	6	Upper	Customer	Customer	KALS	Yes				
EFFDT	Date	10		Effective Date	Eff Date	KD	Yes				
EFF_STATUS	Char	1	Upper	Status as of Effective Date	Status		Yes	Xlat			%date
Values: A	Active			Active	Active				07/09/1997 12:39:29PM		'A'
I	Active			Inactive	Inactive				07/09/1997 12:39:29PM	PPLSOFT	
CUSTOMER_NAME	Char	30	Mixed	Customer Name	Cust Name	AAL	Yes			PPLSOFT	
CUST_CONTACT_NM	Char	30	Name	Customer Contact Name	Contact Name						
STREET1	Char	30	Mixed	Street (Line 1)	Street						
STREET2	Char	30	Mixed	Street (Line 2)	Street						
CITY	Char	30	Mixed	City	City						
STATE	Char	4	Upper	Postal Abbreviation	State						
ZIP	Char	10	ZPCIn	Zip Code	Zip						

Figure 23.6 *Printout of the CUSTOMER record*

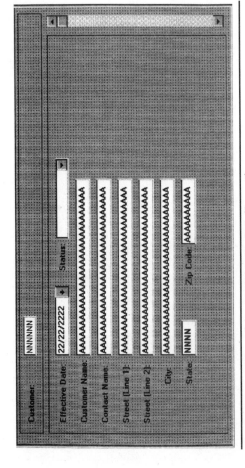

Figure 23.7   *Print of the CUSTOMER_PNL (Page 1)*

Database: FUNGAME2   PS Panel: CUSTOMER_PNL   Version: 1485

Last Changed: 05/06/99 10:58:59PM

Num	Field Type	Label Text	Label Type	Record Name	Field Name	Siz	Alg	On	Off	DSP	INV	CTL	REL	RelNum	CUR	DER	OccLvl
			PTTRN														
1	Frame	Frame	None														
2	Edit Box	Customer	RFT Long	CUSTOMER	CUSTOMER_ID					Yes							
3	Frame	Frame	None														
4	Scroll Bar	Scroll Bar	None														
5	Edit Box	Effective Date	RFT Long	CUSTOMER	EFFDT												1
6	Drop Down Lst	Status	RFT Short	CUSTOMER	EFF_STATUS												1
7	Edit Box	Customer Name	RFT Long	CUSTOMER	CUSTOMER_NAME												1
8	Edit Box	Contact Name	RFT Short	CUSTOMER	CUST_CONTACT_NM												1
9	Edit Box	Street (Line 1)	RFT Long	CUSTOMER	STREET1												1
10	Edit Box	Street (Line 2)	RFT Long	CUSTOMER	STREET2												1
11	Edit Box	City	RFT Long	CUSTOMER	CITY												1
12	Edit Box	State	RFT Short	CUSTOMER	STATE												1
13	Edit Box	Zip Code	RFT Long	CUSTOMER	ZIP												1

Figure 23.7 Printout of the CUSTOMER_PNL (Page 2)

Developing the Project: Customer Secondary Panel

From the design of our Fun-N-Games application we understand that a given toy project can be created for one or more of our customers. Another one of our business requirements is to maintain information about the relationship between our projects and the customers who have requested a project. Recall from our design that we have decided to implement this requirement using a Secondary panel "attached" to the Project panel.

We will refer to this as the Project–Customer secondary panel. The basic information includes the unique Project Identifier, the Customer Identifier, and the Project Request Date (the date that this project was requested by this customer). Please refer to Figure 24.1 for a sample of the completed Project panel, showing the pushbutton used to invoke the Project–Customer secondary panel. Please refer to Figure 24.2 for a sample of the completed Project–Customer secondary panel itself.

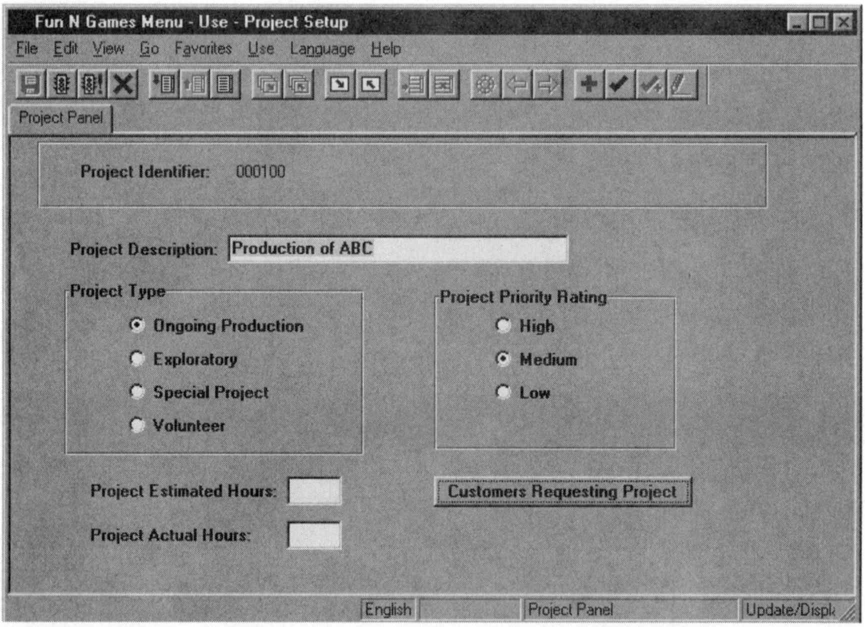

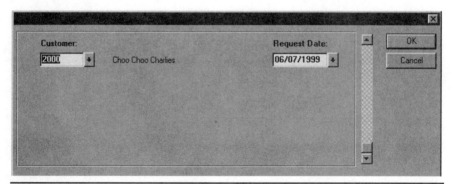

Figure 24.1   *Sample Project panel—notice the "Customers Requesting Project" pushbutton*

Figure 24.2   *Sample Project—Customer secondary panel*

Understand the Data: Project–Customer Panel

The data requirements for the Project–Customer secondary panel are quite straightforward. Several of the fields required for the panel have already been created. Please refer to Table 24.1 for details of the one new field that will be required for the application.

Table 24.1 *Development worksheet – New field required for project –Customer secondary panel*

Field Name	Type	Format	Length	Translate Values (if any)
Project Request Date	Date			

Three fields will be included in the new PROJ_CUST_TBL record. Two of them, the Project ID and the Customer ID, in combination will form a unique key. Notice that although we want the Customer name to appear on the secondary panel, we do not need to include that field in our new PROJ_CUST_TBL record. Instead, we will reference that field from the Customer record on our panel using a related display. Please refer to Table 24.2 for further details of the PROJ_CUST_TBL record field properties.

Table 24.2 *Development worksheet for PROJ_CUST_TBL record*

Field Name	Key	Defaults	Required?	Edits
Project ID	Key		Yes	PROJECT_TBL
Customer ID	Key		Yes	CUSTOMER
Project Request Date		%date		

To complete the data section of our activity, Build the PROJ_CUST_TBL record to create the corresponding relational database table.

Develop the User Interface: Project–Customer Secondary Panel

Now let's take a look at the Project–Customer secondary panel from the application developer's view. Please see Figure 24.3 for a sample of the PROJ_CUST_SEC panel open in the Application Designer tool.

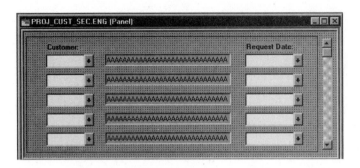

Figure 24.3   *Sample PROJ_CUST_SEC panel open in Application Designer*

We dragged the Customer ID and Project Request Date fields from the expanded PROJ_CUST_TBL record in the Project Workspace and dropped them onto the panel. We inserted an edit box in between these fields and assigned it to the Customer name from the Customer record. The Customer ID field from the PROJ_CUST_TBL record must be marked as a Display Control field and the Customer Name field from the Customer record marked as Related Display. The only other panel control we had to insert was the scroll bar with an occurs level of 1 and an occurs count of 5. The occurs count of 5 allows the application user to see up to five Customers requesting a Project on the panel without scrolling. Please see Figure 24.4 for the Order Panel display.

Now, we must update the panel properties for PROJ_CUST_SEC to indicate that the panel type is secondary panel and to set panel size to auto-size (to shrink the panel). Please refer to Figure 24.5 for the Panel Properties dialog box.

To associate this new secondary panel with the Project Setup "primary" panel, we need to insert a pushbutton on the PROJECT_PNL panel we have already created. This pushbutton will be used to invoke the secondary panel. Please see Figures 24.6 and 24.7 for the Panel Field properties of the pushbutton.

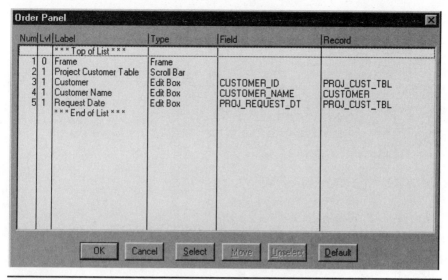

Figure 24.4   *Order Panel display for the PROJ_CUST_SEC panel*

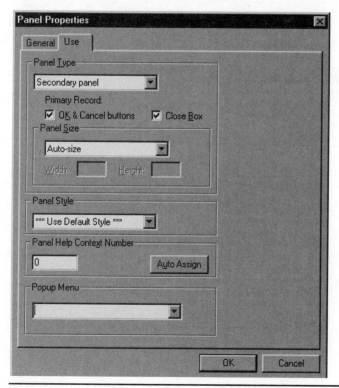

Figure 24.5   *Panel Properties for the PROJ_CUST_SEC secondary panel*

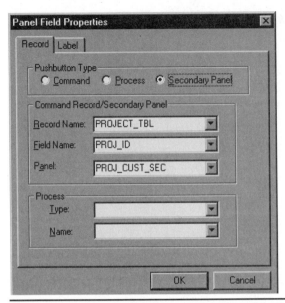

Figure 24.6   *Panel Field properties for the pushbutton on the PROJECT_PNL—*
                   Record tab

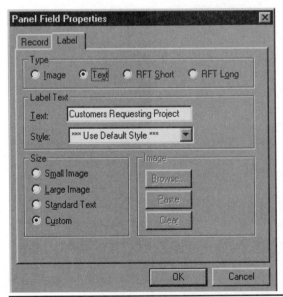

Figure 24.7   *Panel Field properties for the pushbutton on the PROJECT_PNL—*
                   Label tab

Since the secondary panel is now "attached" to the PROJECT_PNL (via the push button) and that panel already belongs to a panel group, we do *not* have to associate the secondary panel with a panel group.

Complete the Application: Project–Customer Panel

We are ready to access our new secondary panel and test it. Interestingly, we do *not* need to go into the Security Administrator tool and give access as there is no new menu item to give access to in this case. Operators who have access to the Project Setup menu item will immediately have access to the newly created Project–Customer secondary panel. Now we can begin to test our secondary panel.

We suggest that you begin to test the Project–Customer secondary panel by relating one or more customers to a particular project. Access the Project panel for an existing project and click the **Customers Requesting Project** pushbutton. This should invoke the new secondary panel, but with no data displayed. Now test the various fields on the panel. Test the prompt on the Customer ID field. You should be presented with a list of all customers. Select a customer and tab out of the Customer ID field. Check that the related display of the customer name is working correctly. Check that the default project request date is the current date, and that you can select another date from the Windows calendar. Ensure that you can save this first row of test data. Test inserting, changing, and deleting rows of data within the scroll bar. Click **OK** to return to the Project panel. As before, you may want to use an interactive SQL tool to query PS_PROJ_CUST_TBL after your online tests to check the contents of the database.

Sample Solution

Here we present our sample solution for the Project–Customer application panel. Please refer to Figure 24.8 for the printout of our PROJ_CUST_TBL record and Figure 24.9 for the printout of our PROJ_CUST_SEC secondary panel itself.

```
Printed: 07/16/99  8:07:06AM                    Database: FUNGAME2     PS Record: PROJ_CUST_TBL     Version: 6444

Field Name      Type  Length  Format  Long Name              Short Name    Key  Req TblEdt AU Dt PC Aud Prompt Table   Default Value
Last Updated Date/Time:  05/07/1999  7:31:38AM
Last Updated by Operator:  PTTRN

PROJ_ID         Char    6     Upper   Project Identifier     Project Id    KA   Yes Prompt            PROJECT_TBL
CUSTOMER_ID     Char    6     Upper   Customer               Customer      KA   Yes Prompt            CUSTOMER
PROJ_REQUEST_DT Date   10             Project Request Date   Request Date                                            %date
```

Figure 24.8 *Printout of the PROJ_CUST_TBL record*

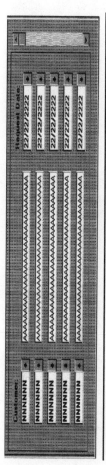

Figure 24.9 *Printout of the PROJ_CUST_SEC secondary panel (Page 1)*

Printed: 07/16/99 8:07:17AM

Database: FUNGAME2   PS Panel: PROJ_CUST_SEC   Version: 1498

Num	Field Type	Label Text	Label Type	Record Name	Field Name	Siz	Alg	On	Off	DSP	INV	CTL	REL	RelNum	CUR	DER	OccLvl
Last Changed:	05/07/99 7:25:44AM		PTTRN														
1	Frame	Frame	None														
2	Scroll Bar	Project Customer Table	None														
3	Edit Box	Customer	RFT Long	PROJ_CUST_TBL	CUSTOMER_ID												1
4	Edit Box	Customer Name	None	CUSTOMER	CUSTOMER_NAME					Yes		Yes	Yes	3			1
5	Edit Box	Request Date	RFT Short	PROJ_CUST_TBL	PROJ_REQUEST_DT												1

Figure 24.9 *Printout of the PROJ_CUST_SEC secondary panel (Page 2)*

341

25

Developing the Employee Panel

Another one of the basic business processes of the Fun-N-Games application is to maintain information about employees. The Employee panel will be the part of our application that will be used to add, display, or change employee information. Employee information includes a unique Employee Identifier (key), Name, Specialty, and Position. Please refer to Figure 25.1 for a sample of the completed Employee panel.

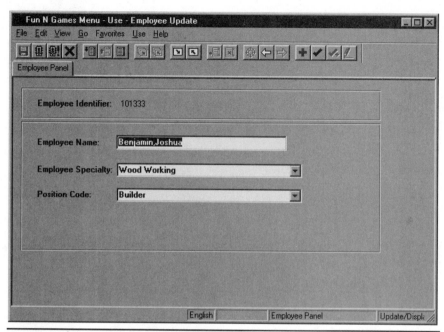

Figure 25.1   *Sample Employee panel*

Understand the Data: Employee Panel

Now we have a good idea of the Employee panel data requirements. Please
refer to Table 25.1 for details of the new fields that will be required for the
application.

Table 25.1   *Development worksheet—New fields required for employee panel*

Field Name	Type	Format	Length	Translate	Values (if any)
Employee ID	Char	Upper	6		
Employee Name	Char	Name	30		
Specialty	Char	Upper	4	METL	Metal Working
				PLAS	Plastic Molding
				WOOD	Wood Working
Position	Char	Upper	4	BLD	Builder
				DES	Toy Designer
				MGR	Manager

These are all the fields that will be included in the EMPLOYEE_TBL record in our application. Please refer to Table 25.2 for further details of the EMPLOYEE_TBL Record Field properties.

Table 23.2   *Development worksheet for employee record*

Field Name	Key	Defaults	Required?	Edits
Employee ID	Key, Search Key		Yes	
Employee Name	Alt Search		Yes	
Specialty		WOOD	Yes	Xlat
Position		DES	Yes	Xlat

As before, we need to Build the EMPLOYEE_TBL record to complete the data section of our activity and create the required database table.

Develop the User Interface: Employee Panel

Now let's look at the Employee panel from the application developer's view. Please see Figure 25.2 for a sample of the EMPLOYEE_PNL panel open in the Application Designer tool.

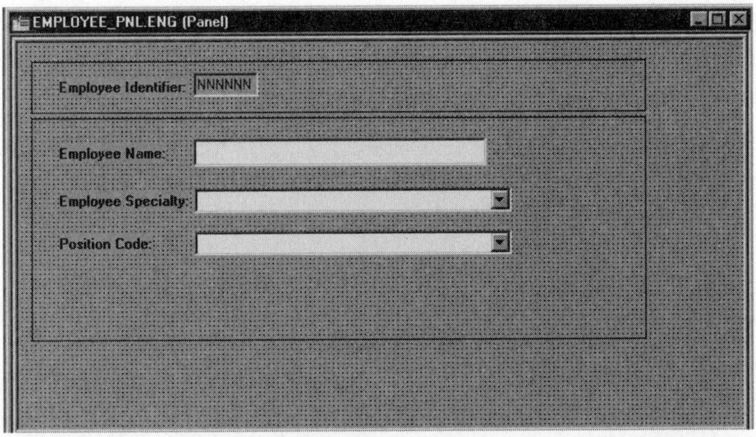

Figure 25.2   *Sample EMPLOYEE_PNL open in Application Designer*

This is certainly one of the simplest panels in our application. We dragged all fields from the expanded EMPLOYEE_TBL record in the Project Workspace and dropped them right onto the panel. Notice that there is no scroll bar on this panel, all fields are at level zero. Please see Figure 25.3 for the Order Panel display.

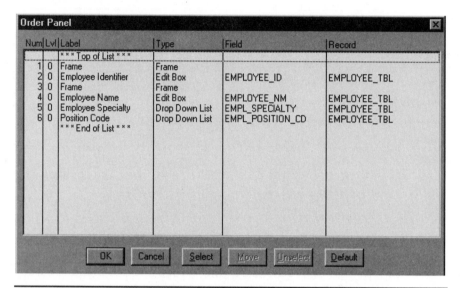

Figure 25.3   *Order Panel display for EMPLOYEE_PNL*

Now, we must place the EMPLOYEE_PNL within a panel group and then associate the panel group with a menu item. We will create a new panel group called EMPLOYEE_PNLGP. Please refer to Figure 25.4 for the Panel Group properties. Note the Search record selected and the actions assigned.

We will now open FUN_N_GAMES_MENU and place this panel group under the Use bar item. Open the Menu Item Properties dialog box to change the Menu Item label to read "Employee update."

Complete the Application: Employee Panel

We must give ourselves access to the new Employee panel to use and test the application. Again, we access the Security Administrator tool to begin the process. Open either the operator you are using, or preferably, the class that is the primary class for your operator. View the Menu Items list and select FUN_N_GAMES_MENU. Initially the new menu item is *not* highlighted in the Select Menu Items dialog box. Click the **Select All** pushbutton to give your class or operator access to the new menu item. After saving the security profile, exit the Security Administrator and Application Designer tools, and log off from all PeopleTools application panels. The next time you sign on to PeopleTools you should have access to the new Employee Panel menu item. Now we can begin to test our new panel.

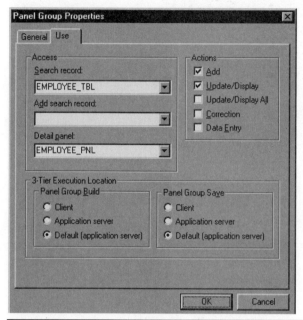

Figure 25.4   *Sample EMPLOYEE_PNLGP Properties dialog box*

We suggest that you test the Employee panel by first adding one or more Employees, each with a unique Employee Identifier. Then test each field on the panel to ensure that the field accepts the correct data type, etc. Check the Specialty and Position fields to ensure that the Translate values are working. You may want to use an interactive SQL tool to query PS_EMPLOYEE_TBL after your online tests to check the contents of the database.

Sample Solution

Here we present our sample solution for the Employee panel. Please refer to Figure 25.5 for the printout of our EMPLOYEE_TBL record and Figure 25.6 for the printout of our EMPLOYEE_TBL.

Printed: 07/16/99 8:44:37AM   Database: FUNGAME2   PS Record: EMPLOYEE_TBL   Version: 6459

Field Name   Type Length Format Long Name
Last Updated Date/Time: 07/05/1999 3:41:00PM
Last Updated by Operator: PTTRN

Field Name	Type	Length	Format	Long Name	Short Name	Key	Req	TblEdt	AU Dt PC Aud	Prompt Table	Default Value
EMPLOYEE_ID	Char	6	Upper	Employee Identifier	Employee ID	KALS	Yes				
EMPLOYEE_NM	Char	30	Name	Employee Name	Employee	AAL	Yes				
EMPL_SPECIALTY	Char	4	Upper	Employee Specialty	Specialty		Yes	Xlat			
Values: METL	Active			Metal Working	Metal Work				05/06/1999 10:24:58PM	PTTRN	
PLAS	Active			Plastic Molding	Plastic Mo				05/06/1999 10:25:09PM	PTTRN	
WOOD	Active			Wood Working	Wood Worki				05/06/1999 10:24:46PM	PTTRN	'WOOD'
EMPL_POSITION_CD	Char	4	Upper	Employee Position Code	Position Code		Yes	Xlat			
Values: BLD	Active			Builder	Builder				07/05/1999 3:40:15PM	PTTRN	
CON	Active			Consultant	Consultant				07/05/1999 3:39:37PM	PTTRN	
DES	Active			Toy Designer	Designer				07/05/1999 3:37:55PM	PTTRN	'DES'
MGR	Active			Manager	Manager				07/05/1999 3:39:53PM	PTTRN	

Figure 25.5 *Printout of EMPLOYEE_TBL*

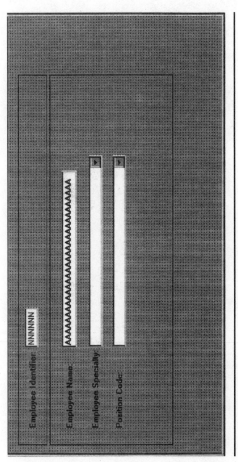

Figure 25.6 Printout of EMPLOYEE_PNL (Page 1)

Printed: 07/16/99 8:44:45AM

Database: FUNGAME2   PS Panel: EMPLOYEE_PNL   Version: 1562

Num	Field Type	Label Text	Label Type	Record Name	Field Name	Siz	Alg	On	Off	DSP	INV	CTL	REL	RelNum	CUR	DER	OccLvl
Last Changed:	07/05/99 3:48:24PM																
1	Frame	Frame	PTTRN														
2	Edit Box	Employee Identifier	None	RFT Long	EMPLOYEE_TBL	EMPLOYEE_ID				Yes							
3	Frame	Frame	None														
4	Edit Box	Employee Name	RFT Long	EMPLOYEE_TBL	EMPLOYEE_NM												
5	Drop Down Lst	Employee Specialty	RFT Long	EMPLOYEE_TBL	EMPL_SPECIALTY												
6	Drop Down Lst	Position Code	RFT Short	EMPLOYEE_TBL	EMPL_POSITION_CD												

Figure 25.6 Printout of EMPLOYEE_PNL (Page 2)

349

26

Developing the Employee Time and Expense (T&E) Panel

Probably the most interesting and important of the business processes of Fun-N-Games is to maintain records of employee time and expense on toy projects, especially custom toys done for specific customers. You will recall that this business requirement is really the original motivation for the Fun-N-Games application.

The Employee Time and Expense (T&E) panel will be the part of our application used to assign an employee to a particular project and then allow an employee to record time and expense for that project. Employee time and expense information includes Employee Identifier, Project Identifier, Assignment Date, Work Date, Work Hours, and Work Expenses. Please refer to Figure 26.1 for a sample of the completed Employee T&E panel.

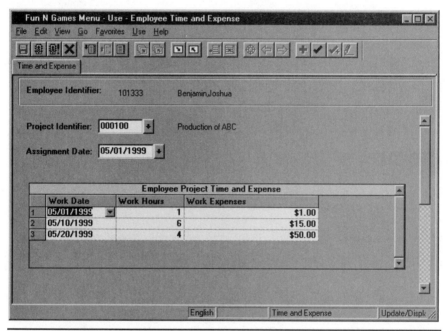

Figure 26.1 *Sample Employee T&E panel*

Understand the Data: Employee T&E Panel

From a review of the Fun-N-Games data model from our original design (Chapter 19) you will recall that there is one table defined to record the assignment of an employee to one or more projects. We will name this the EMPL_PROJ_TBL. There is another table defined to collect one or more employee time and expense records related to a particular project. We will name this the EMPL_TE_TBL. Data from both records will be included on the Employee T&E panel. Notice the "nested" scroll bars on the T&E panel. The "outer" level 1 scroll bar will used to insert one or more EMPL_PROJ_TBL rows for an employee. The "inner" level 2 scroll bar (within the Grid) will be used to insert one or more EMPL_TE_TBL rows for a project.

Aside from the data we have already defined for employees and projects, there are only a few new data fields that will be required for the Employee T&E panel. Please refer to Table 26.1 for field details.

Table 26.1   *Development worksheet—New fields required for Employee T&E panel*

Field Name	Type	Format	Length	Translate Values (if any)
Assignment Date	Date			
Work Date	Date			
Work Hours	Number		2	
Work Expense	Number		6.2	

Please refer to Table 26.2 for further details of the EMPL_PROJ_TBL Record Field properties and to Table 26.3 for details of the EMPL_TE_TBL Record Field properties. You will notice from the key structure that there is a parent-child relationship between these two records, with EMPL_PROJ_TBL as the parent and EMPL_TE_TBL as the child. This parent-child relationship reinforces our understanding of the multiple scroll levels on the Employee T&E panel.

Table 26.2   *Development worksheet for Employee Project (Assignment) record*

Field Name	Key	Defaults	Required?	Edits
Employee ID	Key		Yes	EMPLOYEE
Project Id	Key		Yes	PROJECT_TBL
Assignment Date		%date		

Table 26.3   *Development worksheet for Employee T&E record*

Field Name	Key	Defaults	Required?	Edits
Employee ID	Key		Yes	EMPLOYEE
Project ID	Key		Yes	PROJECT_TBL
Work Date	Key	%date	Yes	
Work Hours		0		
Work Expenses		0		

We will need to Build both the EMPL_PROJ_TBL and EMPL_TE_TBL records to complete the data section of our activity and create the required database tables.

Develop the User Interface: Employee T&E Panel

Now let's take a closer look at the Employee T&E panel, this time from the application developer's view. Please see Figure 26.2 for a sample of the EMPL_TE_PNL panel open in the Application Designer tool.

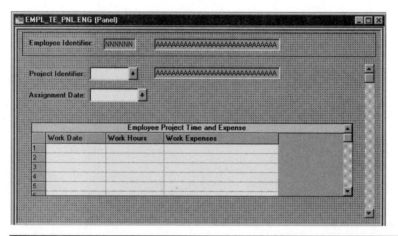

Figure 26.2   *Sample EMPL_TE_PNL panel open in Application Designer*

This is like other panels in our application, with the exception of the grid panel control to capture employee time and expense. We started development of the panel by inserting Employee Identifier and Employee Name from the EMPLOYEE_TBL (our Search record) in the level 0 panel area. We proceeded to insert the level 1 scroll bar and insert Project Identifier and Assignment Date from the EMPL_PROJ_TBL record. Notice that the Project Description field is also inserted onto the panel and set up as a related display, with Project Identifier as the Display Control field. We then saved the panel.

Now we are ready to insert the grid onto the panel. We select a grid from the Insert menu, drop it onto the panel, and size the grid area. We cannot drag fields into the grid, but rather we must double click on the grid to open the

Grid Properties dialog box. First we enter the Main record and the occurs level for the grid scroll bar in the General tab of the Grid properties. Please refer to Figure 26.3 for a sample of this dialog box. We then must Add and define the fields that will become the columns in our grid on the Columns tab. Please refer to Figure 26.4 for a sample of this dialog box.

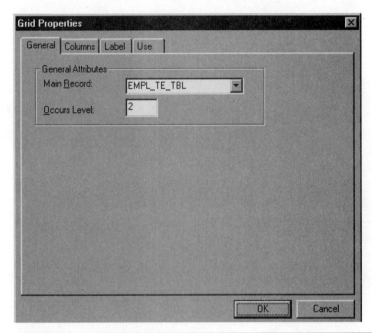

Figure 26.3   *Grid properties for the EMPL_TE_PNL panel—General tab*

Please see Figure 26.5 for the Order Panel display. Note, that while the grid is represented in the Order Panel display as a single panel control we must still obey the panel layout order rules for all the fields in the grid. We can check the order of the fields on the Grid Properties–Columns tab.

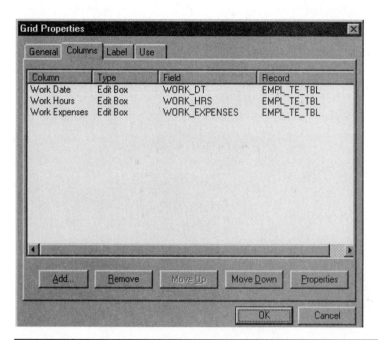

Figure 26.4   *Grid properties for the EMPL_TE_PNL panel—Columns tab*

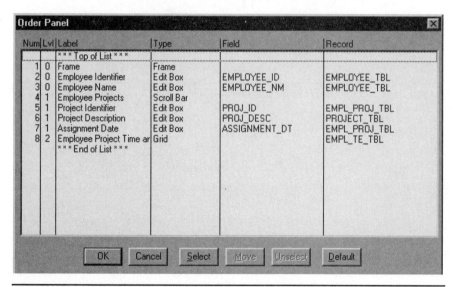

Figure 26.5   *Order Panel display for EMPL_TE_PNL*

We must place EMP_TE_PNL within a panel group and associate the panel group with a menu item. We will create a new panel group called EMPL_TE_PNLGP. Please refer to Figure 25.4 for the panel group properties. Note the search record selected and the actions assigned.

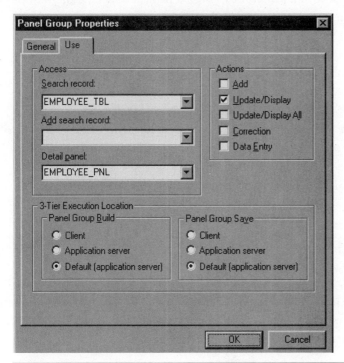

Figure 26.6   *Sample EMPL_TE_PNLGP Properties dialog box*

We will now open FUN_N_GAMES_MENU and place this panel group under the Use bar item. Open the Menu Item Properties dialog box to change the Menu Item label to read "Employee T&E entry."

Complete the Application: Employee T&E Panel

To give ourselves access to the new Employee T&E panel, we must start the Security Administrator tool. Open either the operator you are using or the class that is the primary class for your operator. View the Menu Items list and select the now familiar FUN_N_GAMES_MENU. Click the **Select All** pushbutton to give your class or operator access to the new menu item. After saving the security profile, exit the Security Administrator and Application Designer tools, and log off from all PeopleTools application panels. The next time you sign on to PeopleTools you should have access to the new Employee T&E panel menu item. Now we can begin to test our new panel.

Select one employee and attempt to assign a project. Check that you can select a project from the prompt table on Project Identifier and that the related display of Project Description works correctly. Either accept the default or select an assignment date from the calendar and save the employee to project assignment. Now tab down into the grid area and enter values in Work Date, Work Hours, and Work Expenses columns. Again save the panel, this time to save the Employee time and expense entry. Test inserting, changing, and deleting rows of data in the grid. Also experiment with inserting, changing, and deleting rows of Project assignment data in the outer scroll. You may want to use an interactive SQL tool to query the PS_EMPL_PROJ_TBL and PS_EMPL_TE_TBL tables after your online tests to check the contents of the database.

Sample Solution

Here we present our sample solution for the Employee T&E panel. Please refer to Figure 26.7 for the printout of our EMPL_PROJ_TBL record and Figure 26.8 for the printout of our EMPL_TE_TBL record. Please refer to Figure 26.9 for the printout of our EMPL_TE_PNL panel.

```
Printed: 07/16/99  8:46:33AM              Database: FUNGAME2    PS Record: EMPL_PROJ_TBL    Version: 6444

Field Name            Type  Length  Format  Long Name      Short Name    Key  Req  TblEdt  AU  Dt  PC  Aud  Prompt Table   Default Value
Last Updated Date/Time: 05/06/1999 10:40:16PM
Last Updated by Operator:  PTTRN

EMPLOYEE_ID           Char  6       Upper   Employee Identifier   Employee ID   KA   Yes  Prompt                            EMPLOYEE_TBL
PROJ_ID               Char  6       Upper   Project Identifier    Project Id    KA   Yes  Prompt                            PROJECT_TBL
ASSIGNMENT_DT         Date  10              Assignment Date       Assign Date                                                             %date
```

Figure 26.7 *Printout of the EMPL_PROJ_TBL record*

359

Printed: 07/16/99   8:46:44AM

Database: FUNGAME2   PS Record: EMPL_TE_TBL   Version: 6463

Field Name   Type Length Format Long Name
Last Updated Date/Time: 07/08/1999 12:20:12AM
Last Updated by Operator: PTTRN

Field Name	Type	Length	Format	Long Name	Short Name	Key	Req	TblEdt	AU	Dt	PC	Aud	Prompt Table	Default Value
EMPLOYEE_ID	Char	6	Upper	Employee Identifier	Employee ID	KA	Yes	Prompt					EMPLOYEE_TBL	
PROJ_ID	Char	6	Upper	Project Identifier	Project Id	KA	Yes	Prompt					EMPL_PROJ_TBL	
WORK_DT	Date	10		Work Date	Work Date	KA	Yes							%date
WORK_HRS	Nbr	2		Work Hours	Work Hours									'0'
WORK_EXPENSES	Nbr	6.2		Work Expenses	Work Expenses									'0'

Figure 26.8   *Printout of the EMPL_TE_TBL record*

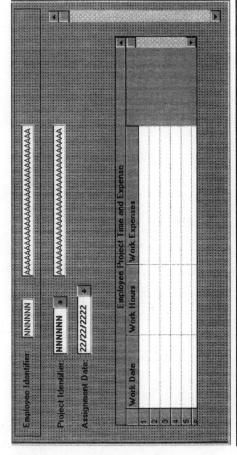

Figure 26.9 *Printout of the EMPL_TE_PNL panel (Page 1)*

361

Database: FUNGAME2   PS Panel: EMPL_TE_PNL   Version: 1563

Num	Field Type	Label Text	Label Type	Record Name	Field Name	Siz	Alg	On	Off	DSP	INV	CTL	REL	RelNum	CUR	DER	OccLvl
Last Changed:	07/08/99 12:18:48AM																
1	Frame	Frame	None	PTTRN													
2	Edit Box	Employee Identifier	RFT Long	EMPLOYEE_TBL	EMPLOYEE_ID					Yes							
3	Edit Box	Employee Name	None	EMPLOYEE_TBL	EMPLOYEE_NM					Yes							
4	Scroll Bar	Employee Projects	None														
5	Edit Box	Project Identifier	RFT Long	EMPL_PROJ_TBL	PROJ_ID							Yes					1
6	Edit Box	Project Description	None	PROJECT_TBL	PROJ_DESC					Yes			Yes	5			1
7	Edit Box	Assignment Date	RFT Long	EMPL_PROJ_TBL	ASSIGNMENT_DT												1
8	Grid	Employee Project Time and Expense Text		EMPL_TE_TBL													1
9	Edit Box	Work Date	RFT Long	EMPL_TE_TBL	WORK_DT	Cus											2
10	Edit Box	Work Hours	RFT Long	EMPL_TE_TBL	WORK_HRS	Cus											2
11	Edit Box	Work Expenses	RFT Long	EMPL_TE_TBL	WORK_EXPENSES	Cus											2

Figure 26.9 *Printout of the EMPL_TE_PNL panel (Page 2)*

27

Developing the Employee Work Summary Panel

As described in the initial design of our Fun-N-Games application, one of the basic business processes is to provide a summary of the work performed by an individual, across all projects. The Employee Work Summary panel will be the part of our application used to display this summary. Note that the panel is display only; there will not be any access to update the information presented to the user. The basic information includes Employee Identifier (key), Project Identifier (key), Project Description, and Work Hours. Please refer to Figure 27.1 for a sample of the completed Employee Work Summary panel.

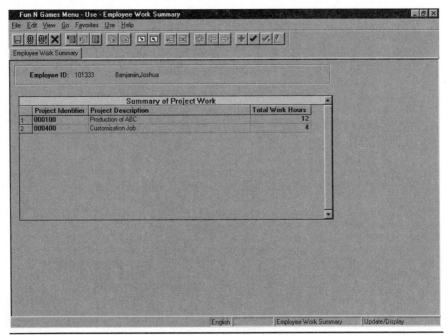

Figure 27.1 *Sample Employee Work Summary panel*

Understand the Data: Employee Work Summary Panel

We have a good idea of the data requirements from reviewing the Employee Work Summary panel. But when looking at the information requirements, note that all this information already exists. Employee ID, Project ID, and Work Hours all exist on the Employee Time and Expense record (EMPL_TE_TBL) and the project description is stored on the Project record (PROJECT_TBL). Therefore, instead of new fields and a new SQL table, what needs to be developed is a View record. Please refer to Table 27.1 for further details of the Employee Work Summary View Record field properties.

Table 27.1 *Development worksheet for EMPLOYEE WORK SUMMARY view record*

Field Name	Key	Defaults	Required?	Edits
Employee ID	Key		Yes	Prompt - EMPLOYEE_TBL
Project Id	Key		Yes	Prompt - PROJ_TBL
Work Hours				

Recall that this view can be built either as an SQL view or as a query view. If an SQL view is used, the fields should be dragged and dropped onto the record definition and then the SQL should be written in the Record Properties Type tab (remember to change the Record type to SQL View). If a query view is used, the fields should *not* be dragged and dropped onto the record definition. The query should be created in the query tool, which can be accessed from the Record Properties Type tab once the record type is changed to Query View.

The tricky part about this view is that an aggregate function is being used to summarize the number of hours worked on each project for each employee. If the hours were not summarized, then for each day that hours were recorded, there would be a row of data in the View record. For either the SQL view or Query view, the resulting SQL will appear as:

```
SELECT A.EMPLOYEE_ID, A.PROJ_ID, SUM(A.WORK_HRS)
FROM PS_EMPL_TE_TBL A
GROUP BY A.EMPLOYEE_ID, A.PROJ_ID
```

To complete the data section of our activity, let's not forget to Build the view for EMPLOYEE WORK SUMMARY. Ensure that your Build options are set to Create View.

Develop the User Interface:
Employee Work Summary Panel

We have seen the Employee Work Summary panel from the user's view. Now let's take a look from the application developer's viewpoint. Please see Figure 27.2 for a sample of the panel open in the Application Designer tool.

The level 0 on the panel is populated from EMPLOYEE_TBL (this will be discussed more when we address the panel group). The employee ID and name can be dragged and dropped onto the panel from EMPLOYEE_TBL in the Project Workspace. The remainder of the panel is built using a grid object. Recall that a grid must be inserted from the menu **Insert/Grid**. Once the grid is inserted the fields are added to the grid as columns. Project ID and Work hours are from the EMPL_WORK_SUMM view we created. The project description is from PROJECT_TBL and is a related display field controlled by the Project ID. Therefore, set Project ID with a Field Use option of Display Control Field (on the Panel Field Properties Use tab) and set Project Description with a Field Use option of Related Display Field. The grid should have an occurs level of 1. Refer to Figure 27.3 for the Order Panel display.

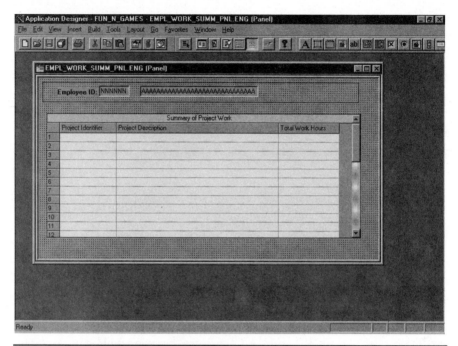

Figure 27.2   Sample EMPL_WORK_SUMM_PNL panel open in Application
Designer

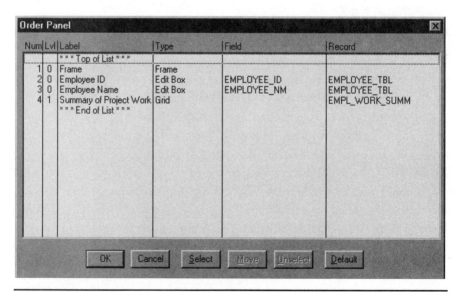

Figure 27.3   Order Panel display for EMPL_WORK_SUMM_PNL

Now we must place EMPL_WORK_SUMM_PNL within a panel group and then associate the panel group with a menu item. We use the existing panel group called EMPL_TE_PNLG. Refer to Figure 27.4 for the Panel Group properties. Note the Search record that we have selected is EMPLOYEE_TBL. This was chosen because we want the user to see a complete list of all employees prior to viewing the panel; this information is stored in the employee record. This explains why our level 0 on the panel is populated from EMPLOYEE_TBL (recall that the Search record populates level 0 on the panel). Also note that the only action assigned is Update/Display because this is a summary panel which does not allow any new entries or updates.

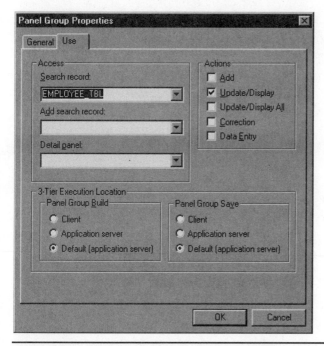

Figure 27.4   *EMPL_TE_PNLG Properties dialog box*

We will now open FUN_N_GAMES_MENU and place this panel group under the Use bar item. Open the Menu Item Properties dialog box to change the Menu Item label (e.g. to read "Employee Work Summary").

Complete the Application:
Employee Work Summary Panel

Finally, we must give ourselves access to the new Employee Work Summary panel in order to use and test the application. We start with **Go/PeopleTools/Security Administrator** to begin the process. Now open either the operator that you are using, or preferably, the class that is the primary class for your operator. View the Menu Items list and select FUN_N_GAMES_MENU. Notice in Figure 27.5 that initially the newly created menu item is not highlighted in the Select Menu Items dialog box.

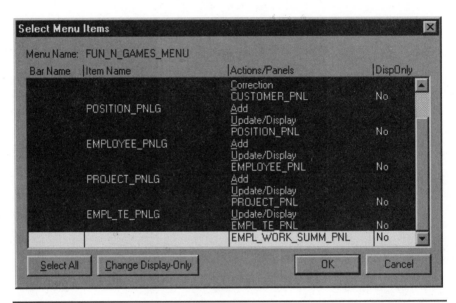

Figure 27.5 *Select Menu Items dialog box*

Just click the **Select All** pushbutton to give your class or operator access to the new menu item. After saving the security profile, exit the Security Administrator and Application Designer tools, and log off from all PeopleTools application panels. The next time you sign on to PeopleTools you should have access to the new Employee Work Summary Panel menu item. Now we can begin to test our new panel.

As before, we will not present a formal test plan or process here. Rather, we suggest that you test the Employee Work Summary panel by ensuring that the summary data "matches" the data found on the Employee Time and Expense panel. Then, ensure that the project description is appearing correctly in the grid. You may also want to use an interactive SQL tool to query the PS_EMPL_WORK_SUMM view after your online tests.

Sample Solution

Refer to Figure 27.6 for the printout of our EMPL_WORK_SUMM View record and Figure 27.7 for the printout of our EMPL_WORK_SUMM _PNL panel.

Printed: 07/15/99 9:05:31PM

Database: FUNGAMES   PS Record: EMPL_WORK_SUMM   Version: 6472

Field Name   Type Length Format Long Name
Record Description: View for Employee Work Summary
Last Updated Date/Time: 07/15/1999 9:05:12PM
Last Updated by Operator: PTTRN

Field Name	Type	Length	Format	Long Name	Short Name	Key	Req	TblEdt	AU	Dt	PC	Aud	Prompt Table	Default Value
EMPLOYEE_ID	Char	6	Upper	Employee Identifier	Employee ID	KA		Yes				Prompt	EMPLOYEE_TBL	
PROJ_ID	Char	6	Upper	Project Identifier	Project Id	KA		Yes				Prompt	PROJECT_TBL	
WORK_HRS	Nbr	2			Work Hours									

Figure 27.6 *Printout of the EMPL_WORK_SUMM record*

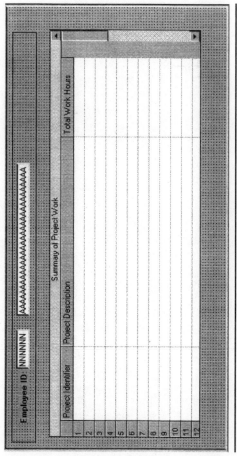

Figure 27.7 Printout of EMPL_WORK_SUMM_PNL (Page 1)

Printed: 07/15/99 8:57:06PM

Database: FUNGAMES   PS Panel: EMPL_WORK_SUMM_PNL   Version: 1547

Num	Field Type	Label Text	Label Type	Record Name	Field Name	Siz	Alg	On	Off	DSP	INV	CTL	REL	RelNum	CUR	DER	OccLvl
			PTTRN														
1	Frame		None														
2	Edit Box	Employee ID	RFT Short	EMPLOYEE_TBL	EMPLOYEE_ID					Yes							
3	Edit Box	Employee Name	None	EMPLOYEE_TBL	EMPLOYEE_NM					Yes							
4	Grid	Summary of Project Work	Text	EMPL_WORK_SUMM						Yes							
5	Edit Box	Project Identifier	RFT Long	EMPL_WORK_SUMM	PROJ_ID							Yes					1
6	Edit Box	Project Description	RFT Long	PROJECT_TBL	PROJ_DESC					Yes			Yes	5			1
7	Edit Box	Total Work Hours	Text	EMPL_WORK_SUMM	WORK_HRS												1

Last Changed: 05/07/99 8:46:03AM

Figure 27.7 Printout of EMPL_WORK_SUMM_PNL (Page 2)

28

Incorporating PeopleCode into the Application

In Part 4 we introduced PeopleCode concepts (Chapter 12), discussed the PeopleSoft application processor and the various PeopleCode event types (Chapter 13), presented PeopleCode syntax and messages (Chapter 14), and useful functions and commands (Chapter 15). Now we will incorporate several small PeopleCode programs into our current Fun-N-Games case application. Specifically, after demonstrating the Fun-N-Games application to our business managers we learned of additional functional requirements that will require us to add logic to the Employee Time and Expense panel.

373

The first additional functional requirement is that users may not enter time and expense entries for a work date that is before the project assignment date. An edit should be placed on the Time and Expense panel to prevent this and an appropriate message should be displayed to the application user. Please see Figure 28.1 for an illustration of the Time and Expense panel with the Assignment Date and Work Date fields highlighted.

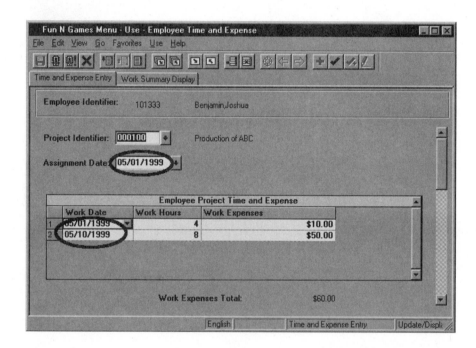

Figure 28.1   *T & E panel—showing the assignment date and work date*

The second additional functional requirement is that users should see a running total of their expenses for a given project displayed on the bottom of the Time and Expense panel. The running total can be calculated from the current expense entries each time the panel is displayed. It should be updated as the application user adds, changes, or deletes an expense entry. Please see Figure 28.2 for the Time and Expense panel with the calculated Work Expense Total field highlighted.

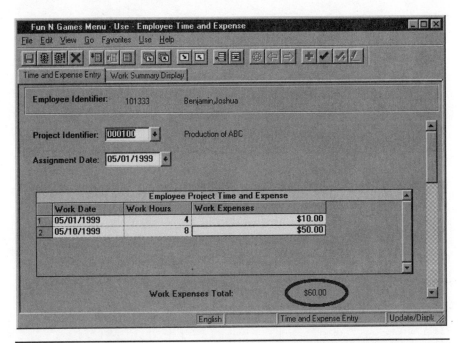

Figure 28.2   *T & E panel—showing the calculated total expense amount*

Requirement #1: Work Date Edit

The first step in developing a PeopleCode program, and often the most difficult step, is to determine where to place the PeopleCode. We need to determine what record and field to place the PeopleCode on and what event type is
appropriate. Given the work date edit requirement, we may start by re-examin-
ing the Time and Expense panel. We find the Work Date field is located in the
grid used to update/display time and expense entries. The Work Date and
other Time and Expense entry fields are being written to the EMPL_TE_TBL
record. Therefore, the Work Date field in this record may be the appropriate
placement for the PeopleCode.

But what PeopleCode event type should we use? Given the requirement to
edit the Work Date field, the Field Edit event type might seem appropriate.
However, we are comparing the Work Date field to the assignment date on the
EMPL_PROJ_TBL record, another field on this panel. Generally, when performing an edit between two fields on the same panel we use the Save Edit
event type. However, if one of the fields in the comparison is display only, then

Field Edit can be used. In our example we will use the Save Edit event on the EMPL_TE_TBL record. Although we can place the PeopleCode on any field in the record (Save Edit code is not field specific) we will place the PeopleCode on the Work Date field.

After deciding the appropriate placement of the PeopleCode, the following steps are performed to insert the PeopleCode syntax onto the record:

1. Open the EMPL_TE_TBL record in the Object Workspace and show the PeopleCode display. Position your cursor on the intersection of the Work Date field and the **Save Edit** event type. See Figure 28.3 for an illustration of this display. Double click on the location to open the PeopleCode program editor.

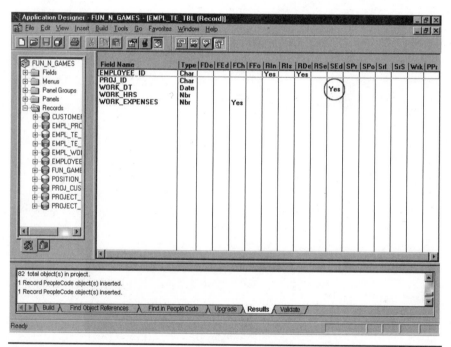

Figure 28.3 *Record EMPL_TE_TBL PeopleCode display*

2. Enter the PeopleCode syntax. Be sure to begin with a comment with background information and explanation of the code. Notice in Figure 28.4 that the code for this example includes an **If... Then... End-if;** statement to compare the work date in the EMPL_TE_TBL to the assignment date in the EMPL_PROJ_TBL.

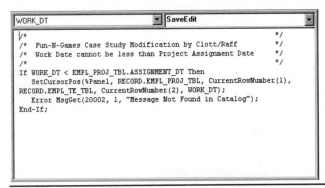

```
WORK_DT                          SaveEdit
/*                                          */
/*  Fun-N-Games Case Study Modification by Clott/Raff   */
/*  Work Date cannot be less than Project Assignment Date  */
/*                                          */
If WORK_DT < EMPL_PROJ_TBL.ASSIGNMENT_DT Then
   SetCursorPos(%Panel, RECORD.EMPL_PROJ_TBL, CurrentRowNumber(1),
RECORD.EMPL_TE_TBL, CurrentRowNumber(2), WORK_DT);
   Error MsgGet(20002, 1, "Message Not Found in Catalog");
End-If;
```

Figure 28.4 *PeopleCode program editor—Save Edit code*

3. If the work date is less than the project assignment date the PeopleCode should set the cursor position to the current row of the EMPL_PROJ_TBL record (project assignment date) and the current row of the EMPL_TE_TBL (work date). The PeopleCode will then issue an error and display a message to the application user.

4. The actual text message has been stored in the Message Catalog. Recall that to add a message we select **Go/PeopleTools/Utilities** and then **Use/Message Catalog/Add**. Notice in Figure 28.5 that we enter a message set number and message number, and then associate our message text and any explanation.

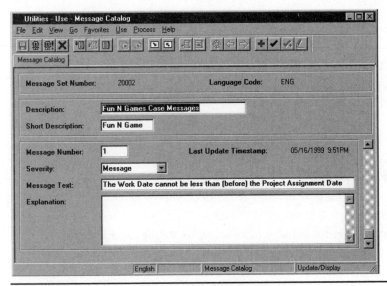

Figure 28.5 *Add a message to the Message Catalog*

5. We should now test our PeopleCode program. We may enter one or more rows of time and expense with a work date less than the project assignment date. Upon a save of the panel, we should see the error message, as displayed in Figure 28.6. Similarly, if the assignment date is changed to make it greater than the work date of one of the rows of time and expense data, then the same error condition will be detected and the same message displayed.

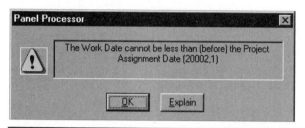

Figure 28.6   *Error message displayed by Save Edit PeopleCode*

Note that if the PeopleCode is entered as a Field Edit event on Work Date the code will prevent a change to a work date less than assignment date but will *not* prevent a change to an assignment date greater than a work date.

Requirement #2: Running Total of Expenses

Again, the first step in developing a PeopleCode program is to determine where to place the PeopleCode, in terms of the specific record fields and appropriate PeopleCode event types. For the requirement to calculate a running total of employee expenses for a given project to display on the Time and Expense panel, we will need to develop several PeopleCode programs.

The running total must be calculated initially from the expense entries found on EMPL_TE_TBL when the panel is first displayed. This can be accomplished with the Row Init event type. Since Row Init code is not field specific, we can place the code on any field in EMPL_TE_TBL. We will follow the convention of placing PeopleCode that is not field specific on the first field in the record definition.

The running total must also be updated as the application user inserts, changes, or deletes an expense entry. The insert of a new row of

EMPL_TE_TBL data in the grid does not actually change the running total until the application user enters a non-zero value into the Expense Amount field. This is equivalent to the application user's changing the value of the Expense field. Therefore, we can use the Field Change event on the Work Expense field in the EMPL_TE_TBL record. This code will also recalculate the running total if an application user changes the expense amount on an existing time and expense entry in the grid.

If an application user deletes a line from the time and expense grid, the running total must be recalculated to subtract the expense amount (if any). The Row Delete event type can be used for this purpose. Again, since Row Delete code is not field specific, we can place the code on any field in EMPL_TE_TBL. We will again place the PeopleCode on the first field in the record.

Finally, before developing the actual PeopleCode programs we will need to create a new Derived/Work record. This record will contain the field that we will use for the running total amount. Recall that a Derived/Work record is used to temporarily store fields for use in the PeopleTools application. In this application, the new work record field will be placed onto the Time & Expense panel for display only. When the PeopleTools panel is closed the value will not be saved to any database table.

The following steps are performed to create the Derived/Work record, place the work field onto the Time & Expense panel, and then insert the PeopleCode syntax onto the record:

1. Add a new field by selecting **File/New/Field** and choosing the number data type. We call this field the Work Expense Total. Enter the desired integer positions, decimal positions, and field long and short names and **Save** the new field as seen in Figure 28.7.

2. Add a new record by selecting **File/New/Record** and insert the Work Expense Total field into the record as seen in Figure 28.8.

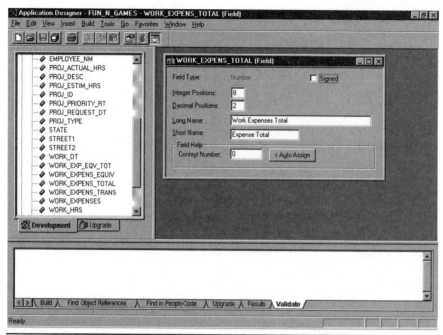

Figure 28.7   *Define a new Work field*

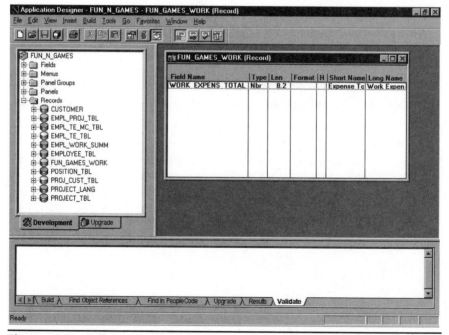

Figure 28.8   *Define a new Work record*

3. Display the **Record Properties/Type** tab for this record and set the Record type to **Derived/Work** record as seen in Figure 28.9.

4. **Save** the new record. We call this record the FUN_GAMES_WORK record. Note that it is not necessary (or possible) to perform the SQL Build step on this record as there will not be a corresponding database table. This record will only contain fields used during the execution of PeopleCode programs.

5. **File/Open** the EMPL_TE_PNL and drag the new Work Expense Total field from the work record onto the panel. The field can be placed anywhere on the panel. We have chosen to put it just below its respective grid column, as seen in Figure 28.10.

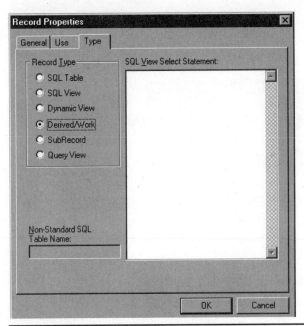

Figure 28.9 *Record properties—Type tab*

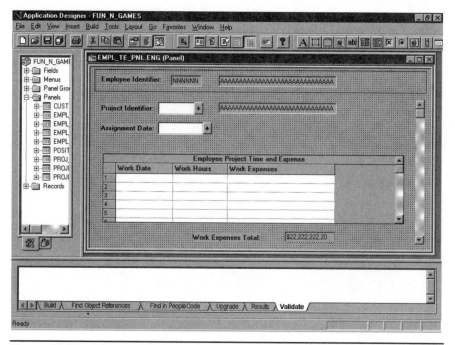

Figure 28.10   *Time and Expense panel with new Running Total field*

6. Open the EMPL_TE_TBL record in the Object Workspace and show the PeopleCode display as seen in Figure 28.11. Double click on the intersection of the first field on the record (Employee ID) and the Row Init event type to open the PeopleCode program editor.

7. The Row Init code is a single statement to calculate the running total by adding the expense amount for each row on the EMPL_TE_TBL to the current value of the running total as the rows are read into the panel buffer. Please see Figure 28.12 for the actual code.

8. The Field Change code is also a single statement, to recalculate the running total when the Work Expense amount changes on a row of data. The statement subtracts the value of the Work Expense amount before the application user made the change using the PriorValue( ) function and then adds in the new value of the Work Expense amount field. Please see Figure 28.13 for the actual code.

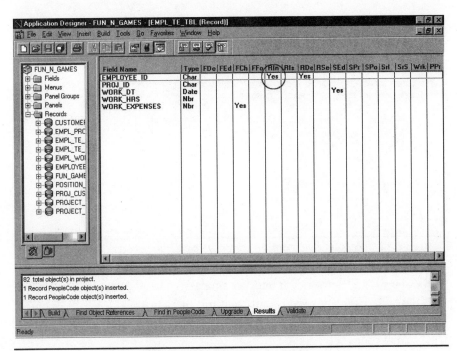

Figure 28.11 *Record EMPL_TE_TBL PeopleCode display*

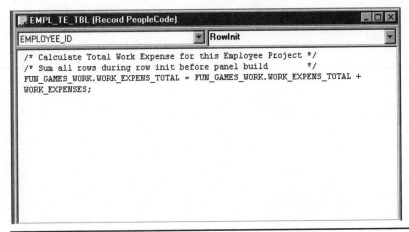

Figure 28.12 *PeopleCode program editor—Row Init code*

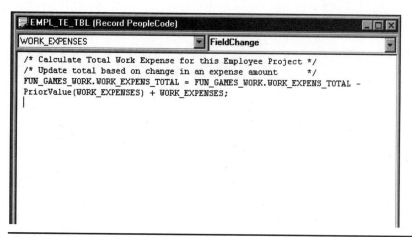

Figure 28.13   *PeopleCode program editor—Field Change code*

9. The Row Delete code is another single-statement program, to recalculate the running total by subtracting the value of the Work Expense amount field for a deleted row. Please see Figure 28.14 below for the actual code.

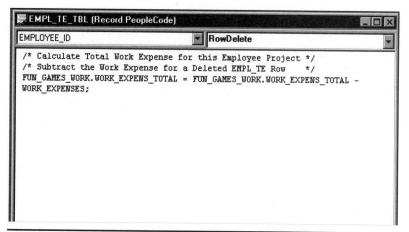

Figure 28.14   *PeopleCode program editor—Row Delete code*

10. Now we should test the Time and Expense panel using a variety of test data cases and conditions. At a minimum, we should test the initial calculation of the running total and the recalculation of the total when an expense entry is inserted, changed, or deleted.

Sample Solution

Here we present our sample solution for the PeopleCode that we incorporated into the T&E application. Please refer to Figure 28.15 for the printout of our EMPL_TE_TBL record that has the PeopleCode attached, and Figure 28.16 for a printout of the modified EMPL_TE_PNL.

```
Printed: 07/16/99  8:57:09AM

                                    Database: FUNGAME3      PS Record: EMPL_TE_TBL      Version: 6463

Field Name       Type  Length Format  Long Name              Short Name      Key  Req TblEdt AU Dt PC Aud Prompt Table   Default Value
Last Updated Date/Time: 07/13/1999 10:13:31PM
Last Updated by Operator: PTTRN

EMPLOYEE_ID      Char  6      Upper   Employee Identifier    Employee ID     KA   Yes Prompt            Y   EMPLOYEE_TBL
PeopleCode-RowInit:
        /* Calculate Total Work Expense for this Employee Project */
        /* Sum all rows during row init before panel build */
        FUN_GAMES WORK.WORK_EXPENS_TOTAL = FUN_GAMES WORK.WORK_EXPENS_TOTAL + WORK_EXPENSES;
PeopleCode-RowDelete:
        /* Calculate Total Work Expense for this Employee Project */
        /* Subtract the Work Expense for a Deleted EMPL_TE Row */
        FUN_GAMES WORK.WORK_EXPENS_TOTAL = FUN_GAMES WORK.WORK_EXPENS_TOTAL - WORK_EXPENSES;

PROJ_ID          Char  6      Upper   Project Identifier     Project Id      KA   Yes Prompt            Y   EMPL_PROJ_TBL
WORK_DT          Date  10             Work Date              Work Date       KA   Yes                   Y                %date
PeopleCode-SaveEdit:
        /*                                                  */
        /*   Fun-N-Games Case Study Modification by Clott/Raff    */
        /*   Work Date cannot be less than Project Assignment Date  */
        /*                                                  */
        If WORK_DT < EMPL_PROJ_TBL.ASSIGNMENT_DT Then
            SetCursorPos(%Panel, RECORD.EMPL_PROJ_TBL, CurrentRowNumber(1), RECORD.EMPL_TE_TBL, CurrentRowNumber(2),
WORK_DT);
            Error MsgGet(20002, 1, "Message Not Found in Catalog");
        End-If;

WORK_HRS         Nbr   2              Work Hours             Work Hours
WORK_EXPENSES    Nbr   6.2            Work Expenses          Work Expenses                             Y                 '0'  '0'
PeopleCode-FieldChange:
        /* Calculate Total Work Expense for this Employee Project */
        /* Update total based on a change in the Work Expense Amount entered   */
        FUN_GAMES WORK.WORK_EXPENS_TOTAL = FUN_GAMES WORK.WORK_EXPENS_TOTAL - PriorValue(WORK_EXPENSES) +
WORK_EXPENSES;
```

Figure 28.15 *Printout of the EMPL_TE_TBL record with PeopleCode attached*

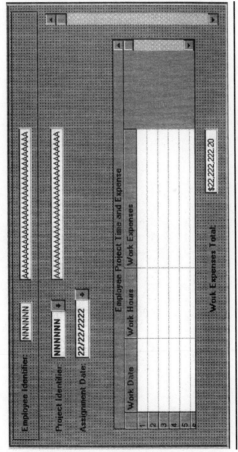

Figure 28.16   Sample printout of modified EMPL_TE_PNL panel (Page 1)

```
Printed: 07/16/99  8:57:18AM

                                    Database: FUNGAME3      PS Panel: EMPL_TE_PNL    Version: 1566
```

Num	Field Type	Label Text	Label Type	Record Name	Field Name	Siz	Alg	On	Off	DSP	INV	CTL	REL	RelNum	CUR	DER	OccLvl
Last Changed:		07/13/99 10:06:10PM															
1	Frame	Frame	PTTRN														
			None														
2	Edit Box	Employee Identifier	RFT Long	EMPLOYEE_TBL	EMPLOYEE_ID					Yes							1
3	Edit Box	Employee Name	None	EMPLOYEE_TBL	EMPLOYEE_NM					Yes							1
4	Scroll Bar	Employee Projects	None														
5	Edit Box	Project Identifier	RFT Long	EMPL_PROJ_TBL	PROJ_ID							Yes					1
6	Edit Box	Project Description	None	PROJECT_TBL	PROJ_DESC							Yes	Yes	5			1
7	Edit Box	Assignment Date	RFT Long	EMPL_PROJ_TBL	ASSIGNMENT_DT					Yes							1
8	Edit Box	Work Expenses Total	RFT Long	FUN GAMES WORK	WORK_EXPENS_TOTAL												
9	Grid	Employee Project Time and Expense Text		EMPL_TE_TBL						Yes					Yes		
10	Edit Box	Work Date	RFT Long	EMPL_TE_TBL	WORK_DT	Cus											2
11	Edit Box	Work Hours	RFT Long	EMPL_TE_TBL	WORK_HRS	Cus											2
12	Edit Box	Work Expenses	RFT Long	EMPL_TE_TBL	WORK_EXPENSES	Cus											2

Figure 28.16 Sample printout of modified EMPL_TE_PNL panel (Page 2)

29

Globalization Activity

We might now consider our Fun-N-Games case application to be complete. We have finished the design and development of the database and the user interface. We have set up application security and tested all the functions of the application. However, if there is a business requirement to adapt the Fun-N-Games application for users who prefer a national language other than English, or there is a need to utilize monetary amounts in different currencies, we need to consider the "globalization" process (please refer to Chapter 18).

For our Fun-N-Games case application, let's assume that most of the application functions are performed by users who prefer English. However, the Project Setup panel must be used by staff in our Mexico facility and these users prefer to work with the panel in Spanish. Users must also have the ability to enter expenses on the Time and Expense panel in any currency and have the application compute the US dollar equivalent amount. We will first step through the translation of the Project Setup panel into Spanish (a non-base language). We will then step through implementation of a multi-currency function for the Time and Expense panel.

Translation

As we step through the translation of the Project setup panel into the Spanish language, we must consider all panel fields and labels, and menu and panel group item labels. We will step through the implementation of a related language record for PROJECT_TBL to maintain the Project descriptions in any non-base language (e.g. Spanish).

1. First, we will translate the field names into Spanish. These will become the Panel Field labels. We will do this all at once using the Translate Fields utility panel, selecting **Go/PeopleTools/Translate** and then **Use/Translate Fields**. See Figure 29.1 for this panel.
2. We select only those fields that appear on PROJECT_PNL using selection criteria entered in the Search Options dialog box as shown in Figure 29.2.
3. We will select Spanish as our target language, and then enter Spanish field long and field short names as shown in Figure 29.3. We then save the Translate Fields panel.
4. Similarly, we must enter Spanish language long and short names for the fields that have XLAT values. We will enter the Spanish names in the Translate XLAT's utility panel for both the Project Type and the Project Priority fields.

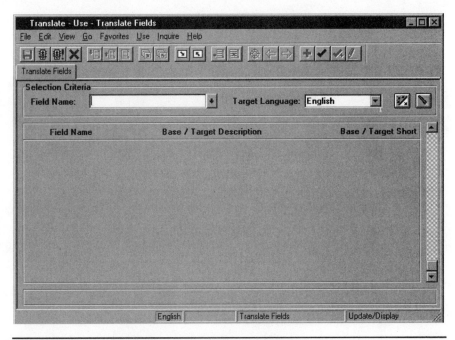

Figure 29.1   *Translate Fields utility panel*

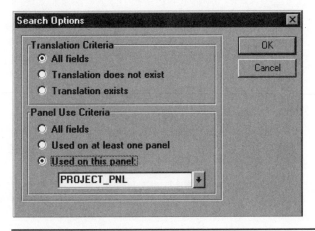

Figure 29.2   *Translate fields—Search options*

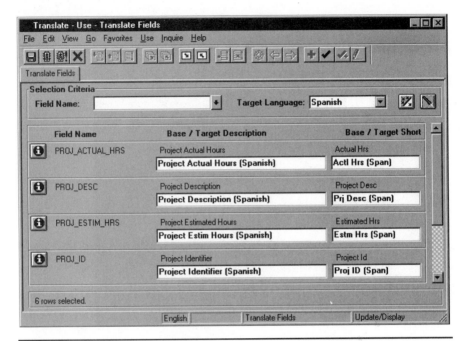

Figure 29.3   *Translate Fields utility panel—with translated field long and short names*

5. We now want to create the translated version of the Project Setup panel. To do this, we must reset our own language preference. We can do this by selecting **Go/PeopleTools/Utilities/International Preferences**, changing our language preference to Spanish as shown in Figure 29.4, and saving the panel.

6. We create a Spanish-language version of PROJECT_PNL by opening the panel up in the Object Workspace. Notice that the Panel Field labels are the translated Spanish names. Move fields and labels about to improve the appearance of the panel. Modify any labels that are not field long or short names (e.g. pushbutton label). See our sample in Figure 29.5.

7. Enter **File/Save As** to save the panel with the same panel name, but select Spanish from the Language drop-down list. Notice that another panel now appears listed in the Application Designer project workspace as PROJECT_PNL (ESP).

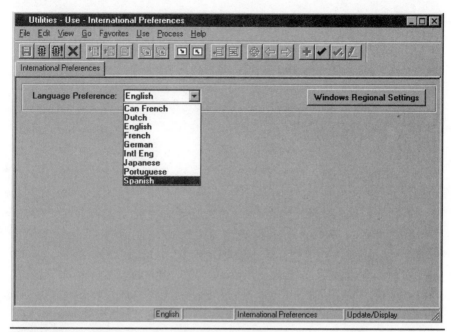

Figure 29.4   *Utilities—International Preferences panel*

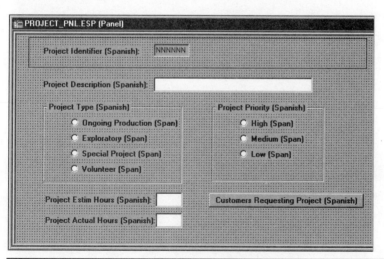

Figure 29.5   *Translated version of PROJECT_PNL in Application Designer*

8. With the Operator language preference set to Spanish, open the panel group and enter a Spanish-language panel group Item label. See Figure 29.6 for an example.

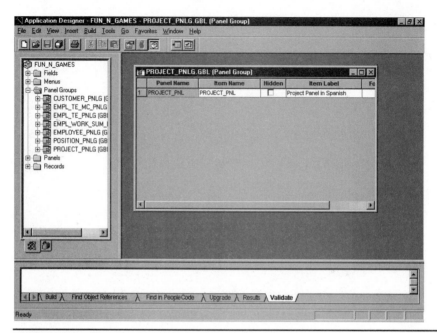

Figure 29.6   *Translated panel group Item label for Project Setup*

9. Likewise, open the menu and enter Spanish language Menu Item labels and a Menu label. See Figure 29.7 for an example.

10. Create the related language record PROJECT_LANG for PROJECT_TBL to store the Project descriptions in a non-base language. Include the key to PROJECT_TBL and LANGUAGE_CD as Key fields and the Project description as the only Non-key data field. See the record definition in Figure 29.8.

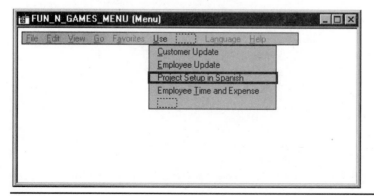

Figure 29.7   *Translated Menu Item label for Project Setup*

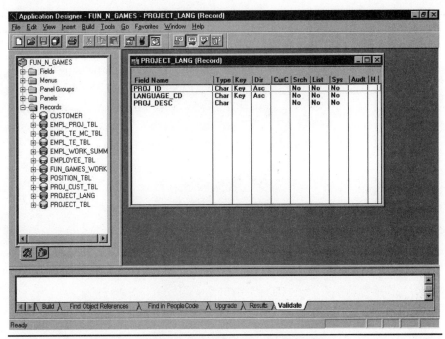

Figure 29.8   PROJECT_LANG record definition—Use display

11. Build the new PROJECT_LANG record to create the corresponding database table. Please see Figure 29.9 for the Build dialog box.

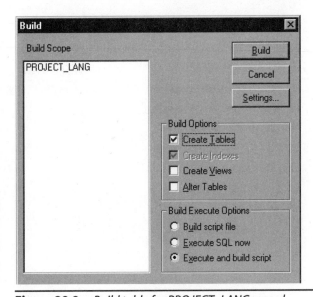

Figure 29.9   Build table for PROJECT_LANG record

12. Modify the properties of the PROJECT_TBL record to indicate that PROJECT_LANG is the related Language record. See Figure 29.10 for the Record Properties Use tab.

13. Test the new Spanish Project Setup panel with Operator language preference set to Spanish (Figure 29.11). Ensure that the Spanish-language version is now executed and that Spanish menu items, the Spanish panel, panel fields, and XLAT values are all displayed. The panel should function just like the base (English) version of the panel.

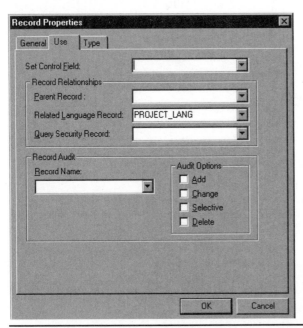

Figure 29.10   *Modify PROJECT_TBL Record Properties for Related Language record*

14. Test the related language record for Project Description. With the Operator language preference set to Spanish, update an existing project and change the name to a Spanish description. Retrieve that project to ensure that the project description is displayed in Spanish. Reset the Operator language preference to English and check that the base language project description is maintained. Note that the project description is now displayed in yellow to indicate that it is a translated value.

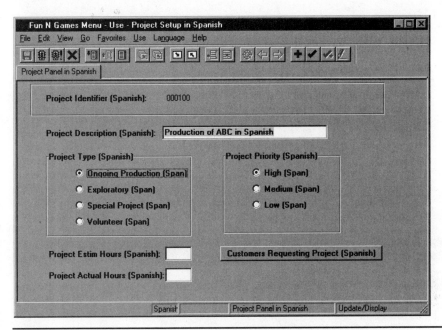

Figure 29.11   *Spanish-language version of Project Setup panel*

Multi-Currency

Our business managers have informed us that there is a requirement to accept expense amounts on the Time and Expense panel in any currency. Here we will have to design and develop a modification to our existing application. To understand this requirement we discuss it with our business managers and determine that if a currency other than US dollars is entered, the application must calculate the US dollar equivalent amount. The panel user must enter the relevant currency exchange rate to be used to calculate the US dollar equivalent. Note that requiring the application user to enter the exchange rate may not be necessary—in a live application you could use the PeopleSoft delivered currency and exchange rate common records, panels, and PeopleCode built-in functions for this purpose. For simplicity, in our case application we will *not* use the PeopleSoft delivered multi-currency functions. We step through the process of implementing this multi-currency requirement into our existing Time and Expense panel below.

1. Define the new field WORK_EXPENSE_EQUIV for the work expense amount in US dollar equivalent that will be calculated by the application. Please see Figure 29.12 for the field definition.

2. Define the new field CUR_EXCH_USD_RT for the currency to the US dollar exchange rate entered by the application user. See Figure 29.13 for the field definition.

3. Modify the EMPL_TE_TBL record to include three additional fields: CURRENCY_CD, CUR_EXCH_USD_RT, and WORK_EXPENSE_EQUIV. See Figure 29.14 for the record definition. Note that the CURRENCY_CD field may have a Prompt Table edit defined against the (PeopleSoft delivered) Currency Code table.

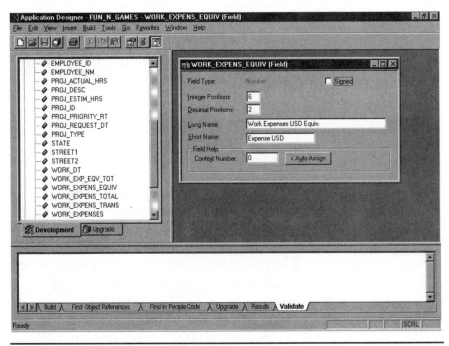

Figure 29.12   *Work Expense Equivalent field definition*

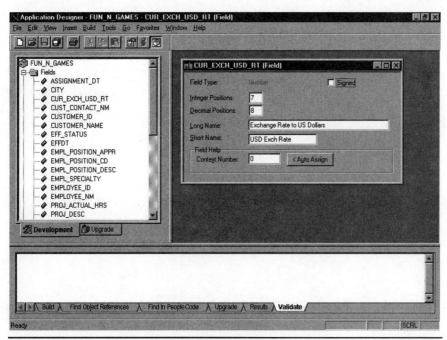

Figure 29.13   *Currency Exchange Rate field definition*

Field Name	Type	Len	Format	H	Short Name	Long Name
EMPLOYEE_ID	Char	6	Upper		Employee II	Employee Identifier
PROJ_ID	Char	6	Upper		Project Id	Project Identifier
WORK_DT	Date	10			Work Date	Work Date
WORK_HRS	Nbr	2			Work Hours	Work Hours
CURRENCY_CD	Char	3	Upper		Currency	Currency Code
CUR_EXCH_USD_RT	Nbr	7.8			USD Exch F	Exchange Rate to US Dollars
WORK_EXPENSES	Nbr	6.2			Work Exper	Work Expenses
WORK_EXPENS_EQUIV	Nbr	6.2			Expense US	Work Expenses USD Equiv.

Figure 29.14   *Modified EMPL_TE_TBL record definition*

4. Notice that CURRENCY_CD will be defined now as the currency control field for the Work Expense field in Record Field properties on the Use tab. Please see Figure 29.15. This will cause the Work Expense amount to be displayed on the panel with the appropriate currency symbol based on the value in the Currency Code field.

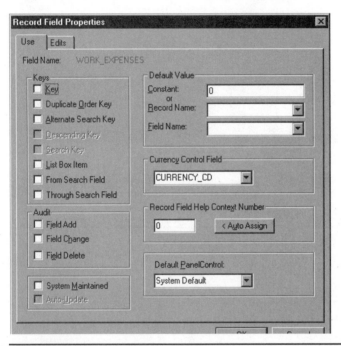

Figure 29.15 *Record field properties for Work Expense—showing the Currency Control field*

5. Build the modified EMPL_TE_TBL to recreate the corresponding PS_EMPL table in the database (do not bother to alter to save test data). See Figure 29.16 for the Build step.
6. Modify the EMPL_TE_PNL grid area to include the three additional fields as columns. Instead of just entering the Work Expense amount, the user will now enter the Currency Code, the Exchange Rate US dollars, and the Work Expense amount. The application will then calculate and display the Work Expense US Dollar Equivalent amount. We will mark the Work Expense US Dollar Equivalent field as display only on our panel. See Figure 29.17.

Figure 29.16   *Build table for EMPL_TE_TBL record*

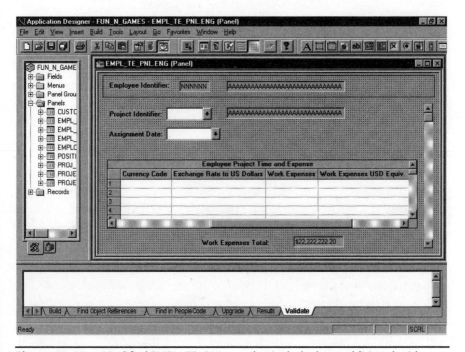

Figure 29.17   *Modified EMPL_TE_PNL panel to include three additional grid columns*

7. We will need to incorporate PeopleCode to calculate the US dollar equivalent amount. This will be FieldChange code placed on the two fields that are used in the calculation: the Work Expense amount and the Currency Exchange rate. Again, in the interest of simplicity in our case application, we assume that all exchange rates are quoted in terms of units of currency per US dollar. Therefore the calculation divides the Work Expense amount by the Currency Exchange rate. We also need to update the PeopleCode that calculates the running total US dollar expense for an employee project assignment in the same FieldChange event. Please see Figure 29.18 for the sample PeopleCode.

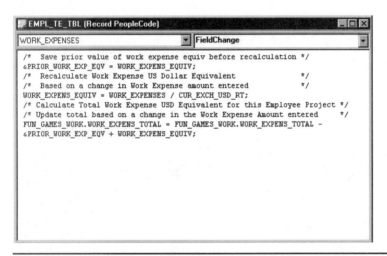

```
EMPL_TE_TBL (Record PeopleCode)                              _ □ ☓

WORK_EXPENSES                          ▼  FieldChange               ▼

/*  Save prior value of work expense equiv before recalculation */
&PRIOR_WORK_EXP_EQV = WORK_EXPENS_EQUIV;
/*  Recalculate Work Expense US Dollar Equivalent            */
/*  Based on a change in Work Expense amount entered         */
WORK_EXPENS_EQUIV = WORK_EXPENSES / CUR_EXCH_USD_RT;
/* Calculate Total Work Expense USD Equivalent for this Employee Project */
/* Update total based on a change in the Work Expense Amount entered    */
FUN_GAMES_WORK.WORK_EXPENS_TOTAL = FUN_GAMES_WORK.WORK_EXPENS_TOTAL -
&PRIOR_WORK_EXP_EQV + WORK_EXPENS_EQUIV;
```

Figure 29.18   *FieldChange PeopleCode on Work Expense in the EMPL_TE_TBL record*

8. Similar FieldChange code must also be placed on the Currency Exchange Rate field. The FieldChange code is required on both fields since a change in the Work Expense amount or a change in the Currency Exchange rate will change the calculation of the new US dollar equivalent amounts. Please see Figure 29.19 for more sample PeopleCode.

9. The RowInit PeopleCode must be modified to use the US dollar equivalent amount in the calculation of the running total of work expense. Please see Figure 29.20 for sample RowInit PeopleCode. We must apply a similar change to the RowDelete PeopleCode.

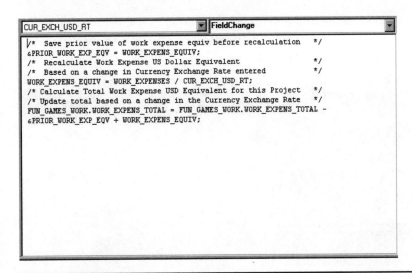

```
CUR_EXCH_USD_RT                    ▼ ||FieldChange                          ▼
/* Save prior value of work expense equiv before recalculation    */
&PRIOR_WORK_EXP_EQV = WORK_EXPENS_EQUIV;
/* Recalculate Work Expense US Dollar Equivalent                  */
/* Based on a change in Currency Exchange Rate entered            */
WORK_EXPENS_EQUIV = WORK_EXPENSES / CUR_EXCH_USD_RT;
/* Calculate Total Work Expense USD Equivalent for this Project    */
/* Update total based on a change in the Currency Exchange Rate    */
FUN_GAMES_WORK.WORK_EXPENS_TOTAL = FUN_GAMES_WORK.WORK_EXPENS_TOTAL -
&PRIOR_WORK_EXP_EQV + WORK_EXPENS_EQUIV;
```

Figure 29.19   *FieldChange PeopleCode for Currency Exchange rate in the
EMPL_TE_TBL record*

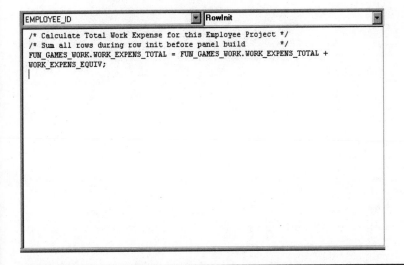

```
EMPLOYEE_ID                        ▼ ||RowInit                              ▼
/* Calculate Total Work Expense for this Employee Project */
/* Sum all rows during row init before panel build        */
FUN_GAMES_WORK.WORK_EXPENS_TOTAL = FUN_GAMES_WORK.WORK_EXPENS_TOTAL +
WORK_EXPENS_EQUIV;
|
```

Figure 29.20   *Modified RowInit PeopleCode on the EMPL_TE_TBL record*

10. Test the working of the new Time and Expense panel. Try various currencies and ensure that the correct currency symbol is displayed for the
amount. Enter various currency exchange rates and check that the calculation of the US dollar equivalent is correct. Insert and delete rows of

time and expense and ensure that the running total of work expenses is still correct. Please see Figure 29.21 for our version of the multi-currency Time and Expense panel.

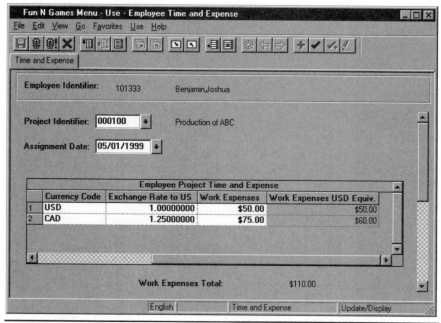

Figure 29.21   *Test of multi-currency Time and Expense panel*

Sample Solution

Here we present our sample solution for the globalization of the T&E application, including the translation of the panel to a non-base language and the introduction of (limited) multi-currency functions. Please refer to Figure 29.22 for the printout of our Spanish-language PROJECT_PNL panel. Please refer to Figure 29.23 for the printout of the PROJECT.LANG related language record.

Refer to Figure 29.24 for the printout of our EMPL_TE_TBL record with the currency code and the modified PeopleCode to compute the currency equivalent amounts. Please refer to Figure 29.25 for a printout of the modified EMPL_TE_PNL panel.

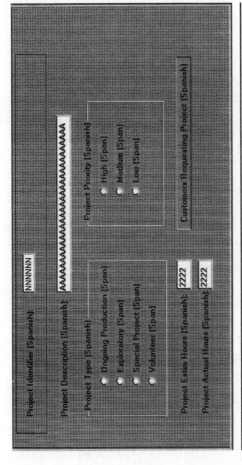

Figure 29.22 Printout of the Spanish-language PROJECT_PNL panel (Page 1)

Printed: 07/16/99 9:01:46AM

Database: FUNGAMES   PS Panel: PROJECT_PNL   Version: 1555

Num	Field Type	Label Text	Label Type	Record Name	Field Name	Siz	Alg	On	Off	DSP	INV	CTL	REL	RelNum	CUR	DER	OccLvl
Last Changed:	06/13/99 11:23:58PM																
1	Frame	Frame	None														
2	Edit Box	Project Identifier (Spanish)	RFT Long	PROJECT_TBL	PROJ_ID					Yes							
3	Edit Box	Project Description (Spanish)	RFT Long	PROJECT_TBL	PROJ_DESC												
4	Group Box	Project Type (Spanish)	RFT Long	PROJECT_TBL	PROJ_TYPE												
5	Radio Button	Ongoing Production (Span)	XLAT Long	PROJECT_TBL	PROJ_TYPE			ONPR									
6	Radio Button	Exploratory (Span)	XLAT Long	PROJECT_TBL	PROJ_TYPE			EXPL									
7	Radio Button	Special Project (Span)	XLAT Long	PROJECT_TBL	PROJ_TYPE			SPEC									
8	Radio Button	Volunteer (Span)	XLAT Long	PROJECT_TBL	PROJ_TYPE			VOL									
9	Group Box	Project Priority (Spanish)	RFT Long	PROJECT_TBL	PROJ_PRIORITY_RT												
10	Radio Button	High (Span)	XLAT Long	PROJECT_TBL	PROJ_PRIORITY_RT			H									
11	Radio Button	Medium (Span)	XLAT Long	PROJECT_TBL	PROJ_PRIORITY_RT			M									
12	Radio Button	Low (Span)	XLAT Long	PROJECT_TBL	PROJ_PRIORITY_RT			L									
13	Edit Box	Project Estim Hours (Spanish)	RFT Long	PROJECT_TBL	PROJ_ESTIM_HRS												
14	Push Button	Customers Requesting Project (Spanish)	Text	PROJECT_TBL	PROJ_ID			Cus									
15	Edit Box	Project Actual Hours (Spanish)	RFT Long	PROJECT_TBL	PROJ_ACTUAL_HRS												

Figure 29.22 Printout of the Spanish-language PROJECT_PNL panel (Page 2)

Printed: 07/16/99   9:08:40AM

Database: FUNGAMES   PS Record: PROJECT_LANG   Version: 6444

Field Name	Type	Length	Format	Long Name	Short Name	Key	Req	TblEdt	AU Dt	PC Aud	Prompt Table	Default Value

Last Updated Date/Time: 05/10/1999 10:39:47PM
Last Updated by Operator: PTTRN

Field Name	Type	Length	Format	Long Name	Short Name	Key	Req	TblEdt	AU Dt	PC Aud	Prompt Table
PROJ_ID	Char	6	Upper	Project Identifier	Project Id	KA	Yes				
LANGUAGE_CD	Char	3	Upper	Language Code	Lang Cd	KA		Xlat			
Values: CFR	Active	01/01/00		Canadian French	Can French				03/21/1998	3:37:38PM	PTGBL
DUT	Active	01/01/00		Dutch	Dutch				03/21/1998	3:37:03PM	PTGBL
ENG	Active	01/01/00		English	English				08/12/1997	5:43:11PM	PPLSOFT
ESP	Active	01/01/00		Spanish	Spanish				08/12/1997	5:43:11PM	PPLSOFT
FRA	Active	01/01/00		French	French				08/12/1997	5:43:11PM	PPLSOFT
GER	Active	01/01/00		German	German				08/12/1997	5:43:11PM	PPLSOFT
INE	Active	01/01/00		International English	Intl Eng				03/21/1998	3:36:57PM	PTGBL
JPN	Active	01/01/00		Japanese	Japanese				08/12/1997	5:43:11PM	PPLSOFT
POR	Active	01/01/00		Portuguese	Portuguese				03/21/1998	3:37:12PM	PTGBL
PROJ_DESC	Char	30	Mixed	Project Description	Project Desc		Yes				

Figure 29.23   Printout of the PROJECT_LANG related language record

407

```
Printed: 07/16/99  9:08:46AM

                              Database: FUNGAMES        PS Record: EMPL_TE_TBL       Version: 6452

Field Name       Type  Length  Format  Long Name              Short Name    Key   Req  TblEdit  AU  Dt  PC  Aud  Prompt Table    Default Value
Last Updated Date/Time: 06/14/1999  7:34:03AM
Last Updated by Operator: PTTRN

EMPLOYEE_ID      Char  6       Upper   Employee Identifier    Employee ID   KA    Yes Prompt                            Y    EMPLOYEE_TBL
PeopleCode-RowInit:
  /* Calculate Total Work Expense for this Employee Project */
  /* Sum all rows during row init before panel build */
  FUN_GAMES_WORK.WORK_EXPENS_TOTAL = FUN_GAMES_WORK.WORK_EXPENS_TOTAL + WORK_EXPENS_EQUIV;
PeopleCode-RowDelete:
  /* Calculate Total Work Expense for this Employee Project */
  /* Subtract the Work Expense for a Deleted EMPL_TE Row */
  FUN_GAMES_WORK.WORK_EXPENS_TOTAL = FUN_GAMES_WORK.WORK_EXPENS_TOTAL - WORK_EXPENS_EQUIV;

PROJ_ID          Char  6       Upper   Project Identifier     Project Id    KA    Yes Prompt                            Y    EMPL_PROJ_TBL
WORK_DT          Date  10              Work Date              Work Date     KA    Yes                                                       %date
PeopleCode-SaveEdit:
  /*                                                    */
  /* Fun-N-Games Case Study Modification by Clott/Raff  */
  /* Work Date cannot be less than Project Assignment Date */
  /*                                                    */
  If WORK_DT < EMPL_PROJ_TBL.ASSIGNMENT_DT Then
    SetCursorPos(%Panel, RECORD.EMPL_PROJ_TBL, CurrentRowNumber(1), RECORD.EMPL_TE_TBL, CurrentRowNumber(2),
    WORK_DT);
    Error MsgGet(20002, 1, "Message Not Found in Catalog");
  End-If;

WORK_HRS         Nbr   2               Work Hours             Work Hours
CURRENCY_CD      Char  3       Upper   Currency Code          Currency             Yes Prompt                            Y    CURRENCY_CD_TBL   'USD'
CUR_EXCH_USD_RT  Nbr   7.8             Exchange Rate to US Dollars    USD Exch Rate        Yes                                                '1'
PeopleCode-FieldChange:
  /* Save prior value of work expense equiv before recalculation */
  &PRIOR_WORK_EXP_EQV = WORK_EXPENS_EQUIV;
  /* Recalculate Work Expense US Dollar Equivalent */
  WORK_EXPENS_EQUIV = WORK_EXPENSES / CUR_EXCH_USD_RT;
  /* Based on a change in Currency Exchange Rate entered */
  WORK_EXPENS_EQUIV = WORK_EXPENSES / CUR_EXCH_USD_RT;
  /* Calculate Total Work Expense USD Equivalent for this Project */
  /* Update total based on a change in the Currency Exchange Rate */
  FUN_GAMES_WORK.WORK_EXPENS_TOTAL = FUN_GAMES_WORK.WORK_EXPENS_TOTAL - &PRIOR_WORK_EXP_EQV +
  WORK_EXPENS_EQUIV;

WORK_EXPENSES    Nbr   6.2             Work Expenses          Work Expenses        Y                                                        '0'
PeopleCode-FieldChange:
  /* Save prior value of work expense equiv before recalculation */
  &PRIOR_WORK_EXP_EQV = WORK_EXPENS_EQUIV;
  /* Recalculate Work Expense US Dollar Equivalent */
  WORK_EXPENS_EQUIV = WORK_EXPENSES / CUR_EXCH_USD_RT;
  /* Based on a change in Work Expense amount entered */
  WORK_EXPENS_EQUIV = WORK_EXPENSES / CUR_EXCH_USD_RT;
  /* Calculate Total Work Expense USD Equivalent for this Employee Project */
  /* Update total based on a change in the Work Expense Amount entered */
  FUN_GAMES_WORK.WORK_EXPENS_TOTAL = FUN_GAMES_WORK.WORK_EXPENS_TOTAL - &PRIOR_WORK_EXP_EQV +
  WORK_EXPENS_EQUIV;

WORK_EXPENS_EQUIV  Nbr  6.2           Work Expenses USD Equiv.    Expense USD
```

Figure 29.24 Printout of the EMPL_TE_TBL record with currency code and modified PeopleCode

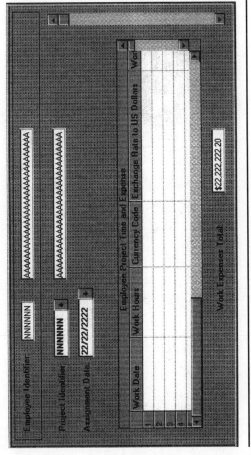

Figure 29.25 *Modified EMPL_TE_PNL panel (Page 1)*

```
Printed: 07/26/99  3:18:49PM                    Database: FUNGAMES    PS Panel: EMPL_TE_PNL    Version: 1559
```

Num	Field Type	Label Text	Label Type	Record Name	Field Name	Siz	Alg	On	Off	DSP	INV	CTL	REL	RelNum	CUR	DER	OccLvl
Last Changed:	06/14/99 7:51:20AM																
1	Frame	Frame	PTTRN														
2	Edit Box	Employee Identifier	RFT Long	EMPLOYEE_TBL	EMPLOYEE_ID					Yes							
3	Edit Box	Employee Name	None	EMPLOYEE_TBL	EMPLOYEE_NM					Yes							
4	Scroll Bar	Employee Projects	None														
5	Edit Box	Project Identifier	RFT Long	EMPL_PROJ_TBL	PROJ_ID							Yes					1
6	Edit Box	Project Description	None	PROJECT_TBL	PROJ_DESC					Yes			Yes				1
7	Edit Box	Assignment Date	RFT Long	EMPL_PROJ_TBL	ASSIGNMENT_DT									5			1
8	Edit Box	Work Expenses Total	RFT Long	FUN_GAMES_WORK	WORK_EXPENS_TOTAL					Yes							1
9	Grid	Employee Project Time and Expense Text		EMPL_TE_TBL													
10	Edit Box	Work Date	RFT Long	EMPL_TE_TBL	WORK_DT	Cus											2
11	Edit Box	Work Hours	RFT Long	EMPL_TE_TBL	WORK_HRS	Cus											2
12	Edit Box	Currency Code	RFT Long	EMPL_TE_TBL	CURRENCY_CD												2
13	Edit Box	Exchange Rate to US Dollars	RFT Long	EMPL_TE_TBL	CUR_EXCH_USD_RT										Yes		2
14	Edit Box	Work Expenses	RFT Long	EMPL_TE_TBL	WORK_EXPENSES												2
15	Edit Box	Work Expenses USD Equiv.	RFT Long	EMPL_TE_TBL	WORK_EXPENS_EQUIV					Yes							2

Figure 29.25 Modified EMPL_TE_PNL panel (Page 2)

Index

About the Authors

Jami A. Clott is an Assistant Director in the Information and Technology Services organization of Ernst & Young LLP. Her background includes experience as a systems consultant, business systems analyst, and functional project manager. Ms. Clott holds a BS in Statistics from Cornell University and an MBA in Information Systems and Management from the NYU Stern School of Business Administration.

Stephen S. Raff is an Associate Director in the Information and Technology Services organization of Ernst & Young LLP. His background includes experience as a programmer, database administrator, and project manager. Mr. Raff holds a BS in Computer Science from Cornell University and an MBA in Finance from the NYU Stern School of Business Administration.

Together, the authors lead the PeopleSoft technical training program for Ernst & Young LLP. They are PeopleSoft accredited technical instructors. In addition to delivering training, they also design and develop custom PeopleSoft training programs. They have taught PeopleSoft application development skills to hundreds of information systems and management consulting professionals at their firm.